"Do you want to think bigger about who you are and what you offer the world? Of course, you do. Then you need to do the work, but you shouldn't do it alone. That's why you must be able to ask for help. Laura's book will show you how to do so with grace and strength. Highly recommended."

—Michael Port, *New York Times* bestselling author of *The Think Big Manifesto*

"People are more involved and more passionate than ever about causes in their life and reaching goals, yet most still are not very good at the most important part: asking for what they want in life! This book offers comprehensive but practical advice on how to connect with, convince, and inspire people to help you succeed in your goals—whether it's business, charitable, personal, or any aspect of your life."

—Paulette V. Maehara, president and CEO, Association of Fundraising Professionals, Alexandria, VA

"In my experience, asking is all about imparting a sense of urgency and making your ask crystal clear and positive, not apologetic or assuming the person will be offended. Laura gives great examples of how to make each ask a positive experience for the asker, as well as for the person being asked."

—John E. Möller, director, Office of Protocol, The University of Queensland, Brisbane, Australia

"I find it a privilege to do the work of Keystone Human Services. Increasingly, when I ask others to share in the work, I approach the ask as an invitation to become part of something significant, something that is relevant to the times and personally meaningful. Everyone wants their life to matter—what better gift is there?"

—Dennis W. Felty, president Keystone Human Services, Harrisburg, PA

"Unless you ask, how can you know that the road is open for business?"

—Maria Isabel De Guzman Vendrell, Certified Yoga
Teacher IYTA, Puerto Rico

"Asking for money is something everyone else is supposed to do—not the artist, the performer. Wrong! While I resist learning how to do the task for myself, it is the only way I can be sure I can fulfill my ideas, my dreams, and my goals of where I want to perform. Read this book with me and we both will learn and get what we want."

—Jay Clayton, jazz vocalist and educator, New York

"When my patients *ask* me questions I am able to individualize their treatment plans and tailor my expertise to their needs. In the end we both succeed."

—Dr. Pamela A. Charles, chiropractic neurologist, New York

"Laura is the wizard of strategic fundraising, and this is a guidebook for all of us to use in everyday matters, whether it's asking for a raise or negotiating with our partner. Seasoned executives as well as newbies in the business world will benefit from this compendium on how to get what you want out of life—just by asking."

—Donna Weaver, founder, WeaverWorks, Yardley,
Pennsylvania; formerly a corporate communications
executive in the apparel industry

"This book is a clear road map for initiating and making the ask in the not-for-profit and business sectors. As the president of an executive recruitment firm, I see this book as an invaluable resource for planning your career and landing your best job."

—Gail L. Freeman, president, Freeman Philanthropic
Services, New York

The

ASK

The

ASK

How to Ask for Support for Your Nonprofit Cause, Creative Project, or Business Venture

Laura Fredricks

Foreword by
Ivan G. Seidenberg

JOSSEY-BASS
A Wiley Imprint
www.josseybass.com

Published by Jossey-Bass
A Wiley Imprint
989 Market Street, San Francisco, CA 94103-1741—www.josseybass.com

Jossey-Bass books and products are available through most bookstores. To contact Jossey-Bass directly call our Customer Care Department within the U.S. at 800-956-7739, outside the U.S. at 317-572-3986, or fax 317-572-4002.

Jossey-Bass also publishes its books in a variety of electronic formats. Some content that appears in print may not be available in electronic books.

Library of Congress Cataloging-in-Publication Data

Fredricks, Laura.
    The ask : how to ask for support for your nonprofit cause, creative project, or business venture / Laura Fredricks.
        p. cm.
    Includes index.
    ISBN 978-0-470-48094-6 (cloth/website)
    1. Fund raising. 2. Nonprofit organizations—Management. I. Title.
    HG177.F68 2010
    658.15'224—dc22

                                                                2009041328

Printed in the United States of America
FIRST EDITION
HB Printing   10 9 8 7 6 5 4 3 2 1

Contents

3 How Do I Know Who to Ask and When to Ask? 53

4 **Who Should Make the Ask and in What Setting?   83**

PART II   How Do I Make the Ask?   111

5 **Asking for a Cause—Small and Large Charitable Gifts   113**

Web Contents

Foreword

I<small>T'S SURPRISING HOW SIMPLE THE FORMULA</small> for success is when you boil it down to its basic elements. You have to know your objectives, think through all the details, have a plan for action, follow through, and follow up. What's more surprising is how elusive these simple principles are in real life, usually because people simply don't know how to ask for what they want and deserve.

Laura Fredricks knows how to ask. I watched her put her methods into action at Pace University, where I sit on the Board of Trustees, in running a major capital campaign. More important for the readers of this book, she knows how to coach others to get the results they want. Her strategies for success apply equally to the business and the nonprofit world, the institutional and the personal spheres, and this book translates those strategies into concrete advice about how to turn your goals into action, no matter what the setting.

Ivan G. Seidenberg
Chairman and Chief Executive Officer
Verizon

*I dedicate this book to everyone who needs to ask
for anything they want.*

Preface

ASKING IS A PART OF EVERY ASPECT OF OUR lives. It should be as natural as walking, having an enjoyable conversation, smiling, and breathing . . . but I know for many of you it is the one thing you dread the most.

During my wonderful experience of speaking and training people on how to ask, using all the tools laid out in the first book, *The ASK: How to Ask Anyone for Any Amount for Any Purpose,* it became crystal clear that in addition to learning how to ask for money to support a nonprofit, hundreds of people asked me if the same principles apply if you are asking for money for a creative project; asking for advice; asking for a promotion, raise, new job title; asking for feedback—in short . . . *asking for everyday living.* Well, this new book will cover it all, from nonprofits that need restricted and unrestricted money, to businesses that need their sales and marketing forces to craft their asks to achieve enhanced sales, to the individual who has dreams, goals, and a strong desire to have the best and most fulfilling personal and professional life possible, with the help of a little financial backing, of course.

The uniqueness of this book is that it will show that there is much to be learned about how to ask in the nonprofit sector, the business sector, and the everyday living sector. By that I mean that so often board members drop the expertise and skills they use in their businesses when they attend a charity board meeting. Why? We have so much to learn in the nonprofit world from their skills and expertise that can help us be more business-like in approaching select donors. Conversely, the business sector can learn a great deal from how fundraisers identify, cultivate, and ask donors (clients in the business world), for money, for an opportunity to invest in the nonprofit and all the satisfying rewards that go along with establishing and solidifying long-term relationships. What boggles my mind is seeing and hearing how many people, regardless of whether they are in the nonprofit or business sector, who *cannot ask for something that is important and personal,* such as medical advice; a raise; a promotion; or financial support for an independent film, a new play, a concert, or art exhibit, because they are afraid of rejection, afraid of offending someone, and most importantly, afraid to examine their views on money and what emotions that brings up for them.

This book will be the bridge across all these sectors that will make asking for anything easy, enjoyable, meaningful, and rewarding. As you can tell, I have written this book in an extremely conversational style, so that it is more inviting and enjoyable for you to learn. Trust me, I take any Ask extremely seriously and I am well aware that in certain circumstances you will need to work with challenging people during the Ask and that this takes time, focus, and dedication. This is why I have organized the book in a very logical and progressive fashion so that you can follow along and experience the sequence of steps that need to be taken before, during, and after the Ask.

If you believe that you and your organization are worthy of the vital resources you need to be successful, read on and feel confident that you will learn how to ask for what you need and deserve.

Acknowledgments

THIS IS GOING TO BE VERY SIMPLE AND VERY honest. I simply and honestly want to thank everyone who has ever hired me to speak and everyone who came to hear me speak. I see your faces, I read your expressions, I hear your questions and remember all of you. For some reason I was born with a photographic memory and I can remember every conversation. (This can be a blessing or a curse—I choose the former!) Without this richness of thought, your participation, your brutal honesty about your challenges, I could not have written to the depth that I hope to have accomplished in this book.

As a dear friend, Patti German, said to me while she was encouraging me to travel and not finish the book until I completed my travels, it was important to listen, to spend time wherever I was speaking, and most importantly to "stay in the second and absorb." Only then could I *"Write with a different lens."* As I write this book I sincerely hope you know how much I appreciate every one of you opening up your schedules, your homes, your families, your backyards, your tours of your communities, and sharing You. I do hope in some significant way I can pay each and every one of you back with this book.

Introduction

ASKING IS SUCH AN ESSENTIAL AND FUNDAMENTALLY IMPORTANT part of anyone's everyday life. Whether you do this for a living as a professional fundraiser for a nonprofit organization; need to do this as a leader or volunteer for the organization; want to do this to support your creative or business venture; or have to learn how to ask for yourself, it is all about how you ask, *the right way* and with *the right steps,* that makes all the difference between getting a shake of the head and a "no" and a nod of the head and a "yes."

This book will walk you through all the steps you need to take in the right order with the right people and the right follow-up so you will see that no matter what you ask for, there is a system. It takes organization, focus, discipline, passion, humor, and most of all a true belief that with your dedication you will make the best Ask possible, which is just as rewarding as getting a "yes" to your Ask.

WHO SHOULD READ THIS BOOK

It would be very easy for me to say everyone should read this book because at some point in time everyone will want to know how they can make the most persuasive and convincing presentation with each and every Ask. In that light, I think everyone will gain a new and special knowledge and will walk away with practical advice and a clear and concise road map on how to make any Ask. There are three particular groups of people that I think would gain the most from reading *and applying* this book:

1. Anyone who needs to ask on behalf of a nonprofit
   - Fundraisers: development officers and directors, annual giving directors and officers, major and planned giving officers, leadership gifts officers and directors, stewardship gifts officers and directors
   - Top administrators: president, chief executive officer, chief financial officer, vice president, vice chancellor, provost, chief medical officer, pastor, priest, and rabbi
   - Board and committee members
   - Donors and volunteers
   - People who are employed by a nonprofit: office managers; program officers; executive assistants; administrative assistants; human resources, accounting, and finance officers
   - Anyone who wants to learn how to fundraise

It is my belief that anyone involved with a nonprofit, regardless of whether it is a primary, part-time, or volunteer position, needs to know how to ask for money. It is easy to see why fundraisers need to know, but now more than ever leadership and volunteers really need the coaching, training, and practical experience in asking for money. Particularly when economic times are challenging, it takes the entire team within the organization to raise money given the scarce resources available. Oftentimes it is the administrative or executive assistant, a former patient, or a volunteer who comes forth and identifies some "new prospective" people who may want to be further engaged in the organization and have the capacity, with the right cultivation, to be a strong supporter. They should not just provide the name and walk away, because their connections to these people is how it all got started. They need to be involved with the cultivation process and oftentimes present during the Ask, so they need to know how to ask.

There are many people who have the desire to learn how to fundraise, which means they need to know how to ask for money. No matter which organization you envision you may want to help—small, medium, large, local, national, international, or if you want to start your own foundation—this book can help you raise the money you need for your organization.

2. Anyone who needs money for a creative project or a business venture

- Independent film producer
- Playwright
- Art collector
- Music producer
- Future small business owner
- Current company that wants to expand
- Inventor of new products
- Venture capitalist looking for other investors

Here, the possibilities are endless for the people in creative fields and business worlds, whether they are just starting out or want to expand their current enterprise. What separates this book from others is the following tip: *asking for a creative or business venture is exactly the same as asking for a gift for a nonprofit organization.* This book will show you how all the steps are exactly parallel and that if you take the time as is normally done in the nonprofit world to cultivate the people you would like to ask, have a solid and convincing business plan (case statements for nonprofits), deliver a solid Ask for a specific amount for a specific purpose, listen, and follow up using creative ways to reach the person, you will make the perfect Ask. Skipping any of the steps and then running to the next potential customer, client, or investor will yield you slim to no positive results.

3. Anyone who needs to ask for themselves

I could list the universe here and still have room to add more people! Every day we find ourselves in the position of needing to ask for something. I have seen the most seasoned fundraisers forget all their skills in asking people for money when it comes down to asking for something for themselves, like a raise, promotion, new job title, new office, or a relocation. In nonprofit board meetings I have seen brilliant minds shut down and not offer their expertise or years of experience because they think nonprofit and for-profit skills are different. Many patients do not know how to ask their doctors for medical advice. Many small business owners do not know how to ask for a loan. Many creative artists do not know how to ask friends, relatives, colleagues, or new contacts to invest in their creative venture. As with businesses learning from nonprofits how to ask, anyone who needs to ask for themselves should also learn the right way to ask . . . and it is all here in this book.

How the Book Is Organized

As stated above, there is a real method, organization, and key steps to take before, during, and after the Ask. Each chapter is your stepping stone to the next level so I highly recommend that you read this book from start to finish. That said, it is jam-packed with sample dialogs you can use and adapt to your own situation. The dialogs are there to serve as examples you can practice with and go over and over at a later time, but I still highly recommend you read the book as you would the first section of a newspaper—front to back. Then the logic of the Ask and the follow-up to the Ask will make much more sense. More importantly you will find that it is not as time-consuming to make an Ask if you see it in this progression, rather than jumping in between the parts.

The book is divided into two parts. Part I is all the preparation you need to do prior to the Ask. Part II includes sample dialogs in asking for a nonprofit, a creative or business venture, and for yourself. It also covers how to handle responses to your Ask, the all-important "follow-through" with each Ask, and what to do when you receive a "no" or a "yes" to your Ask.

Throughout this book is a golden thread I have called "10 Things to Know About Any Ask" as well as exercises to do; each chapter has one of each. There is a lot of information and practical advice provided in these two features.

The book begins in Chapter 1 with a very important question: "What does money mean to you and why do you hesitate to ask?" Before anyone can ask for money they should know what money means to them. It can range from what you have to what you do not have, what you want, and what you cannot afford. I have found that people who can come to grips with answering this question and feeling comfortable with it make very good askers. As important as knowing your own views on money, you need to know the views of the person you want to ask. This chapter will provide some suggested ways you can get that answer by using open-ended, non-threatening questions. Perhaps the most popular reason why people fear, hesitate, and resist asking for money is that they do not want to feel rejected and a whole host of other negative factors. This chapter walks the reader through ways to overcome those fears.

Next, Chapter 2 details the importance of having a plan. Before you ask you have to have a well-defined case statement if asking for a charitable gift, or business plan if asking for a creative or business venture. Now more than ever people want all the details about what you are asking them to support. If you are shaky on the facts or future of your organization or even shaky about why you think you deserve what you are asking for yourself, the person you asked will not feel very confident and will likely give you a "no" to your Ask. This chapter will demonstrate all the essential elements to any Ask—emphasizing the importance of scripting out the Ask, sticking to the Ask time frame, making the transitional phase from small talk to the Ask, making the Ask, then staying silent. It will conclude with a three-step method on how anyone can be prepared for any Ask.

One of the hardest questions to answer is: when is the right time to ask? Chapter 3 will first explore how you can find the right people to ask and then conduct some research to ensure that you are prioritizing your pool of people to ask so that you are working with the best people first. It will also reveal my Readiness Formula that one can use when gauging when to ask. This formula has helped me throughout the years and can be a good litmus test for knowing *when* to ask.

Once we know who to ask and when to ask, the next issues to be resolved are who should make the Ask and what is the best setting for the Ask, which are covered in Chapter 4. In many instances you will be doing the Ask but if you work for a larger organization or any organization that has a president, board, volunteers, and other supporters, the question of who should ask becomes more compli-cated. The first rule is that anyone who asks must know the person being asked well and should have been part of the cultivation process. The second rule is that the larger the Ask, the more someone in a leadership role or someone who made a comparable investment *and who knows the person being asked* should be part of the Ask. This chapter explains these two concepts as well as the importance of one's appearance and body language during the Ask.

Chapter 5 is filled with sample dialogs you can use and adapt for your own purposes. This chapter explores asking for an increase in the annual fund and an increased gift to the endowment. It also shows how to ask for a large capital campaign gift and a larger gift from a board member. Each line of the sample dialogs is studied for ways to improve by using different words, positioning the topics in a certain order, and sticking to the script.

Chapter 6 applies everything in asking for a charitable gift to asking for yourself. So many of us separate our professional lives from our personal lives that we forget to use the skills and knowledge we have when asking for things for ourselves such as a job, a new job title, a raise, or money for a creative project or business venture. Once you read through this chapter I think you will be convinced that with all the preparation work in the previous chapters, these very important "everyday living" Asks will go much smoother and you will feel much more confident in your word selection and your delivery of your Ask.

Doing the Ask may be the most nerve-wracking part but waiting to hear the response to the Ask is the second most nerve-wracking part. Chapter 7 will prepare you to anticipate any response you may receive and will provide suggestions for addressing those responses. Only through preparation and anticipation of the person's response can any asker feel fully confident about answering the response. This chapter also suggests ways to best prepare for the person's response so that the conversation remains upbeat, the dialog flows smoothly, and there are few surprises or unanticipated responses. The responses and suggestions in Chapter 7 apply to any Ask.

Chapter 8 is perhaps one of the most important chapters in the book. As you will see in this book, your Ask and the activities leading up to the Ask account for 25 percent of your time; the follow-up is 75 percent. Why so much time? Because the most common response to your Ask will be "I'll have to think about it." "Thinking about it" can take weeks, months, and sometimes years! This is why you need the tools set forth in this chapter to give you a variety of ways with a variety of people to follow up with each Ask so that it does not get monotonous or boring. There is a system, a timeline, and some solid steps you can take after each Ask that will ensure you receive the answer to your Ask within a reasonable time.

Chapter 9 I call my bipolar chapter because it addresses when the answer is "no" and when the answer is "yes." Naturally, everyone wants to hear a "yes" but you will receive "no's" along the way. This chapter addresses first the more unpleasant response, the "no." But I think you will be surprised and less deflated when you see how this chapter illustrates how "*no now does not mean no later.*" With the right next steps you can pave your way to return at a later time and revisit your Ask. On a much more pleasant note, when the answer is "yes" it is a time to feel really good about yourself, your organization, and the people who will benefit from your hard and persistent work. However, there is more work to be done after that wonderful, positive answer, which we call "stewardship." If you follow the stewardship techniques that this chapter outlines, there will be a very strong probability that the person or persons who gave you a "yes" will want to do more for you and your organization or business and you will have a very loyal giver and investor.

Chapter 10 pulls it all together, providing the highlights to each chapter. It also recounts the "10 Things to Know About Any Ask" and gives the last and final exercise to do.

As an added bonus for the readers you will find a nice selection of resources and references online at www.josseybass.com/go/laurafredricks. The resources include sample case statements and business plans as well as references of books and online sites you can use to create your own case statement or business plan. Resources also include fundraising software, prospect research, and wealth screening companies that you may wish to use for your organization's fundraising plan. Lastly, the online references provide books, articles, and Web sites that I used as research for some of the content and concepts in this book.

It is my hope, my dream, and my desire that after you read this book you will see how asking is a logical and organized process, with a timeline and measurable steps to take. More importantly, I hope that you experience a sense of self-confidence, a willingness to empower others who work with or around you to make the Asks for what you need and deserve!

The

ASK

What Do I Need to Know
Before I Ask?

1

What Money Means to You and Why Ask?

P ERHAPS THE MOST IMPORTANT PART ABOUT asking for money is understanding *your views on money*. Note that I said your views, not how the person you are asking for money feels about money. So often we skip this very important step and dive right into identifying and learning as much as we can about the person or people we want to ask for money that we forget about getting in touch with our own feelings about money.

In this chapter I will go through the important exercise of exploring what money means to the asker because it is often the deciding factor between those who can ask easily and those who find it extremely difficult to ask. This is a very important psychological exercise that anyone asking for money needs to experience. It is essential that we explore our own values of what money means to us, and as importantly, why we feel we deserve to get what we ask for. This feeds directly into why many people hesitate and fear to make an Ask. This chapter will detail the most obvious reason why people hesitate and fear to make an Ask and will provide some creative solutions to overcome those negative factors that prevent an Ask.

What Does Money Mean to You?

The topic of money is almost certain to open a floodgate, releasing emotionally charged memories for many of us. Just say the word "money" and a series of visual images come to mind, ranging from childhood memories of the choices that had to be made within the family, to the current time and how one lives. I always open my training sessions with the question "What does money mean to you?" The surprised looks on many people's faces say to me "Why does it matter?" It matters because if you have a positive attitude and outlook about money, then you know the positive transformational power it can bring to deserving individuals and causes, and it makes the Ask go smoothly. If money is viewed in negative terms, it becomes much more difficult during the Ask because these negative feelings can sabotage an Ask or make it extremely uncomfortable and unnatural when asking for money.

Here are some of the responses I received when asking people who want to learn how to ask others for money what money means to them:

Power	Selection	Responsibility
Freedom	Control	Giving
Choices	Independence	Love
Change	Education	Peace of mind
Opportunity	Security	

These are all very emotionally laden terms, and in preparing to ask for money, they do surface in the mind of the asker. I do not mean to suggest that if you grew up in a wealthy and comfortable household and money was never a problem, asking for money will be an easy task. This is not an issue of whether you grew up or currently possess an abundance, moderation, or lack of money. However, it is important to think about what money means to you right now.

Money can mean the following:

- It can define your stature in life.
- It can determine your success.
- It can be why you need to work and why you work where you do.

- It can determine when and if you can retire.
- It can set the parameters of what you can give to your loved ones now or in the future.
- It can make you reflect on whether you made the right choices in life.
- It can govern how much you can borrow.
- It can govern how much you will inherit.
- It can determine what and how much you can buy.
- It can govern what you do in your free time.
- It can determine where and how you live.
- It can be a factor in your selection of health care coverage.
- It can narrow, widen, or obliterate your vacation plans.
- It can play a positive or negative role in your relations with friends, colleagues, and business partners.
- It can influence other personal relationships.
- It can motivate you to be like others or to have similar things and similar lifestyles.
- It can govern how much you save.
- It can govern how much you can invest.
- It can govern how much you need to take out of your savings and investments to live.
- It can be a positive motivational factor in your life.
- It can determine how much you can give to charity.
- It can be a most stressful topic of conversation.

In short, money affects every aspect of your life, which is why it is so important to come to terms with how you feel about money and how it may influence your comfort level in asking for money.

On that note here is the first exercise:

Exercise #1: Write your own list of what money means to you and whether those feelings would help or hinder your ability to ask for money.

Another very important issue to explore for any asker is "What is your first memory of when you knew it was important to give back and help those people or organizations in need?" I like to ask this question because everyone has a unique story to share about the first time they gave money or raised money. All too often fundraisers do not share enough about themselves personally with donors or those who have the capacity to support a cause or a business venture, and these stories tell a great deal about the character, integrity, and warmth fundraisers have regarding their professions. Since I asked you about your first memory, I shall share mine.

I was in sixth grade, at St. Matthews, Ridgefield, New Jersey, in Sister Mary Rita's class. As with any Catholic grammar school, we sat miserably in alphabetical order (for six years Michael Fick sat in front of me and Carol Grinner sat in back of me!). Sister Mary Rita told us that, tragically, a church had burned down in Newark, luckily no one was hurt, and that we were to do "all that we can" to help raise money to help rebuild the church. Welcome to your first capital campaign, Laura. Sister told us that the eighth grade already raised $62. This was sounding more and more like a challenge grant to me now. The person who raised the most money would receive something that was blessed by the Pope and it would have gold. Now to a sixth grader, if it was blessed by the Pope, this would surely be our "ticket to heaven," and if it had gold in it, then it must be as big and blinding as the largest crucifix possible.

I had the bright idea of walking dogs to raise money. In sixth grade, I was all of four feet, two inches. I probably should have quit while I was ahead. I put a notice up in our local grocery store called the Co-op that said "will walk your dog for 25 cents" with my telephone number. I think I am really dating myself now. A short while later I received a telephone call from a distant neighbor who told me to come right away. I jumped on my green Sting-Ray bicycle with a leopard-skin banana seat (I thought I was very cool back then) and went to his home. I put the bicycle down and the neighbor opened the door. The only thing separating me from death was a screen door because there stood not one, but three Doberman pinschers, much larger than me and quite eager to go outside. I negotiated with him that it would be 25 cents per dog, and knew from that minute on I would be a very good attorney and sharp businesswoman some day.

After a few weeks of this dog-walking activity, I went to school with tons of quarters from my afterschool job of dog walking. Sister Mary Rita called us up one by one and of course counted what each of us had raised. You guessed it, I had won the prize. It was a pink plaque, with a postage-size "gold" inlay of Jesus. I sincerely hope it was blessed by the Pope at that time because I still have the prize and I am still very much counting on it to be my "ticket to heaven." Many years later, here I am writing about how to ask for money. I firmly believe it all began way back then raising money for that church that burned down and all of us at St. Matthews and beyond who helped to rebuild the church and the community.

I share this story with you because each of you has one just like it. First and foremost, these stories are classic, touching, engaging, and it should fill you with confidence that you have wanted to help those in need for a very long time. Second, when and if appropriate, do share your story with those people that you are cultivating and asking for support. The more you share of yourself, the closer they are connected to you and the faster trust and a lasting personal relationship will be formed. Third, it makes the fundraising process so much more enjoyable. Why should you know everything about the people who may support you, your cause, or your business if they do not know your values, your dedication, your commitment, and your inspiration to raise money.

---

10 Things to Know About Any Ask—#1

Know your views on money and the importance of raising money before you ask for money.

WHY DO YOU HESITATE TO ASK?

It is extremely common and in some instances very easy to put off the Ask but it is very important to understand why people fear or hesitate to make the Ask. Exhibit 1.1 is a list of the common issues that can get in the way of the Ask. It is by no means exhaustive, but it does reflect the major reasons why people hesitate to ask.

EXHIBIT 1.1. *Reasons Why People Hesitate to Ask.*

1. I don't know the person's views on money.
2. I am not sure the person has that kind of money to give.
3. I don't know if giving money is a positive or negative factor.
4. Prospect research shows that the person has the assets to give, but why should he give his hard-earned, invested, or inherited money to our organization?
5. I know the person supports other causes; why would she support ours?
6. There are numerous groups that do similar work, so why should he support us?
7. So many people recently have supported disaster relief efforts; what makes us think they will support us in the same way?
8. What if the person feels insulted that we asked for money?
9. What if I ask the person for too much or too little?
10. If I ask her for money, she is going to ask me for money.
11. How can I possibly ask a colleague, friend, or relative for money?
12. What if she says no and never speaks to me again?
13. I just know the person is going to ask me something I don't know. Shouldn't the organization president or CEO be doing this?
14. Why can't I ask him for money in writing instead of meeting him in person?
15. In this economy, isn't it insensitive to ask for money when many people have lost major investments and the stock market has been in a downward swing?
16. I have an insurmountable fundraising goal that is highly unlikely to be met this year so why not do these Asks next year when we have a better chance of making our goal?
17. Won't I lose the person's annual fund gift if I ask for a larger, major planned or campaign gift?

Looking over this list in Exhibit 1.1, you will notice that some common themes pop up. The first theme is fear of not knowing the person you are asking for money well enough before making the Ask. The second is learning what makes one's organization or cause so special that people would elect to support it over other groups. The third is understanding why people would part with their money and having the confidence in making the Ask. The fourth is letting external forces and perceived internal problems postpone the Ask for a future time.

Identifying the most common fears and hesitations, as we have just done, is the first hurdle. Now we need to explore what we can do about them. The following are concrete solutions and exercises you can use to "get beyond" the psychological barriers that can make any asker worry himself or herself out of making the Ask.

Know the Person You Are Asking Before You Make the Ask

Essential to your success is knowing as much as you can about the person before making the Ask. Not knowing how the person was raised and the role that money played in that person's upbringing can make anyone hesitate to ask for money. People's views on money begin at home. How they were raised and the era in which they were raised can be the most important factors influencing their philanthropic giving. People who grew up during World Wars I and II or who lived through the stock market crash of 1929 often have "cautious spending habits" and hence a need to save (Nichols 2001, 43). Even though they may give to a charity, their priority is to save money so that everyone can be taken care of if something happens. People who are extremely religious are likely to tell you that they have always been taught to "give back" and "to help others in need." To them, giving is natural, it is expected, and they want to help others in any way they can. As long as they have the means to do so, they are more than willing to lend a hand to those less fortunate. If someone's parents, extended family members, mentors, colleagues, peers, or friends have supported a charity or several charities, there is a strong likelihood that this tradition will have been passed along, shared, and encouraged.

Conversely, people who have experienced major investments and economic losses such as the economic downturn that started in the fall of 2008, technology stocks and the dotcom fall of 2000 and 2001, or loss of a job at any time are likely to tell you that they need lots of time to recoup losses before considering giving money to a worthy cause or project. Such reasons illustrate that understanding how and when a person was raised can give you a greater insight into his views on money. This chapter opened with examining the asker's views on money; now it is time to learn about views of the person that you want to approach.

You find out people's views on money and how they were raised during the cultivation stages. Cultivation is everything you do up to the Ask (see Exhibit 1.2). It is the series of meetings, events, conversations, and exchanges of correspondence you have with the people you will eventually ask for money. This is the time when you really get to know these people, and in turn they build a long and lasting trust with you and with the organization's leaders and volunteers, or the business' executives and staff. Cultivation is essential before any Ask. While you are sharing information with the people you want to ask for money about your organization and business, its mission, goals, plan, leaders, finances, volunteers, and beneficiaries, you also have the golden opportunity to see, hear, and witness their lifestyle choices. You will know, for example, why they feel they are crusaders for controversial causes; why they sent their daughter or son to a certain school; where and when they vacation; how important religion is to them and their family; why they chose to have or not to have a family; why or why not it is important to volunteer for military duty; how they selected their career path; the importance and value of their cars, homes, second homes, and boats they have selected; how and why they volunteer; which charities they support; and why supporting your creative idea fulfills a dream for them. These things unfold naturally over time if you and others from your organization are passionate and diligent in building relationships with potential funders.

EXHIBIT 1.2. *20 Cultivation Techniques.*

1. Calling the people you want to meet.
2. Meeting with these people at their homes, offices, or a restaurant.
3. Corresponding with them and sending e-mails if you have received approval.

4. Having the people meet the leaders of the organization, board, committee members, administrative officials, staff, and beneficiaries.

5. Giving prospects a tour of the group's facility.

6. Sending the people personal messages attached to the direct mail they receive from your group.

7. Sending the people holiday, birthday, congratulatory, sympathy, and anniversary cards.

8. Asking these people for advice on a particular subject that is important to your group.

9. Having beneficiaries call, write, or visit the people on a frequent basis.

10. *Inviting people to a small gathering of supporters and potential supporters so that they can learn firsthand the magic of your organization and the need for support now.*

11. Asking these people to host a reception, breakfast, lunch, or dinner gathering of select donors and prospects to promote the successes of the group or to inform donors and prospects about the progress of a project or program.

12. Asking people to volunteer for a special event committee, a standing committee, or advisory board.

13. Inquiring whether these people have contacts, colleagues, or friends who would be interested in finding out more about your group or project.

14. Drawing on peoples' writing or communication talents and asking them to write an article for your group's newsletter or magazine.

15. Sending these people newspaper and magazine articles on their interests, such as sports, theater, music, shopping, and literature.

16. Taking the people out for their birthdays or to celebrate some other special event.

17. Joining the people at a concert, play, race, game, hike, or walk when they extend an invitation to do so.

18. Featuring these people on your Web site or group's internal publications (with their permission).

(*Continued*)

(Continued)

19. Inviting the people to give a speech, lecture, or workshop on their area of expertise to the group's beneficiaries, other potential supporters, administrators, or fundraising staff.

20. Having the leaders of the group periodically call, write personal notes, or e-mail people after they have met, just to keep the people informed about the group.

Notice I emphasized number 10. I believe by far this is the greatest, most effective and efficient way to cultivate people to ask for money because it makes them feel special, selective, an insider, and very close to the top leaders and supporters of the organization. If you have a strong, likeable, and charismatic leader for your organization, I strongly suggest that you have her or him host a series of these small, intimate gatherings and follow through with each person as set forth in Chapter 8. This by no means suggests that the other 19 cultivation techniques in Exhibit 1.2 are not important and effective. It is just in my experience, particularly with groups with limited resources, that this is the best cultivation technique.

The easiest way to find out someone's views on money is to ask *open-ended questions* during cultivation such as the following:

"Dan, of all the charities you could support, why do you support us?"

"Kyra, how did you first find out about us and what are you most interested in about our organization?"

I sometimes think that we do what I call "fill in the blank" fundraising, that is, we *assume* we know why someone would want to support the organization or business venture. That can be a dangerous path because when you assume you know why the person may be interested in your organization it starts to become a self-fulfilling prophecy and you can waste precious time and resources cultivating a person towards a particular project, program, or idea when in fact their interests and motivation can be completely different from what you had in mind. Take the time to ask these simple open-ended questions and listen carefully, with full eye-contact, to what the person says. Then and only then will you have the accurate information you need to cultivate the person in the direction of their interest, and you will be that much closer to making the right Ask.

Every Organization Has Its Own Charm

There are over 1.9 million registered charities in the United States (Independent Sector, Nov 7, 2008) and over 78,000 registered charities in Canada (Charity.com, 2008). All these groups are raising money for worthy causes—preserving wildlife, assisting people with handicaps, increasing literacy, reducing homelessness, improving child care, supporting international causes, funding the performing arts, improving education, making health care accessible, promoting research, and defending the environment, to name only a few.

With so many groups to support, fundraisers may wonder why someone would want to support one group over another. Generally, people who have this concern are brand-new to the field, just taking their first plunge into the fundraising pool. The answer to this question is that every organization has what I call its unique charm. It has something that separates it from all the other nonprofit groups and that draws in donors, volunteers, leaders, fundraisers, and administrators like a magnet. It could be that a certain group is taking care of the homeless in a select section of the city, that a theater conducts monthly workshops for children after school hours, or that the rivers are free from waste because a group successfully lobbied local government. Sometimes it is leadership that provides the magic, turning a group from nothing to a huge success. More often than not, it is the select group of beneficiaries the organization serves that makes the group unique and worthy of tremendous support.

Anyone who has concerns that the vast universe of causes might hinder any Ask should remember the following. As the asker, you, in your heart of hearts, must believe in the mission of your organization, be dedicated to speaking on your organization's behalf, be proactive and tenacious for the cause, and most of all, have faith in the organization, even when circumstances, whether within or outside your control, may be challenging. Your commitment to the group must be clearly demonstrated in every conversation and interaction you have with the person you are going to ask for money. If you believe in your group and the person has an initial inclination or strong desire to learn more about that group, then you are halfway there. In time your positive energy will convince the person being asked that, yes, your group is unique, that its charm is different from all the rest, and best of all, that giving, early and often, to this sensational organization is an opportunity not to be missed.

In businesses, the uniqueness comes from the idea, concept, and vision of what you do that no one else thought of and no one else is doing. Even if you want to launch a new play, get a patent on the best invention, or develop software that will make a company highly competitive, you should be able to distinguish yourself from all the rest. The key is to come up with three ways you have something that no one else has, or you can deliver something no one else can, or you do it better, with more personal care and customer satisfaction than the competition. You will hear me reiterate this theme over and over in this book—that for-profit organizations and nonprofits share a commonality to be unique, to provide "customer-" and "donor-" friendly service and attention, which all translates into long-lasting relationships and financial support.

People Like to Give Money

As important as it is to know how and when a person was raised, his or her views on money, and why your organization is so important to him or her, it is also important to know why someone would part with hard-earned money. Exhibit 1.3 lists several main reasons that people give.

EXHIBIT 1.3. *Reasons Why People Give.*

1. Belief that giving is the greatest gift of all.
2. Belief that all the money in the world cannot buy happiness.
3. Belief that there will always be someone less fortunate who needs money.
4. Belief that charity begins at home.
5. Belief that it is the right thing to do.
6. Decision that accumulated assets have made it possible to give.

7. Desire to emulate others who give.

8. Experience of a life-transforming event, such as an accident, near-death experience, or winning the lottery.

9. Instinct that this will be a wise investment.

10. Desire to reduce taxes.

11. Pressure from a friend, peer, or colleague to support a cause that is important to that person.

12. Need to be recognized.

In my experience, most people who give when asked in person do so almost instinctively. It is part of who they are and how they live. They want to make their world a better place for generations to come. People also give because they have a strong interest in sharing. Sharing feels good and makes us feel less selfish and self-focused. How people have been raised governs not only their views on money but whether and when they feel a need to help those less fortunate. Many people I have had the pleasure of working with have always given something, beginning early in life with their religious institutions and then focusing on a handful of groups that mirror their beliefs. Others began giving as a result of a persuasive direct-mail campaign. Yet others have witnessed grave injustice, poverty, or illness that has motivated them to take action.

People give because they reach a point in their lives where they have the assets to give back and it will not impede their lifestyle. Their cushion of comfort makes it possible to support a nonprofit group or groups in a significant way. They saved and planned, and it just took the right time to trigger the gift. Sometimes a gift is spurred by an unexpected windfall, such as winning the lottery, getting a case settlement, or making a superior investment. This over-the-top increase in their personal wealth makes it possible for them to give effortlessly. Giving can also be triggered by a sudden, life-transforming experience, either for the person himself or herself or for a loved one. Anyone who has fundraised for a hospital in particular knows the truth of this statement. Many grateful patients give back because a special doctor, nurse, or ambulance team saved their lives or the life of a loved one.

Fundraisers also cannot rule out emulation theory: some people give because they want to be like someone else or, possibly, want to be perceived as having the assets and lifestyle of a prominent person. These folks will give at a certain level so they can be thought to be as prestigious or charitable as a noted and well-respected peer. This elevates their status in the community, particularly when the gift includes a large naming opportunity. This motivation makes people happy to give because it puts them on an even playing field with some prestigious people. May you have many of these people to ask!

Many times when we ask people for money we say the money will be "an investment" so that the organization can have the present and future means to be in existence; or in the business setting, someone believes that with this financial backing a play can be launched, a new patent can be the greatest new invention, or a new company can be formed that has its own unique place in the industry. These are all attractive, appealing, and highly desirable reasons why people want to "invest," not "part" with, their money.

Although we would all like to think that people support nonprofit causes entirely out of the kindness of their hearts, it would be very naïve to think that other motivations do not come into play. Reducing income and estate, gift, and capital gains taxes are real motivators for some donors. I personally do not think this is a bad thing; in fact, it is a blessing. If some donors could not reduce these taxes, then they would not make charitable gifts at all. It is our job as askers to fulfill their personal and philanthropic goals and desires. Tax breaks for giving to charitable organizations can make it possible for many donors to release precious financial assets to support causes that save children's lives, improve the quality of life for the elderly, or preserve acres of natural resources.

I have also known donors who have been disappointed with themselves for failing to recognize or act on issues that affected their families. Issues such as smoking, drug and alcohol addiction, and mental illness can traumatize any family. These people have thought long and hard about what they can do beyond helping their immediate family, and they usually support prevention programs aimed at the diseases or other problems that have affected them or a loved one. It is important to know the motivation of the people you are asking for money because that will tell you why they want to give and what the act of giving will mean to them.

The need to be recognized can also drive a person to give. Now, at first glance this may appear to be another "negative" reason for giving. We may feel that people should give because they want to help others and they are able to do so. There are people, however, who are proud of what they have accomplished and have the assets to give. They may want to set an example for others like themselves so that these others will also give. This is not a bad reason to give; it is a celebratory reason to give. These donors can set the tone and pave the way for others to give. Most of them want to take on leadership gift volunteer roles. If you have these folks, clone them, and you'll never have a fundraising worry again.

All these reasons why people will give to your group are fabulous motivations. Tuck them in the back of your mind as you are preparing to ask for money. I often tell people to memorize this line:

When you are asking for money, you are not asking someone to give something up, you are giving them the opportunity to invest in your organization and to feel good.

Think of it as offering the person the greatest opportunity to share—because sharing isn't giving anything away, it's spreading it so more people can enjoy it. Think of asking for money as asking for an "investment," because investments usually last for years, and those investments will make it possible for the nonprofit group or business venture to thrive and prosper for many years to come.

Focus on Positive Results, Not Negative Forces That Perceivably Get in the Way

This last category of reasons why people hesitate to ask for money is what I call "the runaway train ideas" that often occur when our minds start to drift and focus on all the universal reasons why it would be better to ask at a later time. Let us take these ideas one by one and turn them into positive, mission-focused affirmations.

"Jack is so hard to reach these days, why don't we just send our proposal in the mail and I'm sure he will get back to us."

People give to people; they do not give to paper. You will have a markedly higher chance of getting money when the Ask is done in person rather than on paper. People cannot see or hear your passion for the cause in a piece of paper. But they may sense from you personally that, yes, this is the right thing to do and it should be done now. A written proposal for an individual is fine if used during an Ask for illustration purposes or as a follow-up to the Ask; it cannot substitute for the initial Ask. This is not the time to hide behind paper. It is the time to believe in your cause and to ask in person.

The same can be said about doing the Ask over the telephone, or in an e-mail or text message. These distance media do not allow the personal exchange needed for the Ask. When you use them, the Ask is one step removed from what it should be, an in-person event. They diminish the quality time you need with the person you are asking for money, and they can make your Ask appear unimportant and not a priority.

There are exceptions, certainly, when it may be impossible or highly inconvenient for you to ask in person. For instance, you may be working with a person and then he moves abroad or so far out of your area that you cannot see him in person to do the Ask. In that case it is preferable to call him/her, specifically state that you regret not being able to do this in person, and ask for the investment. The Ask can then be followed up with further telephone calls, correspondence, or e-mails, but telephone, e-mail, and text message Asks should be avoided at all other times. The bottom line is that except in unusual circumstances, always ask individuals in person for money.

> *"In these troubled economic times, with unemployment soaring and the stock markets at an all-time low, it would be extremely inconsiderate to ask anyone for money."*

We will explore asking for money in economically depressed times in depth later in Chapter 3. For now it is important to know that one cannot and should not wait until the economy gets better to meet with people, hear their stories on how they are doing in this type of economic environment, and speak with them in a sensitive and convincing manner about the importance of why you and your organization are worthy of their support now or in the near future. If someone has been supporting your organization, or you have been cultivating them to give at this time, why in heaven's name would you drop this person and lose all this ground you have gained up until now? Indeed, in very tough economic times there is even more reason to reach out and re-engage with key funders (*Changing Our World,* October 8, 2008). It is also an ideal time to call upon the leadership of the organization to meet with funders and donors one-on-one to stress the fact that your organization needs money to provide critical services now, more than ever (Board Source, November/December 2008).

I often ask the question, "When have we ever fundraised when it was easy?" Even in economically stressed times, our mission, our cause, our constituency, our ideas, our goals and dreams still exist and people do want to know the reasons why it is important for them to start giving or to continue giving in very hard times. Done with sensitivity, Asks should not be postponed during economically challenging times, and this should not be a reason to prevent an Ask if indeed it was the right time for the person to be asked.

> *"We are so far behind in reaching our fundraising goal this year, why don't we just wait until the start of the new year to make these asks?"*

It is a sad but true fact that some organizations are more stringent with reaching fundraising goals than others. It is also equally true that some fundraisers gauge their Asks based on making or not making fundraising goals or reaching a number of Asks each month. I am one of the strongest advocates of asking when the timing is right, as you shall see in Chapter 3, but you must ask when the person is ready to be asked not to fulfill a quota of the number of Asks or to reach a fundraising goal. In my former role overseeing all fundraising activity for two major universities, I always set the goal for front-line fundraisers to see 12 to 15 people in person each month and make three Asks a month. That said, it was more important to me that the fundraising staff showed activity towards these goals, and not that they forced an Ask, or didn't make any Asks because they fell way behind on their goals.

Fundraising goals are goals that hopefully can be reached. They should not command when an Ask is made nor should they be used as an excuse not to carry out on a consistent and well-thought-out fundraising plan, the identification, cultivation, and asking period for any person.

> *"Our annual fund needs to increase to keep up with ever-increasing overhead costs, so maybe we should wait to ask for the larger gift because most assuredly we will lose that person's annual gift."*

I wish I had a quarter for every time a person says that—I would be a very rich lady! Nothing could be further from the truth than thinking that when you ask for a larger gift you are taking away the "unrestricted" annual or direct mail amount. The way to ensure that this never happens is simply to discuss with the person the reasons why it is so important to continue supporting the annual fund and that now they have a wonderful opportunity to continue that generosity by making a gift in addition to their fabulous and thoughtful annual gift. The conversation can go something like this:

> "Kurt, you have been such a wonderful and generous supporter over the past *x* years and your continued support to the annual fund will make it possible for us to continue serving our children with physically challenging disabilities. We are here today to ask you to continue that support and to discuss with you a wonderful opportunity to invest with us to make an even greater impact with these very deserving children. Let us explain."

It could not be any simpler or clearer what you are offering. First and foremost, the person's continued support for the annual fund has to be spelled out. Second, state how a larger gift that will either help more children or will give significant funding for a particular project or program requires a higher level of support. The key is to acknowledge the importance of continuing the annual gift and now that will be coupled with the opportunity to give over and above the yearly gift. In my experience, many people enjoy knowing the benefits and importance of the yearly gift, and if it is explained to them that that support together with the new gift opportunity is so crucial to the existence and growth of the organization, then there should be no worries that the annual fund will ever suffer when making a larger Ask.

CONCLUSION

Asking for money has two emotional components. First, you must know your views on money and then you must know the views of the person you are asking. There are so many emotional factors surrounding the topic of money that can either make it very easy for you to ask, or can get in the way of your asking for money. Once you go through the reasons why you may hesitate and resist to ask and re-affirm that you and your cause, or you and your business, are worthy of support, then you are ready to learn the next steps to crafting the best Ask for each and every person. The more you practice these skills for overcoming fear and hesitation about making the Ask, the easier and more fluid your Ask will be. It is a thrilling moment, and, yes, a bit of a rush when the person looks you in the eye and says, "This sounds pretty good, tell me more." Just remember that there is just as much joy, fun, and reward in asking as there is in receiving.

LOOKING AHEAD

In the next chapter we will explore all the important factors of having a well-thought-out plan of all the details surrounding the Ask. Too many times, people have some of the details in their head but without a plan, script, or roadmap to the Ask, the purpose of the Ask gets lost, misunderstood, or not delivered with conviction or passion and will result in less or no money. In addition to illustrating the importance of having a detailed budget for large projects and business ventures, the next chapter will lay out a three-step method that will make any Ask a great Ask.

Do You Have a Well-Thought-Out Plan of What You Want?

THIS CHAPTER FOCUSES ON ALL THE preparation that needs to be done prior to the Ask. Preparation is everything when it comes time to asking for money. It is extremely important to have a solid plan, case for support, proposal, and detailed budget in certain circumstances for the project, program, or large gift you are seeking. Now more than ever, donors and investors want all the details of what you want them to support. They want a timeline; breakdown of costs; who will benefit from the gift; when the benefits will begin; the revenue projection; and, most importantly, they want to know that this project or program will be sustainable well into the future. No one wants to give money if they think they are the only ones investing in the project or that if no one else invests the gift idea or business venture will disappear. This chapter will illustrate the parallels between a nonprofit's case statement and a for-profit's business plan.

This chapter will detail all the essential elements to any Ask, with emphasis on making sure that each Ask is scripted. Scripts set forth the time frame for the Ask, who speaks and who listens during the Ask, and the four essential elements of any Ask: the warm-up, the actual

Ask, the prospect's comments and concerns, and the close and follow-up. Of key importance is making sure that the person doing the Ask knows how and when to use transitional phrases. Transitional phrases ensure that during the meeting for the Ask, too much time is not spent on "small talk" during the warm-up and that enough time is spent on the actual Ask and listening to the person's response to the Ask. Once these transitional phrases are used, the person doing the Ask can then ask for a specific amount for a specific purpose, and this chapter will provide a few examples of solid asks. It is important to not get caught up in fundraising language that can confuse people when asking for money, and this chapter will highlight the language that is most effective in an Ask.

Finally, this chapter will set forth a three-step method to use in preparation for any Ask. This method pulls in elements discussed in Chapter 1 of overcoming hesitation to ask for money and continues by converting these hesitations into powerful and passionate statements that highlight the importance of the Ask.

THE IMPORTANCE OF A WELL-THOUGHT-OUT PLAN

Many people new to the world of raising money do not realize that there is a great deal of preparation and planning that needs to be done before you can ask for money. I have heard many conversations of how people intend to ask for money that involve no planning or strategy such as the following:

- *"She has family wealth—I'm sure she'll give us money when we ask."*
- *"I want to produce an independent film and I have the telephone numbers for some of the top producers, so I'll call each of them and make my pitch."*
- *"I just read that this donor is giving money to Christian causes in our area so we should approach him right away."*
- *"I have a list of people I can just send an e-mail to and I'm sure that will result in some money for our project."*
- *"My board member, Hank, just had dinner with a wealthy female philanthropist who is recently widowed and has no*

children. Hank thinks we should contact her right away and ask for a large gift."

I am most certain that right now you could add a story or two that would be very similar to the conversations above. There is simply no preparation or thought given to these types of Asks, and they are nothing more than shortcuts attempts to ask for money that most assuredly will result in little or no money.

CASE STATEMENT FOR NONPROFITS

A well-thought-out plan detailing why your nonprofit organization or business venture needs money is the very first step in preparing to ask for money. For nonprofits, that translates into a case for support, the case statement. "A case statement or case for support is the core document sitting at the center of your fundraising strategy" (Ross and Segal 2009, 50). It tells people why your organization exists; why the organization is worthy of support; the difference the organization makes in the community; who or what will benefit; and how the donor will benefit (Irvin-Wells 2002, 16). Exhibit 2.1 details some of the important things a case statement can accomplish.

EXHIBIT 2.1. *Important Elements of a Case Statement.*

1. Justifies and explains the history of the organization.
2. Describes the mission and its uniqueness among similar organizations.
3. States objectives with quantifiable goals and timelines.
4. Identifies the beneficiaries and the quantity and quality of deliverable services it will provide.
5. Presents a community or global problem or need and describes how the organization plans to address the issue now and in the future.
6. Sets forth reasons why someone should support the organization and the benefits the donor will receive in return for support.

It is important for someone who may support your organization to know the history of your organization; who founded it; how it was founded; the year it was founded; where it was founded; if the organization is still on the original site or if it has moved or expanded; and the progress and growth of the organization as a whole to date. People love to learn about history, and oftentimes it is the history of the organization that draws the donor to the organization. Something resonates in the donor and connects them very closely with the nonprofit. If an organization skips educating each donor about its history, it runs the risk of not connecting the donor to the organization in a significant and powerful way.

The history of the organization naturally leads into the mission of the organization and defining why the organization is unique in its mission compared to other organizations. For instance, there are numerous nonprofits worldwide that support children's causes yet each one is very distinct; here are some examples:

- **Save the Children:** Save the Children is the leading independent organization creating real and lasting change for children in need in the United States and around the world. It is a member of the International Save the Children Alliance, comprising 28 national Save the Children organizations working in more than 110 countries to ensure the well-being of children. (http://www.savethechildren.org/about/mission)

- **Invest in Kids:** Invest in Kids aims to strengthen the parenting knowledge, skills, and confidence of all those who touch the lives of children from birth to age five. (http://www.investinkids.ca)

- **Boys and Girls Club of America:** The Boys and Girls Club's mission is the movement's reason for being: to enable all young people, especially those who need us most, to reach their full potential as productive, caring, responsible citizens. A Boys and Girls Club provides a safe place to learn and grow; ongoing relationships with caring, adult professionals; life-enhancing programs and character development experiences; hope and opportunity. (http://www.bgca.org/whoweare/mission.asp)

- **Children's Defense Fund:** The Children's Defense Fund (CDF) is a nonprofit child advocacy organization that has worked relentlessly for 35 years to ensure a level playing field for all children. The CDF champions policies and programs that lift children out of poverty; protect them from abuse and neglect; and ensure their access to health care, quality education, and a moral and spiritual foundation. Supported by foundation and corporate grants and individual donations, CDF advocates nationwide on behalf of children to ensure children are always a priority. The Children's Defense Fund's Leave No Child Behind[R] mission is to ensure every child a *Healthy Start*, a *Head Start*, a *Fair Start*, a *Safe Start*, and a *Moral Start* in life and successful passage to adulthood with the help of caring families and communities. (http://www. childrensdefense.org/site/PageServer?pagename=About_CDF)

The next part to the case statement details the nonprofit's objectives with goals and timelines. This can be achieved by asking three simple questions:

- What exactly does the nonprofit want to accomplish?
- How much does it need to raise to accomplish these goals?
- What is the time frame to raise the funds to accomplish the goals?

Note that the answers to these three questions will provide the framework for the case statement so that it will be crystal clear to anyone who wants to learn more about the plan for the nonprofit to exist and the goals it needs to achieve. The logical next set of information that flows from the goals and the timeline is defining who are the beneficiaries and what services will the beneficiaries receive from the nonprofit. The beneficiaries should be defined in the mission statement, but this part of the case statement expands that concept to include the amount of beneficiaries it is serving now, the amount it wants to serve in the future, and details the services it will provide for the beneficiaries now and in the future. For instance, a hospital that has 300 beds and wants to open a cancer center on the hospital campus may state:

"In addition to providing expert, quality care for each and every patient we currently serve in our in-patient and out-patient services, we intend

to open a state-of-the-art cancer center adjacent to our hospital so that our patients will receive exemplary cancer diagnosis and treatment services. Our oncology program rivals those of the nation's leading cancer centers, enabling patients to take advantage of our expert oncology services, and the latest medical technologies. We anticipate serving over x patients over the next several years."

The last two elements to the case statement are defining the local or global issues the nonprofit will address and why a person should support the particular organization. Defining the need is where many organizations fall short because it can take some time and research to quantify "need." For instance, if your organization provides shelter for the homeless, how many homeless people are in your community each year and why is this need being unmet? If it is due to a decrease or lack of government funding, then that needs to be stated in the case statement. If your organization provides meals for senior citizens and the need to serve more meals has dramatically increased due to the aging population living longer, then that has to be stated.

The more detailed the "need" is explained, the easier it is to make a passionate and persuasive Ask for support. Think about it: if someone gave you very detailed and specific statistics on an issue you cared about deeply, and provided you with facts that showed how this need would increase exponentially unless people like you supported the organization, wouldn't you give the Ask some serious consideration? The point is that preparation in the formulation of the case statement can make the difference between some funding and significant funding.

It is critical that anyone asking for money on behalf of the nonprofit can speak fluidly about the case statement. That includes the CEO, president, trustees, fundraisers, volunteers, and donors who wish to speak about their giving in hopes that it will attract others to give. When you think about it, why should someone support your organization if they do not have these essential background facts about the group? They should exist in a formal board-adopted document, and they should be memorized by anyone who asks for money for the organization.

If your organization is planning to launch a capital campaign, then a case statement is *not an option, it is an imperative.* The case statement for the capital campaign is an expansion of the basic case statement and details what the campaign will address when it reaches its campaign goal. For instance, a college planning for a capital campaign that wants to raise money to increase its endowment for student scholarships and to add a new theater would detail in its campaign case statement why students need more scholarships, how many students will prospectively receive the scholarships, why the college needs a new theater, and what the theater will offer students and the community. It is advisable that any organization detail the prior success it has had raising money. For instance, in this example, the college should state the amount it has raised in restricted and unrestricted money over the last five years, and the success and the amount raised in prior capital campaigns. That will give donors the confidence that the organization's fundraising programs are successful and worthy of new funding.

The References and Resources section online (www.josseybass .com/go/laurafredricks) contains examples and references on case statements.

BUSINESS PLAN FOR BUSINESSES

Nonprofits need a case statement for support. Businesses need a solid business plan so that the business stays on track and, where appropriate, attracts investors. The two are quite similar, which is logical because both seek people (investors) to monetarily support their mission, venture, or particular project or program. This section addresses people who want money to support a project or business venture that does not have a nonprofit 501(c)(3) status. Throughout this book I will be drawing the parallels in asking for money for a nonprofit and a business venture because of the similarities in making the Ask and because there is much nonprofits can learn from businesses, and businesses can learn from nonprofits. I also know that many fundraisers and people involved with nonprofits are businesspeople and creative expressionists who may need to know how to ask for money beyond the nonprofit arena. This section will address people who need money for their personal creative projects, such as making an independent film, writing a new play, backing for a concert or tour, as well beginning a start-up company or getting additional money for an existing business.

As with case statements for nonprofits, business ventures require a well-thought-out business plan. Exhibit 2.2 sets forth the critical elements that should be contained in a business plan.

EXHIBIT 2.2. *Elements of a Good Business Plan.*

1. History of the business or, for start-up companies, the vision for a new business.

2. How the company, product, or concept is distinguishable from the competition.

3. A business model that details the service it will provide or replace; goals for the business with projected revenues; staffing needs; facilities and equipment needed; and potential spinoff opportunities.

4. The need for the service or product and how the business will address the need now and in the future.

5. The target audience of who will benefit from the business venture.

6. Description of the type of investors who may be interested in backing the venture and levels of investment sought.

Like with nonprofits, the history of a company is so important to potential investors. People want to know who are "the founding fathers" of the company; whether it is a family-owned business; how many years it has been in existence; and how long certain employees have been working with the company. Name recognition and branding go a long way when approaching people to invest in the company because there is a sense of security that the company is solid and well managed, has a strong vision, and hopefully is conscientious about the importance of serving the community. People beginning a start-up company cannot benefit from name recognition or branding from a company not yet in existence, but the person starting the business may be well known, which is an immediate attraction for investors. Additionally, people may be attracted to invest in the "latest," "hottest," "most creative and innovative" idea, and they'll want to be among the first handful of investors to help discover and launch the new product.

For creative artists, it is very important that they share their history of past creative endeavors, such as where they have performed or produced, how many CDs they made and sold, who taught them their craft, and who are their past and current mentors. I have been approached by many people in the music and theater industry who want to know how to ask for money, yet they bury or hide their rich history or take for granted that people know or should know all about their accomplishments. The bottom line is to be careful not to skip sharing the history of your business or, for a start-up, what experiences led you to come up with this new concept.

Not knowing your competitors can destroy any business. It may take some research and time analyzing the vast universe of similar products or services but it is well worth the energy. The key is to leverage your company's unique assets and to differentiate your product or concept from all the rest. Again, do not assume that people will automatically perceive that what you are asking to support is so different from what already exists in the marketplace. State in your business plan who may be the obvious competitors and then detail what you do or are about to do that is so different and distinguishable. For instance, if you have a patent on a new design for door locks, your statement might look like the following:

> *"Our technology is a unique differentiator in the door lock product category. While the following companies may be principal competitors, our patented door lock design has the following competitive advantages:*
>
> - *Brand recognition*
> - *Design innovation*
> - *Low cost and high quality manufacturers*
> - *Proven track record for customer service*
>
> *We believe these attributes have monumental advantages over competitive offerings."*

Detailed budgets are a must for any business plan. Once you have defined the competition as we did above, then the service that the business venture intends to create or replace will become quite clear. Next, it is important to set business goals, and here is the fun and creative part. Use some of the following phrases to make your plan come alive:

- "To become the #1 source for career transition advice"
- "To form strategic alliances with leaders in the transportation industry"
- "To perform in all major cities in the United States, Canada and Europe"
- "To have this new play premiere off-Broadway, then be picked up for Broadway"

You are held back only by your enthusiasm and ability to think "big" here, so use your own words and voice to make your goals a reality.

The budget component should also list the potential or projected revenue in the first three years. The projected revenue is usually tied to the previously stated goal. For instance, in the example above, if the newly designed door locks patent projects that a three-year goal is to have 2 million household and industrial customers, then the revenue streams for each year must break down each year of the projected revenue. The budget should state the costs for any staff with salary levels that will be needed to launch or maintain the business as well as facility, manufacturing, and equipment needs with leasing and insurance costs. If the product or idea has the potential to penetrate additional markets or to expand in additional areas, then the budget should explain how and when that would occur.

As with nonprofits, businesses need to spell out the need for the product, service, or idea, which dovetails right into the types of customers that will be served. It is the equivalent to who are the beneficiaries in a nonprofit. Nothing speaks like numbers to make a case for the need for the product, so it is important to quantify the number of people, households, or industries that have benefited or can benefit from the product, service, or idea and then to use some market research to make projections of how many people or what percentage of companies and industries will benefit. Lastly, there should be a solid list of potential investors. This is where I have seen business plans all unravel. It is not wise to assume that once the history, need, business model, and list of potential customers are stated that one can take this business plan and "sell" it to immediate business contacts. A strategy needs to be in place for determining which groups of people or companies are your best prospects for investment. This is very similar to nonprofits that need to ask for major gifts. Nonprofits look at who has the greatest monetary potential *and* who has been educated, involved, cultivated, and therefore ready to be asked for a big gift. In business, a similar strategy should be implemented. We will explore this in detail in Chapter 3, but for now people and companies that have been loyal to you in the past, confident in you and your business team, and who *believe* and want to be part of the success of your product, your idea, your creative dream, are your best prospects for investors.

The References and Resources section online (www.josseybass. com/go/laurafredricks) contains examples of business plans and references on business plans.

---

10 Things to Know About Any Ask—#2

The Ask without a well-thought-out plan will result in no money.

THE SCRIPT FOR EACH ASK

Now that we have a well-thought-out plan for what it is we want to ask, the next step is to develop a script. A script is a road map that askers should use to rehearse the Ask so that they are well prepared to do it. Some people may resist the idea of using a script, claiming that it is too formal, they know the prospect well, and a script diminishes the personal closeness needed for the Ask. Remind these askers that the script is for rehearsal purposes and that when it comes time to do the actual Ask, the script will be in their heads; they are not reading from paper. Exhibit 2.3 outlines the essential components of the script.

Time Frame for the Ask

Everyone has to have a clear understanding of the amount of time needed for the Ask. If a time frame is not placed on the Ask, you run the risk of using your precious time for catching up and, in the worst case,

---

EXHIBIT 2.3. *Essential Components of the Script.*

1. Time frame for the Ask.
2. The warm-up.
3. The Ask.
4. The anticipated response.
5. The close and follow-up.
6. Who speaks and who listens during the Ask.

---

never getting to the Ask because your allotted time with the person has expired. I have been in situations doing a joint Ask when too much time is spent "catching up" on previous conversations with the person about to be asked and updating personal and professional lives. When it is almost time to leave, the Ask is blurted out. Let me tell you, this is not a pretty situation and diminishes the value and the importance of the Ask. When time is not apportioned properly for the Ask, it oftentimes leads the person being asked to give a fraction of the Ask amount, or worse, an "I'll think about it" response that takes ages to close.

As a rule I believe that the Ask should not take more than 25 minutes total. I divide the time as follows:

- The warm-up: five minutes
- The Ask: six minutes
- The person's response: ten minutes
- The close and follow-up: four minutes

If you have an hour with the prospect, terrific, but again, do not use the first half-hour for small talk. Stick with the time frame I have just outlined, and then, if you have time left over after all the points of the Ask are covered, go back to catching up with the person.

The Warm-Up

The warm-up, or pleasant conversation time, is needed to break the ice. You do not want to enter the person's home or office, shake hands while saying hello, and then blurt out the Ask. You need some time with the person to get back in touch. For instance, if the last time you met with the person he told you he and his wife were taking a cruise around the Mediterranean Sea, ask about the cruise. If the person's daughter just had a baby boy, ask how the family is doing and if he has any pictures of the grandson. Using your database, go back and review the person's file. This is where you get the information for your warm-up. Askers cannot possibly remember all the details of every person they are about to ask for money without this review, and they do need to know these details so they can easily weave them into the warm-up.

The most important point about the warm-up is that the person is reacquainted with the asker or asking team. It can and should be a bonding moment. Five minutes should be plenty of time to relax, smile, and share a story or two so that everyone is comfortable. This is exactly the right atmosphere in which to begin the Ask.

The Ask

The Ask has several essential components, as listed in Exhibit 2.4. It is important that each Ask be scripted because that is your insurance that each component of the Ask will be covered.

EXHIBIT 2.4. *Essential Components of the Ask.*

1. Making a compelling case for the organization and the need for support.

2. Using transitional statements that specifically reference the person's interest or prior support, or both.

3. Asking for a specific amount and for a specific purpose.

4. Detailing the benefits of the gift or the business venture.

5. Remaining silent.

THE COMPELLING CASE The compelling case is derived from the case statement or the business plan explained and illustrated previously in this chapter. Now you see the value and importance of having a well-thought-out plan. In this plan is the compelling case for why your cause or your business needs funding. It is a simple and succinct statement that focuses the person being asked for money on the purpose of the meeting, and it rekindles the person's interest in and dedication to your group. It also sets forth why the organization needs support now and at what level. If there is no urgency or no organizational goal that needs to be met and funded, what difference does it make whether the person gives now or years later? The answer is no difference, which is why the asker needs to emphasize the reasons why the group needs funding now.

Examples of Stating a Compelling Case: The following are some suggested statements for conveying a compelling case for your organization:

- "Rachel, our college was just ranked in the Top 10 Best Values in *Money* magazine. We feel the timing could not be better for us to launch a comprehensive campaign. Let me share with you some of the goals for the campaign."

- "Marissa, our women's clinic just received a substantial foundation grant that must be matched by private sources. We have such a loyal following, we are extremely confident we can meet this matching sum over the next three years."

- "Anthony, our young writers series attracted over 200 youths this summer. Although the conference was underwritten, we want to take this to the next level and hold conferences twice a year and give scholarship aid to deserving participants."

- "Lisa, our biomedical research institute just completed a five-year strategic plan. We had 20 experts from around the world help us draft this plan, which calls for raising over $15 million in public and private sources. Among our top priorities is to increase our endowment so that we can guarantee our critical research will last well into the future."

- "Steve, I think you feel as strongly as we do that our newly patented athletic foot measurement is a state-of-the art design that will accurately measure the length, width, and arch of any athlete's foot to suggest the best comfort when purchasing sneakers."

- "Tatiana, you have been attending my art exhibits for quite some time, and thank you for letting me know that you think the current exhibit should be part of a tour overseas. Your connections in the art world could really open some doors right now. Imagine how many art lovers abroad would really enjoy this exhibit as you and many others have."

When making the compelling case, the asker or asking team needs to be direct and to create a context in which the donor can find out how she fits into the just-described new plans for the organization.

TRANSITIONAL STATEMENTS Askers use transitional statements to focus on the person's key area or interest with the group. Such a statement is a natural handoff from a compelling case statement because it hones in on the specific areas that pertain to the person and the Ask. In the examples of compelling case statements given earlier, for example, the asker is positioned to explain to Rachel what the campaign will do for the college, what the areas of funding are, and how Rachel's interest in scholarships would fit squarely within the campaign goals. Marissa is in a position to hear the details of the foundation's matching grant and how her prospective gift to the women's clinic will help meet the match for that grant. Anthony can now be asked either to help support another conference or to contribute to the newly formed scholarship fund for the young writers series. Lisa is ready to hear an overview of the strategic plan; ideally, right then and there she will also be handed a copy to take home, and she will be ready to be asked to support the biomedical research endowment. Steve has the opportunity to learn about a brand new product and be one of the initial investors. Tatiana can be an influential partner that will take the art exhibit on tour. In other words, the asker has the person's attention, and it is time to transition to the person's participation. *The transitional statement is a precursor to the actual Ask.* Remember, you do not want to blurt out the request for money too quickly; the person may feel attacked and uncomfortable. You want to make a natural and smooth transition to the Ask.

Examples of Transitional Statements: Here are some examples of transitional statements that askers can use to focus the conversation with the person on the Ask:

- "Amy, you have been an exemplary donor, and your gifts have inspired so many others to support us. We cannot thank you enough. The last time we met, you expressed an interest in helping us acquire better vans to transport our disabled residents. We have an opportunity that matches your interest, and we would like to share it with you now."

- "Josh, having been a trustee for a number of years, you can appreciate and celebrate how far we have come over the past five years, but as you also know, there is much work left to do. We share your concern that there is not enough space in our facility to help the number of homeless we serve. We are coming to you first with our idea on how we can expand and meet these growing needs. Permit me to share the plan with you."

- "Leslie, your support for our mentoring program has put us on the map as the model for these community programs. We have the chance to take the program to a national level that is exciting and equally challenging. Let me take a few minutes to share with you what needs to be done to make that dream come true."

- "Scott, volunteers are our best publicists, and we would not be here today without your leadership and dedication. We are truly blessed to have you as such an important part of our group. You have said on several occasions that our group needs to have a more powerful voice in government. With your help we can make that a reality. Let us explain."

- "Adrienne, as you know I just formed my own software company and we have designed a new program for the state lottery system. I have the business plan that I would like to share with you. You of course would be the first person I would approach about this new business venture. I hope you are as excited as I am about the possibilities for the both of us to collaborate on the project."

These transitions let the person know that the organization and company did its homework, that it listened to the person and matched his interest with the right gift opportunity or business opportunity to meet his desire to support the organization or company. You have the person's full and complete attention, which is exactly where you want to be at this point in time. The person will be curious to know exactly what you have in mind. And now it is the ideal time for the Ask.

THE ASK AMOUNT AND PURPOSE Each Ask must state the amount and the purpose of the Ask. This principle may seem painfully obvious, but many, many Asks are done without requesting a specific amount. If you do not ask the person for a specific amount, she may supply her idea of an appropriate sum, and it may be well below what you are anticipating or dreaming she will give. Why make this an unnecessary guessing game or mystery? Stating a specific amount conveys a feeling of inclusion because the person has been selected to "join" and to "support" the organization. It sends the signal that the organization thought long and hard about how she could play an important role with the special event; the fund drives for the annual fund, major gift, or planned giving areas; the capital campaign; or business venture. *Failing to request a specific amount can diminish the personal value of the gift.* It can leave the person with the feeling that "it doesn't matter whether the group gets the money from me or from someone else."

As important as asking for a specific amount is asking for a specific purpose. Simply asking the person for $10,000 to support the organization will probably not do much good. She is likely to want to know more precisely what the money will be used for. If the Ask is for an unrestricted gift, then let the person know the group needs unrestricted funds to cover operational expenses. If the gift is for a restricted fund, then let the person know that it will be placed, for example, in the endowment fund and will generate approximately 5 percent interest to be used for the scholarship fund. If the money is to invest in a start-up company, then tell the person they are among the first to be asked and this new company has all the potential to spin off into major markets. *The bottom line is that the Ask must be specific and straightforward.*

Examples of Specific Asks with Specific Amounts: Here are a few examples of specific Asks:

- "Glenn, we would like you to consider a gift of $25,000 for a named, endowed scholarship at your school. We can work with you and whomever you desire on the terms of the scholarship."

- "Alex, we invite you to consider an investment of $1,000 to help sponsor our community fair."
- "Fred, we ask this only of our top donors. We would like you to join with other top donors and consider a leadership gift of $1 million to support the construction of our new surgical wing."
- "Jay, we ask you today to be our lead investor for the new overnight mail delivery company we just formed. Your investment of $4 million can get us up and running within the year."

The Ask should be articulate, crisp, and concise. Two simple sentences are all you need to make an effective Ask, one that states the Ask amount and the purpose of the Ask.

BENEFITS OF THE GIFT   This is a prime time for launching into the benefits of the gift if you are asking for a charitable gift. Notice that the asker or asking team needs to speak about the benefits of the gift, not the financial needs of the organization. People want to hear how the gift will help others, not how the organization will reach its fundraising goals. If a person is asked to make a scholarship gift, it is much more effective to say that the students need and deserve the opportunity for a great education than it is to stress the goal of increasing the scholarship fund. Remember, even if the gift will construct a new wing, add an additional studio, or pay for new laptops, ultimately the gift will help people. Let the person know how many beneficiaries the gift will help and the difference the gift will make to the beneficiaries. If you have written testimonials from beneficiaries or pictures of beneficiaries, bring them with you and share them with the person.

Benefits are also a two-way street. The gift not only aids the beneficiaries but also satisfies the person's interests. The person gains the knowledge that the gift will fulfill his aspirations to help the organization. If the gift also helps the person to meet his own financial goals, make sure this point is highlighted. For instance, if the person can donate his second home, which he wanted to sell anyway, and can get many tax benefits from doing so, then the asker or asking team has to celebrate with the person that this is a win-win situation for him and for the organization's beneficiaries.

BENEFITS OF THE BUSINESS VENTURE It is perhaps easier and clearer to detail what the investor is going to receive once the investment is made. Similar to nonprofits, this is also a win-win situation because the asker is giving the person a chance to experience something new, to get in on the ground floor and see a company or a product develop, which oftentimes benefits many people. For instance, if new non-invasive laser equipment can make it possible for doctors to heal patients quicker and more efficiently without major surgery and post-surgery recovery time, this is an amazing thing to invest in and the people being asked need to be explained the benefits of this new equipment as well as the thousands of people who will benefit. If the business venture has a specific revenue projection stream over time and the percentage the investor is anticipated to receive, then those facts need to be stated clearly. Leave nothing to presumption.

The harder benefits to detail are those that are not material or monetary. There are many Asks that do not come with monetary incentives or rate on return. For instance, particularly in the arts, people can ask friends and colleagues to support a concert, tour, new film, dance performance, or a new CD without making a major investment and without the thought that they will get something in return. The asker is asking on behalf of herself in the hopes that the person being asked will join in the dream, and the benefit is the joy of experiencing this new art form together. But there is still a benefit here—people do want to help people fulfill their dreams and the key is to spell out the joint benefit the asker and the person being asked will receive. Many times people do not want anything back for their monetary support. The joy is in giving, period. If the asker lights up, has such energy and commitment in the Ask, and the person being asked sees and feels the importance and happiness many people will receive from the final product, chances are very good the person will give, and will be very happy to give.

REMAINING SILENT The cardinal rule after any Ask is that the asker or asking team must remain silent. *The next person to speak should be the person being asked.* This is extremely hard for askers to do. The asker or asking team is usually very excited and filled with energy, and the temptation is to keep the conversation going by elaborating on the details and benefits of the Ask. However, if you speak now you run the risk of second-guessing the person's reaction, and then you will not hear in the person's own words how she feels in this moment after being asked to invest in your organization. It is the person's immediate reaction that lets you know, right away, your next strategy. We will explore in great depth in Chapter 7 the myriad reactions people have to being asked for money, and what to do and say to keep the gift and investment opportunity on track. For now, it is important to know that in order to get the person's thoughts, ideas, and concerns, the asker or asking team needs to be silent after the Ask is made. A suggested way to emphasize this point is to place a great big blank space in each asker's written script right after the Ask. This is what I call a visual pause in time. It serves as a visual reminder that silence is a good thing and a necessary thing at this point in time.

The more you listen to the person, the better idea you will have of their major concerns. This is the best preparation of how you will handle your reaction to their response. Silence gives you a golden opportunity to hear the person's concerns, to hear the questions she may have, to hear her silence and hesitations indicating that something is getting in the way of yes, and to hear about the financial and personal issues that may influence her decision.

Many people may think that listening is relinquishing control because as long as you are talking you can steer and shape the direction of the conversation. However, listening can be one of the most effective ways to maintain control. Think back to a committee meeting or speaker series you attended when the person doing the presentation stopped, paused, and reflected silently for what felt like an extremely long time. Everyone in the room was probably fixated on the speaker, waiting in great anticipation for what the speaker was going to say or do. It is by means of this very same silent control through listening that you will gain the insight you need to uncover how the person really feels about the chance to support your group in the special way you have suggested.

The Anticipated Response

As mentioned, Chapter 7 deals in depth with how to respond to the many different reactions and responses the asker or asking team will get. As I stated in Chapter 1, many people do not like to ask others for money because they fear the person's reaction and worry that they will not be able to handle the person's questions and concerns. People will have a variety of reactions, verbal and nonverbal, and the asker or asking team needs to do some homework to anticipate the person's reaction. Out of the 25 minutes allotted to the Ask, I suggest that you devote the most time, at least ten minutes, to dealing with this reaction, because it is the pivotal part of the Ask. If the person has more time and the questions and concerns are complex, then give him all the time he can spare so that he can state his concerns and you can address them the best way possible. It is not necessary that everything be covered in this initial meeting, and in most instances a lot more information needs to be explored and exchanged before the person can make a final decision.

The Close and Follow-Up

After the person's concerns and issues have been aired and addressed as best as possible during the Ask, the asker or asking team needs to bring the meeting to closure. The close contains several key elements (see Exhibit 2.5).

EXHIBIT 2.5. *Key Elements of the Close.*

1. Thank the person for taking the time to share this exciting opportunity.
2. Thank the person for listening to you.
3. Restate the gift or business opportunity and its benefits.
4. Give the person a date when you will get back to her with further information in response to her questions or concerns.
5. Ask the person if he has any additional comments or concerns.
6. Speak with the person as though she will make the gift.
7. Where appropriate, ask the person, if and when the gift or business investment is made, how she would like to be recognized.
8. Set the date and time when the asker or asking team will meet with the person again.

Thank the person for his time, not only for allowing the asker or asking team to share the exciting proposal but also for listening. As difficult as it was for the asker to stay silent after the Ask, it was probably just as hard for the person to listen to an entire presentation without interrupting or stopping the Ask midstream.

The asker must also restate the funding opportunity and then one or two of the benefits. It is not necessary to repeat every point made, just highlight one or two. This will ensure that both the asker and the person heard and understood all the elements of the proposal.

If the person raised a question that could not be addressed during the Ask or if he requested back-up information, tell him when you can get the information to him. This shows the person that the asker or asking team has listened carefully and that together they are moving the proposal forward. Set a realistic but short time frame. If the request requires expertise and research, then a week or two is OK. If, however, you have the materials, data, statistics, or other information readily available at your organization, then I suggest you tell the person you will send it in a day or two. *No more than one week at the very most should go by without getting something back to the person.* Remember, out of sight is out of mind and if too much time goes by before you send or deliver in person additional material, chances are the person being asked will lose enthusiasm and interest in your proposal.

This is also a good time to ask the person if there is anything else he needs to know or if he has any other comments or concerns not raised previously. It is important that the asker or asking team pause here in silence again to let the person mull over all the information that has just been shared. If the person needs more information, then repeat the commitment to get the information or answers to the person as quickly as possible.

A positive voice is a very powerful and effective tool. Speak with the person as if he has said yes to the offer or will do so very soon. This will keep the meeting on a steady upbeat and continue the enthusiasm and momentum. It is very easy to lose this momentum during the final portion of the Ask. It can be draining and straining, but you cannot lose any steam now. This is why it helps if your voice is upbeat, energetic, and positive, because that will carry the tone of the meeting.

Telling the person about the recognition opportunities associated with the Ask can be done during the discussion of the benefits or at the close of the Ask. I think it is important that the asker or asking team be flexible in discussing recognition benefits. Sometimes people want to focus just on the mechanics of the Ask, such as how and when it can be funded, or on the ways in which the money will bring about change and help a good cause. They are not ready to hear about recognition because they have not yet said yes or because recognition does not interest them. In other instances recognition may be part of the total benefits package, so the asker or asking team should share those benefits with the person during the Ask. For example, if you feel the person is leaning toward supporting your special event, tell him that his name or company name can be in the program, on a banner, or in a public announcement. If the person is leaning toward being a backer for an artist's opening show, tell him how the press releases for the upcoming show will list the investors. If the person has been asked for a specific major or capital campaign gift and your organization has recognition levels or naming opportunities at that level, let the person know. Whatever his response you will learn something, because discussing recognition benefits during either the Ask or the close gives you a sense of how serious the person is about funding the opportunity. If the person chimes in during the conversation with a question about naming opportunities for your organization's rooms, wings, lobbies, or solariums, that is a good sign because you have the person's wheels spinning in a positive direction. If, however, the person says, "That's getting ahead of us now," or, "It is premature to discuss this," then it shows that the person will really need much time before deciding on the opportunity.

The last element of the close is the most important. *Do not leave the room until you have set a date and time to meet again with the person.* This will be detailed later in Chapter 8 but needs mentioning now. Some people may be unwilling to commit to the next meeting. All too often they will say, "I'll get back to you on that," "I don't have my calendar with me now," or, "I need some time, so I don't want to set a date yet." These are all perfectly understandable reasons not to set a date, but to the extent one can be set, at least in terms of days, weeks, or the next month, do so. It will be much harder to pin down a date with the person once you have left the meeting. Without being pushy or overly forceful, set a date or prospective time frame when you can meet, ideally in person. This will keep the Ask in the forefront of the person's mind.

Once you are back in your office, send the person a thank-you letter, keeping it as personal and in the moment as possible. Reference elements of your conversation with the person, and if you have set a date for the next meeting, reiterate the time and place. If you have not set a date, tell the person that you will call soon to set one. Most of all thank him, thank him, and thank him again for all he does for your organization and for his time and interest in your group.

Finally, be sure to record the meeting for the Ask in a contact report, using your fundraising or business software, and to gather and send any additional information, data, statistics, or research the person requested.

Who Speaks and Who Listens

The last part of scripting the Ask is to make sure each asker knows what she or he is to say and cover in the Ask. If one person is doing the Ask, then there is no question about who will carry out all the elements. *However, when two or more people are part of the Ask, there is a risk that one will trip over the other in giving information or that each may think the other is going to do the actual Ask.* It is very important that the asking team have in writing which asker covers which areas. Here is an example of how easy it is to script who speaks and who listens:

> *Joyce:* Does the warm-up and compelling case statement (5 minutes).
>
> *Keith:* Does the transitional phrases and the Ask (6 minutes).
>
> *Joyce and Keith:* REMAIN SILENT UNTIL THE PROSPECT SPEAKS.
>
> *Joyce and Keith:* Address the person's concerns. Keith will cover all aspects of the proposal; Joyce will cover all questions about the organization (10 minutes).
>
> *Keith:* Restates the opportunities and benefits, including recognition; asks if the person has any final questions or comments; and proposes a date and time to meet or speak to follow up on the Ask (4 minutes).

That is all you really need. Do take the time to write it down. It is one thing to all be happy and smiley in a meeting before the Ask and to agree to divide up the time and tasks for the Ask; *it is another to see this agreement visually.* Remember, your volunteers lead very busy lives, and it is very easy to forget who does what and when. Furthermore, the asking team may be prepped a day, a few days, or a week before the Ask, and it is not surprising that people forget these important details by the time of the Ask. So write down the timing details in the script, and you will have crafted a masterpiece! I highly encourage you to take the time before the Ask to refresh your memory on the script so that you will be 100 percent prepared to ask.

It is time for our second exercise:

Exercise #2: Write your own script for something that you want to have funded. Be sure to include all the elements listed in Exhibit 2.3.

FUNDRAISING LANGUAGE

You will notice throughout this book that so far I have rarely used the word "prospect" and that I have mostly used the word "person." It is certainly common and it is not a crime to use "prospect" but when it comes to the Ask, you are asking a "person." I have found that people being asked for money do not like that people consider them as "prospects" so I have become much more comfortable with limiting the use of the terms "prospect" and "suspect." They are so common in the fundraising world, particularly when we speak about researching who would be the best "prospects" to ask, as you will see in Chapter 3.

"Prospects" are people who have the potential to give money and have an interest in the organization, and "suspects" are people who may be interested in the organization, but whose interests have yet to be confirmed (Ciconte and Jacob 2001).

Asking is all about knowing and liking the person you are about to ask and hopefully having the opportunity to make her feel good about giving money to a worthy cause or business venture. Using the terms "prospect" or "suspect" are fine if you are in a prospect management meeting with a group of people trying to decide who you should focus on and in what order. It is so common in the nonprofit world we hardly give it a thought. However, once you become so comfortable using these terms it is difficult to drop them and it is very embarrassing if you use them with the people you are going to ask for money.

I do use the term "fundraiser" throughout this book because I think whether you are raising money for a charitable cause, seeking money to back a creative adventure, or asking for money for a business project, you are a fundraiser—you are seeking funds and asking for money!

I'll share with you an example of why I feel sensitive about how we speak about "people" in fundraising. I was out with a fundraiser co-worker and we were meeting with a joint friend who is not in the fundraising world. My co-worker said, "Wow, I had the greatest day today. I met with an older couple who have no children." Our friend said, "Oh, that's a shame the couple didn't have children." My co-worker said with glee, "No, that's fantastic. It means more money for us."

Oh boy! Do you see how this could really get out of hand? Please be very cautious and conscientious with fundraising terms and the way you speak about people you are cultivating and asking for money.

THREE-STEP METHOD PRIOR TO ANY ASK

Now that we have our case statement or business plan, the elements needed for any Ask, and how to script the Ask, here is a three-step method you can use prior to any Ask:

1. What are the specific details of the Ask?
2. What are the top three reasons you think the person you are about to ask will hesitate or say no to the Ask?
3. How can you turn around these three reasons to make a positive and passionate statement about your Ask?

This is an all-new approach that I thought would help in preparing for the Ask. First, you have the specific details of the Ask if you did the exercise of forming your case statement or business plan. Congratulations, you can move easily on to step 2. List the top three reasons why you think the person will hesitate or say no to the Ask.

For example, you are currently the major gift officer for your organization and your boss, the director of major gifts, leaves to take another job. You want to ask the executive director who supervises the director position for a promotion. The specific Ask is that you want to be promoted because of your prior successful track record of raising major gifts; you know the donors and have strong relationships with them; you love where you work; and you want to advance as a senior member of the development team.

What are the three reasons why you feel the executive director may say no to promoting you? Here are some that I came up with:

1. The executive director wants to do a search to find "the best candidate."
2. You are unsure the executive director knows your work because you reported directly to the director.
3. It is a challenging economic time and with pending budget adjustments the director position may be eliminated.

Here is how you tackle these fears head on, one by one. The key is to have the executive director know you and your work better and that the director position is vital to the continued success of the program:

1. Request a meeting with the executive director and tell her that while she may be thinking of doing an outside search for the director's position, you feel the best candidate is someone with a proven track record at the organization, knowledge inside and outside of the organization, established and solid personal relationships with current donors, and a zest to find new people who have the potential to support the organization. That person is you and you want to be given serious consideration for this position, whether or not a formal search is conducted.
2. Have with you all the statistics you can about the gifts you brought in; the number of visits you average a month; the number of cold calls you do per month; and how much you

enjoy cultivating and asking great people for money. Share a story about a person you met initially who had no intentions of giving and how you brought this person to the organization and to special events, introduced her to some beneficiaries, and in time the person made a great gift. Tell the executive director that you have some new ideas for the major gift unit that you would be happy to share at an appropriate time.

3. Be sensitive to the executive director's position that there may be budget cuts that translate into services and supplies being cut back and/or eliminating a position. Put yourself in your executive director's shoes. Hard decisions may have to be made but eliminating positions as you *both* know would impinge on raising money and that will hurt the institution. Tell the executive director that if you get the director position you have or can help get good candidates for your position so that there will be a full complement of fundraisers in a relatively short time so that fundraising will not suffer from open positions.

That is all it takes. This exercise is so important because it is empowering and puts you in a positive and powerful position to make your Ask. Try it—I think you find that it is well worth your time and you will have great results.

CONCLUSION

The Ask is all about preparation, and the best place to start is formulating the case statement or the business plan. Each contains the history of the organization; the uniqueness among similar organizations; products or services; beneficiaries and the quantity and quality of deliverable services; the need for funding now; the universe of people who may be interested in funding the Ask; and what the person will receive in exchange for funding. Writing and rehearsing a script for each Ask, particularly when two people are doing the Ask, will ensure that the Ask will be delivered with convincing clarity and that the person being asked has a precise idea of the amount you are requesting and the purpose for the Ask. Sticking to a 25-minute Ask for the warm-up, transitional phrase, Ask, silence, and close will set the right framework so that you do not run out of time during your meeting before doing the Ask. Doing the three-step method exercise prior to any Ask will give you confidence to ask for anything you need and will keep the Ask in a positive tone, which will inevitably lead you to the answer you want.

LOOKING AHEAD

Now that we have all the preparation elements under way, the next thing we need to know is who should be asked and when should they be asked? It is not always that easy knowing how to prioritize people or groups of people based on who has the greatest likelihood of making the gift or funding the project sooner rather than later. The next chapter will address the types of research that can be done to identify your best people to give money, which will then lead into the magic question of when to ask. Through my readiness formula, readers will have a solid idea of judging and gauging the best time to ask for money or any other need.

How Do I Know Who to Ask and When to Ask?

T HE TWO QUESTIONS IN THIS CHAPTER TITLE can be among the hardest to answer when making an Ask. In fact, in my experience, not knowing the answers or spending way too much time trying to calculate the answers often leads to postponing the Ask for a dreadful period of time. We are going to divide this chapter into two parts. The first part will be "Who to Ask," and we will walk through the prospect research that can be done at a distance and then up close and personal, prioritizing our pool of people to ask. The second part will be "When to Ask," and through the readiness formula askers will have a solid checklist of things that need to be known prior to making an Ask.

WHO SHOULD BE ASKED?

The obvious answer to this question is anyone who has a likelihood of giving you a "yes" answer to your Ask for money at a certain level and who know you very well and are ready to be asked. How you get to the point of knowing all the factors necessary to avoid early or premature asks that most certainly lead to little or no funding is key. Let us start with a few things to avoid when judging your best people to ask, as detailed in Exhibit 3.1.

EXHIBIT 3.1. *Common Mistakes in Judging Who Should Be Asked.*

1. These people are all $5,000 donors so let's hold an event for them, and then send them a mailing asking them for $5,000.
2. This person has so much money we should ask her right away for a big gift.
3. I heard he just gave a lot of money to back this new project; I just know he can do the same for us.
4. A board member gave me this person's name and contact information and said we should move on her quickly and ask.
5. Even though my friend, colleague, or relative is probably really interested in supporting us, we can't ask because it will be embarrassing for the both of us.

EVERY PERSON MUST BE TREATED INDIVIDUALLY

It is so tempting yet so dangerous to "lump" people into categories of giving levels, and then cultivate them in the same manner as people in this level. For example, if you have a category of $2,500 donors and you want to move them up to the $5,000 or $10,000 level, your cultivation efforts can look the same. You group them at special events, send them handwritten notes on publications, list them together in your annual report, and your efforts become routine. I am not suggesting that these are not terrific cultivation techniques but I am saying that they need to be seen and spoken with on an individual basis. For example, donor Samantha may be so happy as life continues to go her way, with her new business, the birth of a grandchild, and secure retirement benefits. She knows about your group, and her family has a history of giving. Donor Rachel is new to your organization but she always makes an initial $2,500 gift to see how the organization will follow up with this new gift. As you can see, the "cultivation curve," as I call it, is much different for these two donors, and each will need very different next steps to get to the $5,000 and $10,000 levels.

Just as there is no exact right time to ask, there is no exact length of time that determines how much cultivation each person needs before she is asked. Some people take a few months; others take years. Fundraisers need to take a look at their top-tier list and make sure that each person is being cultivated to the degree required for that person. One cannot add up the cultivation time or actions taken and use that sum as a yardstick to measure the time to ask. For example, fundraiser Len may have an overall list of fifty people and a short list of five top people whom he has seen or taken to events for the past year. Some of those five may be ready to be asked, but others may tell him that they love his organization but circumstances are not good for giving at this time. *What a mistake it would be if Len set up the Asks according to the amount of time he and others spent with each person, rather than listening to what each person has told Len about his or her level of commitment to the group.*

Sometimes a fundraiser just joining a group discovers that certain people have been cultivated by everyone in the group for long periods of time or have been cultivated intermittently without being asked to give. This is more common than you might think. Fundraising staff, like many other professional staffs, have a fair share of turnover. Now here is a frightening fact. *The average length of time a fundraiser spends with any one organization is less than two years* (Hugg 2006). This is an appalling statistic! How do you even know who you are working with if you are only at an organization for 18 months! Groups that have higher turnovers in staff are especially vulnerable to an ebb and flow in their cultivation efforts. When the fundraising positions are filled, people are given attention, and when there are gaping holes in staffing, many people are dropped, or worse, ignored. Fundraisers new to the group can look at past records and contact reports for these people and surmise that with all this activity, steady or intermittent, certain people should be asked. Under certain circumstances this may well be true, but *the new fundraiser still needs to get to know these people before asking.* Any asker who does not know the person about to be asked very well should never do the Ask. Where is the personal relationship that is needed with any cultivation effort leading to the Ask?

The focus should always be on the quality of the contact, not the quantity of the contact. People do not take too kindly to new fundraisers, people they don't know, who quickly ask them for money. Once this happens it will take a long time to start over and to form a long and lasting relationship. The rule is to take some time to get to know the people who have the best potential to support your organization when entering a new fundraising position.

WEALTH DOES NOT ALWAYS TRANSLATE INTO TRANSFERRING WEALTH

This is a very difficult concept to swallow. No doubt in your fund-raising career and especially if you are seeking money to back or to launch a business venture, you will discover, uncover, and be introduced to people of wealth in varying degrees. As we stated in Chapter 1, money means different things to different people and wealth can be defined in a variety of ways. One million dollars may be extreme wealth to one person, while that may just be "seed money" to someone who has the capacity to give several millions. The "wealth trap" to avoid is the following: the assumption that people who have a lot of money are the best people to approach for money.

---

10 Things to Know About Any Ask—#3

A person of great wealth does not always give great wealth.

It is such a natural instinct to identify, research, and target people of wealth as the best candidates to ask for money. In some instances this works out very well but A does not always translate into B, meaning that people of money will not always give money. As you'll read throughout this book, along with other reference materials, conferences, and seminars, it takes lots of cultivation, as well as a match between your organization and their genuine interest in your organization, before the person of means will even consider investing in your organization.

During the early stages of cultivation with the people who have an interest in your organization, your mission, or your business plan, it is very likely that these people will begin to discuss money and gifts they have given to your group or other groups, and money they may have invested in outside projects. This is a wonderful thing to embrace. It is not, however, an automatic high sign that it is all right to ask for money. The fundraiser needs to have a series of conversations with the person about what he or she would like to give, when, and for what purpose. Again, under certain circumstances with certain people this may indeed be the ideal time to ask, but askers must have a firm grip on the amount of money to ask for and the purpose for that money. Otherwise, they run the risk of asking for too little because they do not have enough information about the person and her ability to give.

In your fundraising career you will most certainly come across people who have either given modest gifts to your group or who have an affinity for your group and who also have enormous wealth. The CEO or president of the group or the person supervising the fund-raising staff and volunteers may apply great pressure to "move on this prospect" because of the wealth indicator. *The fundraiser still needs a well-thought-out strategy before these people can be asked.* Such a strategy usually involves a series of high-end cultivation moves such as:

1. Arranging for the person to meet and socialize with the head of your organization and your board members
2. Placing the person on the board or a committee
3. Honoring the person at an organizational event
4. Introducing the person to the group's beneficiaries
5. Giving the person several private site tours of the group's facilities
6. Asking the person to host or attend a select high-end reception
7. Keeping the person in close contact with the group's existing top donors

These people are extremely bright, very busy, and most of them have earned their wealth through successful business ventures. In a recent study on trends in million-dollar giving, people of "self-made" wealth, such as entrepreneurs, investors, or developers, gave more gifts of $1 million or more from 2000 to 2007 (Advancing Philanthropy Jan/Feb, 2009). People who made these gifts gave "in response to a request for a specific purpose, whether it [was] a capital campaign, endowing an activity within the institution or creating a new program or project." This echoes and supports why asking for a specific amount for a specific purpose as previously detailed in Chapter 2 is crucial.

Wealthy people will not give until they are 100 percent convinced that your organization is worthy of their investment. It would be a big mistake for anyone in the organization to ask these wealthy people for money prematurely, perhaps out of a fear that they might consider giving to another group so "we have to ask first." They need time and attention, and you have to earn their trust, respect, and loyalty.

Board and committee members can and should be sources for uncovering people who have wealth and may be interested in your group. These board and committee members can and should broaden the group's base of support by attracting new people who may be interested in volunteering or giving to your group. Often board and committee members reveal their connections or information formally in committee meetings or peer-screening activities—where they are given a list of people and asked whether they know any of these individuals and might help in involving them more closely with the group—or informally in conversations with the group's CEO, president, or top fundraiser. These board and committee members should be thanked by the group's leadership and top fundraisers. This is not the time, however, to think about quickly asking these wealthy new people for money. If a board or committee member has this expectation, then it is up to the leaders or top fundraisers to inform and educate the board or committee member that any wealthy person needs time, attention, and a strategy well before the Ask.

The only exception to this principle occurs when these new people are being considered for a board position and board guidelines require each member to give at a certain level each year. For instance, many universities, hospitals, and cultural organizations require board members to give anywhere from $10,000 a year to six- and seven-figure gifts a year. It would be entirely appropriate under these circumstances for the prospective board member to be asked to meet that requirement.

RESEARCH CAN HELP TO PRIORITIZE WHO TO ASK

Just as there is no substitute for a well-thought-out plan of what you want as we explored in Chapter 2, there is no substitute for research on the person you want to cultivate and ask for money. "Prospect research" is the "continuing search for pertinent information on prospects and donors" and a "prospect profile" is a "research report detailing the pertinent facts about a prospective donor, including basic demographic information, financial resources, past giving, linkages, interests, potential future giving (Ciconte and Jacob 2001, 415).

Every fundraiser should have a profile on the person she intends to ask for money in the future. Exhibit 3.2 details all the elements that should be in that profile.

EXHIBIT 3.2.   *Contents of a Person's Profile.*

1. The person's addresses, employment history, age, education, family members, religion, hobbies, recreational activities, travel and vacation habits or preferences, outstanding honors, recognitions, memberships, committee work, and board appointments with your group or other groups.

2. The person's giving history, including pledge payments paid and pledge payments unfulfilled to your group and others.

3. Acknowledgment and stewardship for each gift the person has already made to your group.

4. The person's wealth indicators, such as salary, stocks and bonds, company shares, business ventures, real estate, family foundation, and inheritance.

5. The person's attendance at your events (and the dates of that attendance).

6. Communications, marketing pieces, e-mail blasts, and direct mail the person receives from you.

7. The person's contacts with any member, volunteer, or beneficiary of your organization (with details and dates).

8. Any publicity, good or bad, about the person or the person's business or family.

9. The person's motivation to give or prospectively give to your group.

10. The strategy behind asking the person now for money.

Every person who is going to be asked for money should have his own up-to-date prospect profile in your group's database. A list of the fundraising software any group can use to store and track this profile information is listed in the References and Resources section online (www.josseybass.com/go/laurafredricks), and a good source to constantly check for new software providers is the *Chronicle of Philanthropy*. I am sensitive to the fact that many smaller, grassroots nonprofits may not have the resources of a prospect researcher on the staff or the budget to engage a large firm to do prospect research on the organization's database. Listed in the References and Resources section online (www .josseybass.com/go/laurafredricks) is a variety of software companies that can tailor their services to any size organization, and keep in mind that smaller groups can hire an outside person on a consulting basis to do a prospect profile on a person-to-person basis.

The person's record should contain the basics: addresses for home or work, e-mail address, age, employment history, family members, giving history, outstanding pledges, religion, board or committee appointments, recognitions and honors, and a record of the organization's gift acknowledgments and stewardship for each gift already received. It should also contain information about other groups the person has supported or volunteered with or that have recognized or honored the person. The profile should reflect any organizational mailings, such as newsletters, magazines, and invitations, the person receives or does not receive; any committee work; and attendance at any of your events. Any publicity, good or bad, about the person or the person's business or family should be in the profile. Hard copy of any articles in the print media should be scanned into the record.

Research—From a Distance

With the "wealth" (no pun intended) of information there is via the Internet, prospect research has become fast, easy, reliable, and accessible. The References and Resources section online (www.josseybass .com/go/laurafredricks) lists the prospect and donor research and identification companies, and a sampling of search engines that can be used to obtain the "hard data" research you need on the people you want to cultivate and eventually ask. Using these tools, you can get all the public information you need to put together a profile. The profile should contain the person's wealth indicators, such as salary, stocks and bonds, company shares, real estate, a family foundation, and inheritance. These indicators are used to gauge the level of gift or the amount of the investment the person might give when and if she so desires. After all, one should not be asking for a certain amount when there is no indication that the person has the capacity to give at that level. These are the hard data items that should be updated frequently so that the organization has an accurate database.

Additionally, the organization with a large number of potential supporters may find it beneficial to do an electronic screening of a portion of its donor base or perhaps its entire database. Electronic screening uses a number of filters, such as a person's job title, where she lives, her public stock holdings, and her board or foundation affiliation, to rank the best givers for the organization. It can be an enormous help, especially to organizations that have many donors, to have some guidance on identifying the best people, the ones they should be focusing their time and attention on as potential substantial givers. (The References and Resources section online [www.josseybass.com/ go/laurafredricks] lists companies that provide wealth screening services.)

Again, smaller organizations may not have the need to do a wealth screening since the number of people in the donor base is small enough to find out this information in person, as we shall see in the next section of this chapter. If this is the case, the organization can use "peer screenings" to have board and committee members share any pertinent information about prospective top donors to the organization. This is of no cost to the organization and can be a great resource of new information.

Research—Up Close

All the research in the world can never substitute for the things you will learn about "your new best friends" during cultivation and your personal visits, telephone calls, e-mails, text messages, cards, and letters. The best research is the personal visit because then and only then will you have a chance to experience, through listening and seeing, all the very important details of the people you want to educate and further engage in your organization.

You will probably know some facts about the people you want to approach. In some instances, they may be friends, family, or colleagues. We will deal with the potential awkwardness of asking people in this category later in this chapter. Most of the time, there will be known facts, such as that the person gives generously to certain groups; that she holds a certain office; who the family members are; and other obvious bits of information. That is all wonderful background, but when you do your personal visits during cultivation be open-minded and a good listener. So many strong leads on whether a person would be a really good donor are missed during cultivation because we are too preoccupied with driving the conversation, updating the person on information on our organization, and saying silently in our heads "how can I get this person to give more?"

I always encourage fundraisers to ask the following two questions in person with the people they want to cultivate at some point *early* in the cultivation stages:

1. How did you become interested in our organization?
2. Out of all the organizations worldwide, why did or would you support us?

These are jewels, because they will reveal the person's passion for and knowledge of your organization; where their "heart-strings" are; if and when they will give; and most prominently, what is important to them. Without this information fundraisers begin to "fill in" the answers without letting the person tell you the answers. Once you have the answers, you can then begin to lay out a roadmap of how you want to cultivate them. For instance, if you work for a hospital and in response to the above two questions Steve tells you "my mother was a patient here many years ago and I never forgot how the doctor came and got me out of the waiting room to discuss her care" and "after that experience and reflecting on it many years later, I thought it was time to say 'thank you' with a small gift," there you have it. You now know you need to get Steve back to the hospital for a tour, possibly explore the particular reason his mother was in the hospital, see if he remembers the doctor's name, try to get that doctor or another doctor now in that unit to meet with him, and thank him for sharing his memory with you.

The personal visit serves as good research only to the extent to which it is recorded. It is essential that anyone having contact with a person who may be a potential funder and supporter make a contact report that is entered into the group's database. These reports should contain details of conversations with the person (either in person or on the telephone), letters or e-mails exchanged between anyone affiliated with your group and the person, and the contacts made during events. Exhibit 3.3 outlines the contents of a contact report.

EXHIBIT 3.3. *Essential Contents of a Contact Report.*

1. Significant portions of conversation about the person's life, work, hobbies, education, religious beliefs, and political and philosophical opinions.
2. Whom the person knows or has met at your organization.
3. The person's opinions about your group's events, newsletters, and outreach to supporters.
4. What information the fundraiser shared with the person.
5. Any follow-up that needs to be done in the immediate future.
6. The next step for the person, with dates.

In essence, you want to capture the moment so that you do not lose any details useful for future reference. For instance, if the person attended an open house at your organization and spoke with the organization's president, that conversation should be recorded. Similarly, if the person met with a fundraiser and at the beginning of the meeting the person was sharing details about the most recent family vacation or a board retreat, those facts should be recorded in the contact report. All too often, wonderful conversations revealing important details about the person go undocumented, to the detriment of the group. Be vigilant with your contact reports, because when it comes time to ask someone for money, it is impossible to recall all these details. The contact reports serve as your refreshers, so that you can recall all the wonderful encounters and conversations you and others have had with the person.

Additionally, with fundraisers changing jobs frequently, contact reports are a must. Institutional history will be lost forever if contact reports are not recorded. It is a tremendous disservice to your donors if they shared their time, talent, advice, and goodwill by meeting with one fundraiser and those meetings do not get recorded, then in less than two years they are back to square one, having to exchange the same information with a new person. If you supervise front-line fundraisers or if you are a team of one, be disciplined and record your contacts with the people you want to engage in your operation.

As important as what the person has said is what the fundraiser has shared with the person. Any updates; reports on gifts; regards from the CEO, board members, volunteers, or potential investors for the business project; or publicity on the new idea must be entered. Remember, the purpose of the contact report is to preserve institutional history so that anyone can pick up the file or go into the database and see the most current and accurate conversations with that person.

The most important elements in the contact report are:

1. The follow-up that needs to be done

2. The next steps

What good is meeting with the person if he asked for certain things to be done and then that request is ignored? For instance, a fundraiser might meet with a person and she might ask for information on the organization's bequest society. If the fundraiser fails to record this request and no one follows through on it, the person is likely either to be upset or to assume the organization isn't interested. Chapter 8 will discuss the importance of the follow-up in depth. The contact report should serve as a to-do list for any fundraiser, so it will be very clear what needs to be done next and with whom.

I am a strong advocate of the following procedure. Every contact report should have a section titled "Next Steps" that lists the next actions to take in the cultivation process for each person. Without it, folks, you may as well have not seen that person. Every person needs follow-up, so the contact report needs to spell out what needs to be done: "Send more information about X," "He wants clarity on our giving levels," or similar directives to do any of the myriad things that pop into people's minds. Build this "Next Steps" section into your contact reports, and you will ensure that you follow up with all that needs to be done before, during, and after the Ask.

A word of caution is necessary here. Highly confidential or highly personal information the person reveals needs careful consideration. Use your discretion and common sense in determining how much of this information you include in the contact report and how you phrase it. The guideline is that the donor has the right to see his file at your organization. If he walks into the organization and asks to see the file, will he be extremely upset and will he view it as a breach of confidentiality if certain information is recorded in the database? I suggest that highly sensitive information be stated in neutral terms. If the person is going through a very messy divorce, simply state that the person has some family issues. I am not suggesting that you leave this important information out of your contact reports entirely. I am suggesting that you be extremely careful and sensitive about the information that will be shared with others in your organization. For guidelines about donor confidentiality see the Association of Fundraising Professionals Code of Ethical Principles and Standards, Adopted 1964; amended Sept. 2007 (www.afpnet.org).

Prioritizing Your Top People to Ask

Using one or both of the research methods described above, you should have a good idea of which group of people should best be asked first and in what order, followed by the next best group of people. I always found it useful regardless of the size of the organization to have what I call a "Top List" and "Next List" group of people to work with in order of priority. The Top List would have the following characteristics:

1. People who have in the past given the largest gifts, who have been stewarded and cultivated well and have the assets, as revealed through prospect research, to make additional gifts

2. People who have yet to make a gift but have the capacity to make a large gift and are interested and involved with your organization

3. People who have yet to make a gift but have the capacity to make a large gift *but need to be cultivated*

4. People who have come close to making a gift at the highest level and have the capacity to make a gift at the highest level

Notice that in number 3 above, the emphasis is placed on the need to be cultivated, which avoids the traps in Exhibit 3.1, that newly identified people of wealth will not automatically give to you just because they have money. They need to have information about your group or company; they need to know about the leadership, mission, vision, and beneficiaries; and they need to know what their support will ultimately do for you or your organization.

The Next List would consist of the same as above, but at the second highest level for your organization. For example, if your group's highest level to date is $100,000, then people who have given or can give at that level would be in the Top List. Those people who have given close to $100,000 or have the capacity to do so would be in the Next List.

The number of people that comprise the Top List and Next List varies depending on the size of the organization. If you are seeking money for a business venture and you only have a handful of people that you feel have the capacity to back the enterprise and would be very interested in the project, then maybe your Top List would consist of two or three people, and your Next List, one person. For nonprofits the size of the lists varies with not only the size of the organization but also the amount of time a fundraiser has to devote to major gift fundraising. For example, if someone is in a medium-size group, it is critical that you, working as a major gift officer, quantify the amount of time each month that you can actually identify, cultivate, ask, follow up, and steward each person. I have no doubt that in addition to all these activities the major gift officer is also responsible for helping or doing special events, which we all know can take an enormous amount of time staffing committee meetings, preparing reports, and attending numerous internal meetings each week.

There is no magic formula for how many people should be on your Top List and Next List. The goal is to have as many people as you can work with *comfortably and evenly*. I am not trying to discourage anyone from working with the maximum amount of people. It does no one any good to say you are working with x amount of people if all the people on the list are not being cultivated and moved along to the point of being asked and stewarded to their next level of support. We all have the tendency to work with the "most enjoyable people" for a longer time than we do the people who are hard to reach, difficult to schedule for meetings, or who appear too busy to take our calls or respond to our letters. That is why I say work with the right amount of people comfortably, especially considering your other responsibilities, and evenly so that everyone on your list gets your attention in even amounts.

In my experience working at both a medium and a large organization, where I devoted all my time to major gift fundraising, I had a Top 25 list and a Next 25 list. Like many of you I also had other responsibilities but as a major gift officer, my primary responsibility was to raise large amounts of money. This served me well because I knew everyone on both lists and had the time to work with each of them, comfortably and evenly. Set up a number for both lists and if you find you can work with more people, add them. Similarly, if there are people on either list that you cannot have meaningful contact with for a number of weeks or months, then you are probably working with too many. I often get asked "what do you mean by meaningful contact?" By that I mean you visit with them, call them, see them at special events; send cards, letters, handwritten notes on your publications; or that you set up meetings with your leadership, beneficiaries, and staff members within your organization to meet with them. Remember from "Every Person Must Be Treated Individually" earlier in this chapter, each person on your Top and Next lists is what I call "their own mini campaign." Each person needs attention at varying levels and at varying points in time. As long as you have these meaningful contacts and a strategy and plan for each person on your list and you are executing these plans, you are working with the right amount of people in priority order.

Exercise #3: Make a list of people who would be in your Top Tier and Next Tier lists and analyze if you have too few or too many to cultivate evenly.

ASKING FRIENDS, RELATIVES, OR COLLEAGUES DOES NOT HAVE TO BE STRESSFUL

It is very easy to avoid thinking about asking friends, relatives, or colleagues, those people close to us who we have a personal relationship with, for money. This can fit squarely into why people fear or hesitate to ask as discussed in Chapter 1. The fears can be:

1. The Ask will damage or ruin the personal relationship.
2. It will be an embarrassing moment for the both of us.
3. I have to work with this person every day and they will think less of me.
4. If I ask them for money, then they will turn around and ask me for money.

We can focus on these fears, or choose to look at it another way. In many instances, you have been sharing the good work of your organization, the start of your new business, or the success of the business. Your closest people around you are your friends, relatives, and colleagues so it is natural that they probably already know and have expressed genuine interest in your fundraising activities.

The best way to ask these people who are intimately close to you is to be honest. Here are some simple, honest, and open examples of how you can ask the people who are close to you:

"Robert, you know how I have been working over the past few months trying to finish the final plans I have for the new product. Right now I have one and possibly two people who are seriously considering backing the product with x investment. This may be an awkward moment for the both of us, but I would feel horrible if you were interested in investing yourself and I did not ask you. Robert, are you interested in hearing more about these investment opportunities?"

"Ana Marie, I think I heard somewhere that you should never mix family and business, or is that business and politics? Kidding aside, you know that I love what I do raising money to combat breast cancer, and this is National Breast Cancer Awareness Month. You know our aunt and late grandmother battled with this disease, which motivates me each day to raise the money for this great cause. I never thought I

would ask this but would you be interested in making a gift to fight breast cancer? I'm really OK with whatever you decide."

"Anthony, we both have been running this marathon for four years. Front Runners asked me to be their area volunteer after I gave them $2,500 so that they could promote athletics to inner-city children who no longer get gym classes. Can you believe gym is no longer required in school? Anyway, I was thinking with the rise of obesity in children and all, this would be a start to helping those kids. You and I work together, and we work out together. This may be totally out of line but giving that $2,500 made me feel really good and I was thinking maybe it would do the same for you. Do you want me to tell you more about where the money goes and why I gave it to them?"

I believe that the more honest and open you are, the more the conversation will be natural and unobtrusive. Notice in the above three examples that the asker gently and easily weaves in what is being asked, as well as why it may be awkward, but the emphasis is that it would be a missed opportunity if the person did not ask. As long as you keep the focus on sharing an idea your friend, relative, or colleague may want to support, your Ask will go well.

If you are still afraid that if you ask the person will in turn ask you for money, you have to use the same honesty if you really are not interested in the idea of supporting the organization and say, "I support many groups and right now, unfortunately, I am not interested," and always thank them for thinking of you and for their courage for asking. You can also say, "I admire that you are asking me but right now that would not be a priority for me," and thank them for asking you. I am most certain that this is easier said than done; however, please do not resist asking people you know for money just because you think they will ask you. You don't know that they will and if they do, now you are prepared.

WHEN SHOULD YOU ASK?

If I had a dollar for every time I was asked this question, I would be very, very wealthy. There is no one definitive "right time" to ask for money but there are many guidelines and principles that can help you define the right time to ask. Whether you are new to the fundraising field or have been actively involved in the splendor of fundraising, it is the personal interaction you have with the people you are cultivating and eventually asking for money, that dynamic connection, that makes this process so enjoyable. You will meet and get very close to people of all ages and from many geographical locations. Many will have definite opinions about giving and where they fit within your organization's hierarchy of giving. This is why the timing of the Ask is crucial. The best time is the moment when there is a true understanding and appreciation that the person's gift and investment will be instrumental and transforming for the organization or the business.

The Readiness Formula

Here is a formula I created that has guided all my Asks:

EDUCATION + INVOLVEMENT + CULTIVATION + INCLINATION + ASSETS = THE RIGHT TIME TO ASK

Over the years I have found that if I stick with this formula, I am pretty much on the mark to know when it is the right time to ask someone for money. As we examine each element of the readiness formula, keep in mind that people will have varying degrees of education and involvement and that each may require a different quality and quantity of cultivation. Generally, the elements of the readiness formula are proportionate to the size of the Ask. In most cases the larger the gift Ask, the more education, involvement, cultivation, and inclination a person must have before she will make a large gift to your group. Again, these elements are guidelines, not hard and fast rules, and you need to apply them one by one with each person to judge her readiness to give.

EDUCATION People should be well educated about your group or your business. The person you are about to ask for money should know most of your case statement or your business plan detailed in Chapter 2. The level of education needed will vary from person to person. Obviously, the larger the Ask, the more education the person should have about your group. I call this the sliding scale theory. For instance, if you are going to ask someone for a five-, six-, or seven-figure gift or investment, then she has to be well briefed on all aspects of the group. People do not relinquish their hard-earned dollars in such amounts unless and until they are totally convinced that giving to your group is a sound investment. Conversely, if you are asking someone in person for a smaller amount for a nonprofit, the person you are asking should know about the good work your group does, how the money she is about to give will support the group's beneficiaries, and that you will report back to her on the success of the overall fundraising effort. If you are asking for a smaller amount for your business, the person should know how your business is doing overall, why this amount is needed, and when they can see results of their investment. Either way, the person probably does not need the high degree of cultivation required for larger asks.

INVOLVEMENT Ideally, people you want to ask should have some level of involvement with your group. Some folks love to read all the literature you send them or to visit your Web site regularly. They then call or meet with the fundraiser to offer suggestions on areas of improvement, or they let the staff know what a great and creative job the organization is doing of keeping everyone informed. That is one level of involvement, and it is also a sign of high-level education about your group. On the next level are the people who come to all your group's special events. Every organization has a set of people, and you know who they are, who show up in response to every invitation. They love to mingle with the group leaders and are genuinely fond of the fundraising staff. Events are a way to keep them active in and informed about your group. The next level includes the people who volunteer for the group, as speakers, event hosts, or committee or board members, for example, and those who are honored by the group. This is high-end involvement. The sliding scale theory applies here as well. *The larger the Ask, the more involvement is required.* For example, if you are considering asking someone for a major gift, it would be ideal if that person spoke before your beneficiaries or served on an advisory board. This level of commitment to helping your group paves the way for the person to then support the group in a significant way. If you are asking someone for a large business investment, they should visit your place of business if there is one, meet all the partners and decision makers, and be asking some very key questions about the future plans and continued success of the business. On the opposite end of the scale, your good friends who read all your publications, visit your Web site, and attend a few events, but who have not been asked to speak before your group or to serve on a committee or board may not be ready to make a major, planned, or capital campaign gift. People who may be moderately interested in your business but are not asking key questions and who have not read the literature you have given them or visited your Web site likewise may not be ready to make that large investment. These people have not yet demonstrated a sufficiently high level of involvement. They may, however, be ready to make a larger annual gift, be willing to take a top-tier level of sponsorship for one of your special events, or give an initial smaller amount to the business, but they are not involved to the point of wanting to give you or your cause more.

CULTIVATION Cultivation is a two-way street. It is the series of steps you take with each person to learn as much as you can about him, and he in turn needs to know as much as he can about your organization. It requires that the fundraiser, leaders, volunteers, or business partners carefully plan a series of activities that will educate and involve the person with the organization or business (see Chapter 1, Exhibit 1.2). Cultivation is essential because without it the chances are highly unlikely that your people will give.

The more creative you can be with cultivation, the better. One of the best cultivation techniques is to learn the person's hobbies or recreational activities and, whenever you have the chance, to send him some article or small gift that reflects these interests. For instance, almost everyone has a person they want to cultivate who is an avid golfer. If you see a humorous article or editorial about golf, clip it out, place a handwritten note on it, and send it to that person. If you are in an airport and you see a golf ball that is a clock with legs, and you have a budget for these small prospect gifts, buy it and send it to the person on her birthday. If sports are not the person's forte, turn to books, wine, cooking, music, skiing, or travel. The possibilities are endless. You can send them send reviews on a favorite author, a bottle of wine you think they would enjoy, an article on a new chef, a music review, Web sites on the latest ski equipment, or a new travel magazine. The whole point to cultivation is that you get to know the person as best you can so that you will be in a position to know when it is the right time to ask for support.

The sliding scale theory is a bit different when it comes to cultivation. Generally, people who are going to be asked for a large gift need more cultivation. They need to know, trust, and like the fundraiser, leaders, and volunteers. They have to be convinced that they are about to give to an organization that is transformational and that will be successful well into the future. This is what I call *giving to a forward-moving train*. People need to feel that the group is on track and moving well on the road to success. That said, I have worked with people who have given very large gifts who did not require much cultivation. Some people do not like you to "waste" the organization's money on them, so they decline invitations to receptions, lunches and dinners, or breakfast meetings, and they do not want you to send them anything with your group's logo on it. This is admirable, but it can make it more difficult for the fundraiser to cultivate these folks. In this situation I usually resort to periodic telephone calls, holiday and birthday cards, and e-mail where appropriate. This is the level of activity that makes these people comfortable. You must remember to use these, albeit distant, forms of communication to exchange information about your group and to gather information about these people. In your call, for example, ask them how they are doing at home or at work, ask them to call you, or tell them you will call just to see how they are doing. This is not the ideal situation because naturally you would like more face-to-face time with these folks, but you have to tailor your cultivation activities to match the person's comfort level.

As long as you stay active with each person, and there is a steady stream of information flowing both ways, your cultivation efforts will help you judge when it is the right time to ask. Perhaps the best benefit of cultivation is that it can provide fundraisers with constant feedback so that they know the person well, know that that the person's interests in the organization have not changed or strayed, and know that they are in the right position to fully appreciate the right time to ask for a gift.

INCLINATION People can be educated, involved, and cultivated to their comfort level with you and your group, but without the inclination to give, they simply will not give. Inclination is akin to motivation. The person must have the motivation, the inspiration, to support your group and your cause. Now, if the fundraiser has done his or her homework educating, involving, and cultivating the person, all signs should lead to sparking the person's inclination to give. A good example is what happens when a group selects a particular person to honor at a special event. It is a thrilling moment for the honoree, her family, and her colleagues as they experience the admiration and gratitude the group bestows. If the event is a fundraiser, then the honoree usually supports the group at the event by giving at a top sponsorship level. After these events most honorees are or should be in line to be asked for a follow-up major gift to the organization. These people are at their peak of inclination right after being honored. This event has brought them within the group's inner circle and as long as these people stay in close connection with the group, their inclination will be to make a gift at a significant level.

The reverse situation is that because each person has her own set of circumstances, good and bad, personal and professional, that she has to deal with day to day, it can appear that she should give but the inclination is simply not there. For instance, you might have a top person who could be a spokesperson for your group because she is so highly educated about it, has served on several committees, and has hosted and attended many of the group's functions. All the stars seem aligned for an Ask, but then this person tells you that her health has taken a turn for the worse or that she is in the middle of moving her mom into an assisted living facility or that her company was just acquired by a larger firm and jobs and locations have yet to be settled. Despite the education, involvement, and cultivation this person has enjoyed, it is highly doubtful that she is inclined or motivated to give at this point in time. There are just too many complications in her life right now. Supporting your organization is not a priority, hence, she has no inclination or motivation to give right now. It won't be until things settle down for her that you may be able to get her back on track with your group through further cultivation, and rekindle her inclination to give to your group.

The best way you can determine if a person is "inclined" to give is what I call the *pre-Ask conversation*. You know it is my job in this book to make "asking" as simple, easy, and effortless for anyone to ask, and this is a prime example of making a difficult judgment easy. All you need to do to determine inclination is ask the following question:

"Laura, when and if you were able to do something that was meaningful and significant to you with our group/business, what would that look like?"

I love this open-ended question for many reasons. First, the word "money" is nowhere to be found in this question. It is open-ended for a reason. You want the person to "open up" and honestly tell you what they would do that is meaningful to them. If they answer that they want to volunteer, or attend more events, or meet more people within the organization, that is a sign that they need more involvement. It is also an indication that they have not been thinking about either giving at a higher level or giving at a significant level and that more cultivation and a giving strategy needs to be formed (every person is their own mini-campaign) and executed with this person. Second, you will know from the answer where you fit in that person's priority list for giving. You may well hear that Laura is thinking of making a large business investment or that her college has been speaking to her about a capital campaign gift. This is great information because you have more to flesh out the person's profile. This is not to deter you from continuing to cultivate and eventually ask this person for money, but it does signal that you will need to sell and win over this person by making your work, your mission, your beneficiaries, your business important and so worthy of consideration for support in the very near future.

Third, hopefully you will hear the ideas and areas of support that are most important to her. This is what is called the *match,* matching the person's key interest in your group with a funding opportunity. For example, you may be working for an environmental nonprofit and you have been speaking with Cynthia about a great, new, exciting project that will take the concept of "going green" within the organization to the next level. This new project may be the template for multiple organizations to drastically reduce the amount of paper and chemical waste. Up until now, Cynthia has been energized, informed, and very interested in having this project succeed. But when you ask her the pre-Ask question, she turns to you and says:

"Trevor, I believe and admire the leadership of your organization. While this new project is great, I think I would just do something that

helps the whole organization. It is important that this operation stay
fiscally strong to do the environmental work the government simply
will not address."

Now you have the match. You know that when and if Cynthia were to do something for your organization it would be to benefit the overall good work, most probably an unrestricted gift. Pre-Ask conversations are ideal for nailing down the exact match between the person's interest in your organization and a giving opportunity.

ASSETS You cannot ask a person for money at a certain level if he does not have the assets to give away. It does not get much clearer than that. The person you are about to ask for $25,000 to name a room in a rehabilitation unit must have the means to make that gift without depleting his bank accounts, stock holdings, real estate, or life insurance. As I stated earlier in this chapter, you can find out a great deal about a person's assets through prospect research. Prospect research can be done even in a one-person shop as long as you have a computer and access to the Internet. If you have the budget, check out some of the prospect research providers; they may save your group a ton of time and be well worth the investment for you.

Crucial asset information should show that a person is living well, that her family members are provided for, and that she does not have any large debts or outstanding pledge payments to other groups. Fundraisers do not want to be blindsided during an Ask; they don't want the person to turn to them and say, "Sounds good, and I would love to do it, but I've committed $100,000 over several years to the Big Sisters so my money is tied up right now," or, "I just lost my job, and the recent hurricane destroyed my parent's home." The rule is that you need this background information to estimate how much money you think the person can give to the organization at this point in time.

Three notes of caution about using prospect research to judge the amount for an Ask. First, prospect research does not reveal every single asset a person possesses. Chances are the people you are cultivating probably have private holdings such as bank accounts, mutual funds, and stocks and bonds. Unless the person tells you how many shares of XYZ corporation he bought or traded or the size of his mutual fund holdings and bank accounts, you do not have the person's total asset portfolio.

Second, as emphasized in this chapter, the best prospect research is done in person through cultivation. During your meetings, conversations, and easygoing quality time with people you are cultivating, you will get to know and experience their lifestyles. You will know whether they spend their money on cars, boats, real estate, or vacations or on their children, stepchildren, and grandchildren. Many fundraisers make the quick assumption that if a person has wealth, as evidenced by expensive homes and hobbies, then they have the assets to give large gifts. It could very well be that their assets are supporting their expensive lifestyles and that they do not have the additional money to make a large gift to your group. I know many people who want to live long and live well, and that does not translate into giving large gifts to nonprofit organizations or large investment businesses.

Third, assets should not be mistaken for inclination. If your top people are sitting on piles of money and appreciated stocks and real estate and they have a modest lifestyle, this does not automatically translate into an inclination to share their wealth with your group. Someone at the leadership level in your group may well question why a person who has the capacity to give is not supporting the group. Quite simply, if this person has already been educated, involved, and cultivated and has the assets, then this person just might not be inclined or motivated to give. Some people never get to the point of being inclined to give. This could be why they have so much stored-up wealth! The bottom line is that fundraisers can do only so much with educating, involving, and cultivating; they cannot instill the inclination or motivation that will make the person share her assets. Now you see how all the elements of the readiness formula are dependent on each other.

Having Some but Not All of the Readiness Elements

What if you and the group's leaders or other members of your fundraising team think that a person has almost all the elements of the readiness formula and you all really feel the time is right to ask. For instance, what if you know the person is educated about the organization, her involvement is minimal, but she has said in conversations with you and others that she may be inclined to do something more for your group. You sense through conversations and research that she has the assets to make a major or planned gift. Then, yes, ask this person for a gift. Likewise, if you have been discussing your business plan with a potential investor, and she definitely knows about the project, goals, and competition, and has been modestly receptive to your meetings and telephone calls but her questions about the types of investments lead you to believe you need to ask now, then ask. The readiness formula just provides elements and guidelines for you to use. You do not need to know 100 percent for each element. As long as you, the leadership, or business partners have gone through the exercise of checking the elements of the readiness formula, you should be in a good position to make the right decision.

Asking for Money in Hard Economic Times

While I could write a whole other book on this topic, and as I am writing this book we are going through the recession of 2009, I felt it was important to address why and how you should still ask for money in hard economic times. If the person you want to ask for money has all the elements of the readiness formula, or if you would have asked for money at this point in time but the economy took a turn for the worse and there is no way of determining when it will recover, it is my firm belief that you should still ask, *with all the gentleness, empathy, and understanding* as possible.

First, do not do what I call "fill in the blanks" fundraising. In hard economic times it is very easy to assume that everyone is doing poorly and that the economic crisis will postpone all types of spending and giving. The key here is to get out *early* to your top people, meet with them in person, and ask them how they are doing. Thank them over and over again for their past support if they gave previously and share stories often of how their gifts were instrumental in sustaining, improving, and changing the lives of so many people or causes. Listen to their stories. Offer to help in any way you or your organization can to the extent possible. In tough economic times, people just want to be heard and feel that the organization is not ignoring them. In short, *be present* for those people who are important to your organization or business.

Second, not everyone does poorly in hard economic times so this is why it is so important to meet with them one-on-one and listen carefully to how they are weathering the challenges of the economy. Many people get extremely creative in hard times and that opens new opportunities that might not have been available to them previously. Many are new business ventures that can turn out to be quite lucrative.

Third, and this is the most important, in hard economic times *people want to feel good, which translates into giving and supporting their community.* I have seen this happen time and time again. I came to New York City in 2002, right after the disastrous events of September 11, 2001, to be Vice President of Philanthropy for Pace University. Pace University's downtown campus is only a few short blocks from ground zero. The university wanted to launch a capital campaign at that time and great consideration was given to postponing the campaign because the sentiment was that it would be insensitive to ask for large gifts in the wake of this horrific event. We did wait until 2003 to launch the campaign but the outpouring of support was overwhelming. Alumni and outside supporters wanted to see this university get back on its feet, to maintain its academic excellence well into the future, and in six years we raised over $92 million. I use this example but there are many others, such as the outpouring of support after Hurricane Katrina and the unfortunate hurricanes and earthquakes that followed that event.

Please memorize this line for me:

In very hard times the only thing people can control is their community.

They want to know their religious organizations are OK; they want to know their hospitals, schools, ambulance, police, and firefighters are there for them; they want to know when they drive/commute home that their small businesses are still there—in short, they want to feel "secure."

They cannot control terrorism; they cannot control weather disasters; they cannot control an economic crisis; they cannot control when their retirement funds will rebound; they cannot control interest on savings. They simply feel out of control. By giving and staying involved with local nonprofits, supporting local businesses, and feeling that they can maintain a quality of life for themselves, family, friends, and colleagues, they feel better about themselves.

How you ask during these times makes all the difference in the world. Again, if you feel the person is ready to be asked and they have not been tremendously set back by the economy, then do your Ask in the following manner:

> "Andrea, thank you for sharing so much about your family and your business. As I said, if we at the Cancer Institute can do anything to help you, please let me know. You and I have been discussing for quite some time your interest in making a $50,000 gift for our cancer research unit and we sincerely hope that this is still a priority for you to do. Andrea, can we discuss now how together we can make that gift happen? We have some ideas that may make it easier for you to be able to do it, knowing the challenges we all face in this economy. As you have said many times, 'If we don't have our health, what do we have?' and you above all know the need for this research only escalates every day."

> "Colin, thank you so much for your time today. We know how busy you are. We felt it was important to continue our conversation on how you wanted to hear more about investment opportunities with the company. We all know this is a tough economy and yes, so many small businesses are having a hard time staying in business, but we think you share our vision that our new business can actually help some of these small businesses stay alive, which is great for the community. Colin, we don't know if you can do this now, but let's talk about some of the ways over a period of time that together we can make this possible."

These are just some sample dialogs you can use. The point is to be sympathetic, not apologetic, because if you really believe in what you are asking for, hard times or not, it is worthy of support. Additionally, these examples are using very inclusive words like "together we can make this possible," "how we can make that gift happen," and "you share our vision" so that the person does not have to shoulder this decision now, alone.

Remember, in hard economic times people want to feel good so give them a reason to give; have a clear, calm, and convincing voice; and be ready to have some options on how they can make the gift or investment happen over time. I think you will do very well if you follow these small but important steps. Besides, if you do not ask, chances are there are many other nonprofits or business propositions right behind you that will, and now you and your cause are no longer a priority because your Ask is not even "lined up in the queue" for that person. Avoid sitting still during uncertain times when people are ready to be asked because your cause, your business, and you deserve funding before, during, and after any challenging time. Staying positive always wins the day.

CONCLUSION

In order to be the most successful with any Ask, you need to know who to ask, in what order to ask, and when to ask. Doing prospect research—if you have the resources to invest in private companies that specialize in this type of research; if you have someone full-time on your staff that can be your prospect researcher; or if you can hire a consultant who can research pertinent information that will provide you with a full prospect profile—can be tremendously helpful as you shape your cultivation strategies for each person. If money is not available for these services, keep in mind that the best prospect research is in person. When you sit down with your top people and ask open-ended questions, you will learn how this person feels about your organization so that you know how to engage and involve them to the point of asking them for money. Prioritization of the best people who have the best capacity to support your organization or business can easily be done by creating top tier and next tier lists so that all your cultivation activities are streamlined and you are focusing on the best people in priority order. Do not avoid asking friends, relatives, or colleagues for money if you think they would be interested in supporting what you do, because oftentimes they want to help you but you have not asked them. To avoid potential embarrassment, just be honest and state it may be uncomfortable but you believe in your cause and it is important to ask them if they want to be included in your charitable work or business venture.

The readiness formula can guide you when you are at the point of finding out if this is the right time to ask someone for money. Keep in mind that each person must be treated individually. Some people take months to ask, others years, and some, if you are very lucky, can be asked very soon after they are educated, involved, cultivated, and inclined. The best source of gauging when a person is ready to be asked is your instinct, so if you feel a person is ready to be asked, ask. Do not let a troubling economy put off your Ask if you feel the person is ready to be asked. Again, just be sensitive and honest and believe that what you are asking for is deserving of their support, even in tough economic times. People do want to feel that they can make a difference in hard times which may make it an ideal opportunity for you to ask and be flexible in how they can make the gift or investment possible.

LOOKING AHEAD

In the next chapter we will explore the last part of the preparation before getting to all the sample dialogs in Part II. The next chapter will outline who should make the Ask and what is the best setting for making the Ask. Deciding each of these questions naturally depends upon the nature of the Ask and the amount of the Ask. What is ideal for one person is not necessarily ideal for the next. There is no one formula for who should ask and where the Ask should be conducted, but there are many guidelines for making the Ask by the right person in the right setting that can make all the difference in the world.

CHAPTER

Who Should Make the Ask and in What Setting?

ELECTING THE RIGHT PERSON TO ASK MAY not be as obvious as it seems. Even if you are a nonprofit shop of one person or two people, or a solo business owner, sometimes you may need a person of leadership, another donor, volunteer, former customer, or satisfied beneficiary to be with you on the Ask. The nature and the amount of the Ask will determine who makes the actual Ask. Equally important is where the Ask is conducted. There are many things to avoid in selecting the right setting for your Ask, and this chapter will explore how you can have the right person make the Ask in the right atmosphere.

WHO SHOULD MAKE THE ASK?

Once you know the timing is right to ask a particular person for money, your next big decision is selecting the person or persons that will make the Ask. In some instances this will be an easy choice; in other instances it will be harder because the organization's leaders, members of the fundraising team, and volunteers do not always agree on who should do the Ask. Luckily, there are a number of organizational factors that will guide you during the selection process. As the initial step, one must look at the nature of the Ask. What is the Ask for and what is the Ask amount? The best rule of thumb is the higher the Ask amount, the more imperative it is to have someone in a leadership role at the organization to do the Ask. For instance, if you are working for a nonprofit and a high-end Ask would be $500,000 or more, then the president, CEO, or a board member would be ideal people to make the Ask. Exhibit 4.1 illustrates the ideal characteristics of any asker.

EXHIBIT 4.1.   *Ideal Characteristics of Any Asker.*

1. The asker is known, liked, admired, and respected by the person about to be asked.

2. The asker played a major role in cultivation.

3. The asker is comfortable, relaxed, and confident with the Ask.

4. The asker has given at the same level that is being asked.

5. The asker has given at a level in relation to his abilities that is comparable to the level being asked of the person in relation to her abilities.

6. The asker has demonstrated a strong commitment to the organization and is fully knowledgeable about the organization.

7. The asker knows the details of the gift or business opportunity and can clearly articulate the need for support.

8. The asker has the time to prepare for the Ask, do the Ask, and *carry out the necessary follow-up* to the Ask.

9. The asker keeps everyone involved with the fundraising process fully informed on the details of an Ask and the follow-through.

10. The asker has fun doing an Ask and can feel the rewards of asking for money for the organization.

A Charismatic and Confident Personality Goes a Long Way

As we go over each one of these elements, keep in mind the sliding scale rule. The larger the Ask, the more important it is that the person doing the Ask should possess all these characteristics. Large Asks, for a major, planned, or capital campaign gift, or large business investments, for example, require that the person doing the Ask have the background, confidence, and stature within your group to ask for significant funding. Charismatic personality, energy, demonstrated commitment, and loyalty to your group are a must for any large Ask. Conversely, it would not be the end of the world if the person asking for an annual gift, special event support, or smaller business investment opportunity possessed eight out of the ten characteristics. These smaller gifts are requested more frequently than larger gifts are, and even though, ideally, you would want any asker to possess the same qualities as someone asking for a transformational gift, the reality is that the Ask for a smaller, albeit very important gift, will go very well as long as the person has a majority of these qualities.

I think the best way to analyze the elements of a good asker is to take the point of view from the person being asked. Anyone being asked would like to be asked by someone who is known, well liked, admired, and respected. Mutual respect and admiration between the person being asked and the asker should set the tone for the Ask. The asker must have had some part, preferably a major one, in cultivation. All the meetings, events, correspondence, telephone calls, and e-mails during cultivation are the foundation for crafting the Ask. Yet I have known organizations to give part or all of the Ask to a person who has had little cultivation time with the person being asked. The results were not good. Put yourself in that person's shoes: how would you feel if someone with whom you have had very little contact asked you for a major gift or investment for an organization? You would not be experiencing the close, meaningful, and personal setting that is needed for any individual Ask. Strive to have all your askers play a major role in cultivating all the people you intend to ask.

Every Asker Must Give First

It is essential for anyone asking for money on behalf of an organization to make their own gift or investment comparable to the size they are about to ask for. Think about this. Why should anyone give you their hard-earned money if the person asking them has not made a similar commitment? Giving solidifies the asker's commitment to the organization. It is one thing to talk a good game; it is another to make a personal monetary commitment. No asker should be in the position of asking anyone else for any amount without giving first. People who have given first will always be more successful in asking for money because they have demonstrated their commitment to and investment in the group. The asker can easily say with conviction:

"Joan, join with me in this great investment."

"Russell, I support this group, and it is worthy and deserving of your support as well."

"Sandra, I have made a five-year pledge to this group because I wanted to invest in its future. Please join me and other top supporters and consider making a gift now. Our combined support will be no less than transformational."

For nonprofits it is essential that there be full board participation. What constitutes "full board participation" ranges from each board member giving at the same level; each board member giving a "stretch" gift, that is, an amount that would be a high-end gift for their income level; or raising for the nonprofit the equivalent amount of what they have been asked to give. For instance, if a board sets a threshold that every board member must make a yearly gift of $10,000 or more, there may be some board members who cannot give at this level and their responsibility then is to raise $10,000 yearly for the nonprofit.

The ideal way to make this happen is for the board to adopt a giving amount that is codified in the nonprofit's bylaws, and then for the president or CEO of the nonprofit along with the board chairperson to ask, in person, each board member for their yearly gift. I did say this was the "ideal" way because I have seen way too many instances where board members have no idea they are supposed to give, or know they are supposed to and never make their yearly commitment because no one ever asks, or worse, they are sent a letter asking for their yearly amount and no one ever follows up. If you have this situation where you work, and you are not the president, CEO, or chairperson of the board, then it is your obligation to remind this leadership group that prospective donors will ask "Does your board contribute 100 percent yearly?" and that it is imperative that you as the fundraiser be able to look that person in the eye and say, "Yes, and that is why we are asking for your support now, because our board backs this organization and we want you to join them."

When I headed the fundraising team for several nonprofits, I made it a point to have not only full board participation, but also full yearly giving to the nonprofit from every member of the fundraising team. This included administrative staff. I did ask them in person, and I stated that we can raise so much money by delivering the powerful message that not only does the board give 100 percent but so does the fundraising staff, which signifies we are all deeply committed to the financial strength and future of this organization. Now it was not the amount they gave, it was the fact that they did. I told my staff "I don't care if you give the difference between the cost of a regular coffee and a latte, the fact that you gave means more." It made the fundraising team more committed and I honestly never got the feedback that their extra uncompensated hours of work should count as their gift. If I had, I still would have asked for the difference between the coffee and the latte. So try it where you work and see if your fundraisers respond positively.

Even if there is total agreement that one must give before one asks, there is always a great deal of discussion in the fundraising arena about how much a person should give before asking and when and if he should ask someone for a gift or investment that is larger than the one he has given. There are no hard-and-fast rules on this issue, but there are some guidelines. First, whenever possible, have the asker give at the same level being asked. It just carries more weight, more cachet, and it puts the asker on par with the person being asked. That said, some of your most dedicated and ideal askers do not always have the assets to make large gifts or investments. It would be a shame if these people were discouraged from asking for money on behalf of the group, because they could be your best cheerleaders for drawing in new supporters. In these instances, have the person give at a level that is comparable for him to the gift being asked (Irwin-Wells 2002, 82). For instance, you may have a board member whose top gift is $50,000. This board member has served your organization for years, recruited new board members, and used her expertise to improve your group's financial investments. She knows and has cultivated the person about to be asked, who should be asked for a high-end gift of $100,000. The board member should ask this person for that gift because she has made what is for her an equally meaningful high-end gift. Just remember that if asker Ann made a "stretch" gift and she is the right person to do the Ask because she is closest to the person being asked, then even if the Ask amount is much higher than the amount the asker has given, asker Ann should do the Ask because she has demonstrated her commitment to the organization by making her own "stretch gift."

Every Asker Must Have the Time Before, During, and After the Ask to Follow Through

Asking for money is a multifaceted activity. One does not just ask, sit back, and wait for an answer. *It takes a commitment of time before, during, and after each Ask to see the gift come to fruition.* Moreover, one does not ask and then walk away and let someone else work with the person being asked until the gift or investment is received or completely rejected. People expect that the person who asked them for money will continue to meet and speak with them and discuss the gift opportunity and investment with them. (We will go into great depth on this topic of following through after the Ask in Chapter 8.) They do not take too kindly to being handed off to someone else after the Ask is made. If a CEO, president, or board member does the Ask or is part of the Ask, most likely it will be acceptable to have a staff fundraiser or volunteer available to provide additional information or materials for the person being asked. That person will also expect, however, to hear from the top askers again, following up on the Ask. The asker must be aware that the amount of time needed to continue to work with the person after each Ask is three times greater than what was needed for the preparation and actual Ask. If this follow-through is lacking, the Ask will lie in limbo, with no resolution.

If you are doing the Ask alone, then make sure you have the time after the Ask to follow through. As we shall see in Chapter 8, it can take weeks, months, and even years to close the Ask. The harder thing to gauge is, if you do the Ask with someone in a leadership role, whether you can know for certain if this person will have the time or make the commitment after the Ask to follow through. *The best thing you can do is to sit down with your asking partner with a calendar.* If you are going to do this joint Ask in October, then make sure she has time in November through January to follow up. Take the calendar and have her show you which days and time slots each month she will block out to do all the necessary follow up steps. Go one step further and then let your asking partner's administrative assistant know that these dates and times are blocked off so that you do not lose this precious committed time to follow up. This may seem overly simple but I guarantee if you do not do this prior to the Ask you will find yourself in the position of chasing after your asking partner to the detriment of the person being asked. The person being asked *expects* to hear from both of you so you need to set aside the time to make that happen.

If you do a joint Ask, it is very important that the information obtained before, during, and after each Ask is shared with both askers, and in some instances if it is for a large nonprofit, the fundraising team. All too often people ask for money and then do not share how the Ask went, the questions the person had, or the request for more time to consider the offer or for further information. The conversation during the Ask, observations about the person's reaction to the Ask, and the next steps to be taken after the Ask need to be shared with everyone involved with the preparation for the Ask and recorded in a contact report in the organization's database as discussed in Chapter 3. An organization does not do one Ask and then wait until there is closure on that Ask before asking for another gift. Multiple Asks will be going on simultaneously, and the best structure for keeping full and accurate records on each Ask is the group's database, so that leaders and fundraisers can accurately recall at a later time all the dynamics that occurred during the Ask and the next steps that need to take place to get the gift.

The Reward Is in the Ask

To ask for a gift of money is a privilege, a wonderful expression of commitment to and ownership of the organization. Getting a yes to an Ask can be a rush, but *asking for the gift can and should be just as rewarding.* This should not be a dreaded activity or a tense time. It is a time to share and celebrate the group's achievements and what the group can achieve for future generations, with help, support, and love from others. Best of all, the Ask can and should be fun. If it is fun for the asker, it will be a fun and positive time for the person being asked. People should see and experience the joy their prospective gifts will bring to the group's beneficiaries. The more upbeat and energized the asker can be, the more open and willing the person will be to consider the gift.

---

10 Things to Know About Any Ask—#4

When you ask for money you are not taking something away; you are giving someone the opportunity to feel good.

Four Eyes Are Better Than Two

Whenever possible, use two people; this number is ideal for any Ask. This team can be more effective because two people "have twice the talents and strengths of one" (Irwin-Wells 2002, 83). Team members can use their individual strengths when making the Ask and can feed off each other's energy and enthusiasm. While one member of the team is speaking, the other member can and should be a human sponge, absorbing the eye contact, body language, and tone of voice of the person being asked and can judge her level of comfort. I always use the expression "four eyes are better than two." With two people making the Ask, there is less chance that the team will miss something the person said, suggested through intonation, or expressed through body language. The bottom line is simply that there is strength in numbers, so every chance you get to do a joint Ask, take it.

The best way to experience the benefits of a team Ask is to do an Ask by yourself; then do one with another asker. As long as you both are prepared and well scripted as we discussed in Chapter 2, it will be crystal clear that your comfort level and confidence rise when you do the Ask with a partner. This is a wonderful exercise to try. Do an Ask with a partner. Right after the Ask, sit down and go over all the details that you and your partner heard and saw. I guarantee you that your notes will be comparable for some parts of the Ask, but for others you and your partner will have different versions.

For example, James, a director of development, and Kate, a director of direct mail, might jointly visit Vince at his home to ask for an enhanced gift. Vince has been a consistent giver through direct mail at the $200 level, but has the potential to make a larger gift of $1,000, which would place him in the group's Benefactor's Circle. It has been agreed that Kate will start the dialog, thanking Vince for previous important contributions to the direct mailings, and then James will spell out the need for increased gifts to this fund so that the group can do three specific new things to help its beneficiaries. James then asks Vince for the $1,000 gift. Vince says that he needs some time to consider his finances, and James agrees to call him within two weeks.

After the visit the directors sit down and compare notes. Kate had noticed piles of magazines, unopened letters, and other direct appeals on Vince's desk. She was also a bit distracted by Vince's dog, who had wanted to play with her. James missed all that because he was carrying most of the conversation, but he did see lots of construction taking place in Vince's backyard. He wondered whether the cost of these renovations might be a factor in Vince's need to think over whether to give a $1,000 gift now. Kate had missed all that because from her vantage point she could not see the backyard. This small example illustrates how two people can paint a much more complete and accurate picture of the Ask, a picture necessary to appropriate follow-up.

The team approach also has the advantage of letting the person know that she is important to the organization. Even when the Ask is not a top Ask for the group, the fact that two people are doing the Ask says that the group thinks very highly of the person being asked. It sends the message that the organization does not take the Ask lightly and that this is an important moment for the person and the organization. She will feel elevated because time and attention have been devoted to her, and that sets the stage for a very effective Ask.

EXECUTIVE LEADERSHIP AS PART OF THE ASK As mentioned before in this chapter, under the sliding scale theory, the larger the Ask, the more a person of leadership should be present. This can be the president, CEO, or board member. A president or CEO can carry the most weight for any Ask. Generally, it is a good idea not to exhaust their time with smaller Asks. You want to be respectful of their time, as the organization's day-to-day operational needs are their main focus. The exception would be if the person being asked has the capacity to give a large amount eventually, in which case it may be a good use of the leadership's time to ask for a smaller, interim amount and have them work this person up to that larger gift. This would be an effective use of the leadership's time because having them present, speaking with the strongest authoritative voice about why the organization is worthy of funding now, will probably result in getting that larger gift in a shorter amount of time. I have done this on several occasions very successfully but again, this would be the exception to the general rule of saving the executive leadership's time for high-end Asks.

Similar to the president or CEO, board members lend prestige to the Ask. Their volunteerism and financial support for your organization will be among the most powerful and influential factors in any Ask. According to the Advisory Board Company, support of the leadership, board, CEO, and senior executives ranked number four out of the five most important factors to the success of hospital fundraising (Advisory Board Company, January 2008). I would expand this and say that it probably applies to most organizations. This executive leadership presence alone heightens the level and importance of the Ask. The "dream team" of Asks would be the president or CEO and a board member, but save this asking team for your highest of Asks.

Asking board members to go on the road and ask for gifts with other members of your organization also serves to give the board members a realistic view of how challenging it can be to get the appointment to see potential donors and investors and then to ask for money. It is one thing to sit in a meeting, removed from your top and next tier lists of people who have the potential to give your organization money, and think that it is an easy task to ask for money. It is another to be a part of that process. Some board members may think their group has such a rich pool of people to ask for money that it should be raising more money. This is easy to say in a meeting; it is not so easy to experience when these wealthy people say no to the Ask or take months or years before unleashing a large gift to the group. Board members need this experience so that they can better understand and appreciate the fundraising process.

Because board members together with the CEO or president are the leadership for a group, they need a little tender loving care as they embark on the wonderful journey of asking people for money. I have some words of wisdom on this subject. First, obviously, be conscientious about board members' time. The organization should not be asking them to do more than they can handle. As previously mentioned in this chapter, it is so useful to sit down with each board member and carve out some time in the calendar year when they can assist you with your Asks. This will ensure that each board member does not volunteer to do more Asks than she or he can handle and that the organization has realistic expectations of each board member's time. Second, *nothing succeeds like a quick success.* During board members' early Asks, try to have them ask people who are likely to say yes to the Ask. A yes will empower them and make them feel as though they are good at asking, and they will then be more willing to do Asks for a longer period of time because their rate of success is pretty good (Lysakowski 2004). Third, have the fundraising person do all the administrative work required on each Ask, such as scheduling appointments, preparing letters to the people from the board members, and reminding the board members when it is time for them to call or visit a potential giver to keep the Ask viable. Some board members use their own support staff for these activities, which is terrific. In other cases, however, make sure the fundraising staff stays on top of the cultivation process; otherwise, the Ask will never be scheduled and there will be no follow-up.

Fourth, to the extent your organization has the budget for it, offer training on how to ask for money, preferably from an outside consultant. Even the most seasoned board member, one who has asked for gifts for your group and other groups, can always benefit from training and role playing. Moreover, beyond knowing the potential giver and the organization inside and out, board members also need to know the larger picture of the philanthropic climate. How are other organizations doing? Is giving on the rise, stalemated, or declining? How does a declining economy affect restricted and unrestricted giving? Which groups are doing better than others? Which constituencies are doing better than others? How do other groups attract younger donors? Consultants or members of the fundraising team should carve out some time, before or during a board meeting or at a retreat perhaps, to focus on the skills and techniques of the Ask, role playing for the Ask, and updates on current national and global fundraising trends.

Lastly, many of your board members will be closely connected to the community and will have influential friends and family who can widen your group's base of support. This was addressed in Chapter 3, but it bears repeating here, especially when it comes to board members. These people are particularly hesitant to ask for money from people who are close to them; it seems awkward and uncomfortable to them. Use the sample dialogs illustrated in Chapter 3 to overcome these fears and hesitations. Additionally, share the following statistic with them as a motivator for them to ask their colleagues, friends, and family to be more involved with your group and in turn to give. The *Chronicle of Philanthropy*'s list, "The Philanthropy 50: America's Most Generous Donors in 2008," *cited the organization's leadership as the major factor in their decision to give* (*Chronicle*, January 29, 2009). Many people on this Top 50 list of givers knew the leadership, especially the board members, very well, which inspired these large gifts. Also, in a University of Pennsylvania report, 23 out of 33 respondents said that knowing someone on the board or from their peer group ranked a four or a five on a scale of one to five (five being the highest) in importance of their giving (The Center for High Impact Philanthropy at the University of Pennsylvania, September 2008). Surely this will help to encourage many board members to take the leap and to ask those closest to them to support your group. Ask your board members to include their circle of close friends in this effort. Not to do so is a missed opportunity for your organization to expand its donor base.

People asking for money to support or invest in a business should use the same principles as stated above for nonprofits. The best board members to go on the Ask are the ones who are engaged, are knowledgeable about the "sell," have made their own investment, know the person who is about to be asked, and have the time to follow up after the Ask. And it should be for a high-end Ask. Again, the same rules of the game apply for businesses as well as for nonprofits.

The larger issue for both is what if you have very reluctant board members who do not want to participate in the activities before, during, and after the Ask either by themselves or with another person from the organization? There are some guidelines I can share with you that have helped me tackle this very issue. First, I have a saying: "take the best, leave the rest." We cannot expect that every board member has the skill set and desire (and you need both) to make Asks. There are plenty of tasks a board member can do if she absolutely resists asking for money. Second, with the right training, many board members change their minds and at least try to do some Asks. Third and most importantly, give the board members a small number of people to cultivate and eventually ask, and an assigned staff person even if you are a shop of one to help coordinate the activities. Again, small quick successes go a long way in gaining a board member's confidence to help ask for money.

Over the past few years I have done many board trainings, particularly covering what every board member needs to know about fundraising in economically challenging times. At the end of the training I give them a checklist of things they can do, and they must check off at least three activities. After all, what good is a training if it cannot be implemented immediately? Exhibit 4.2 shows the list I hand out.

EXHIBIT 4.2. *Ways Every Board Member Can Help Raise Money.*

1. Help identify potential new supporters.

2. Send handwritten notes to potential supporters on why they should meet with development staff.

3. Go on personal cultivation visits alone, or with executive leadership or development staff.

4. Host small gatherings of potential supporters at the organization's site, your home, or office to explain the organization's mission and/or business plan.

5. Take prospective givers on tours of the organization.

6. Meet with prospective givers at special events and tell them why you are a board member for this organization.

7. Volunteer to speak at special events.

8. Ask for money, with staff support, at the right time for a specific amount for a specific purpose and be available to follow up with each Ask.

9. Send handwritten notes thanking the people you met with for their past support.

10. Make thank-you telephone calls to recent supporters.

Name: _____

Best Months, Dates, Times for the Selected Activities:

_____

_____

_____

_____

There is really something for everyone to do, and I think if you use this list, tailor it to your organization, and add things for board members to do that will be beneficial to your organization, you will invigorate and energize your board members. Make sure you add the end part about listing best months, dates, and times for the activities because without this commitment, all the promises of doing some of these activities will surely be lost.

> Exercise #4: Set aside a portion of your next board meeting to distribute the Ways Every Board Member Can Help Raise Money checklist and follow up with each board member.

DONORS AS PART OF THE ASK   No doubt you will have a group of top donors who may want to help raise money for your group. This can be such a blessing because potential supporters do not want to feel alone when they give. Even though potential givers know that they will not be the only ones asked for money, at the moment of the Ask they can feel very alone and that if they give, they may be giving to a "black hole" with no one else contributing. If you have a donor on the Ask who can speak about why she gave, what hesitancies she may have had, how she overcame them, and best of all, how thrilled she is to see results and feel terrific about her giving, this would be a powerful Ask.

Some of these donors may be appropriate for a joint Ask, and some may not. The fact that they have made a significant gift or series of such gifts is not a signal that they should automatically be made part of any Ask. However, if they possess most of the ideal characteristics of a good asker, as spelled out earlier in Exhibit 4.1, and if they know and have a personal relationship with the person being asked, then, yes, they should be involved with the Ask. Conversely, I caution groups not to include a donor on the team making the Ask when that donor has not cultivated or does not have a past, positive history with the person. This is not the time you want to bring in someone brand new just to tell her giving story and then assist with the Ask. Where is the trust between the donor and the person being asked? No Ask should involve someone brand new to the dynamic of the asking process. The point of the Ask is to have a pre-established personal and trustworthy relationship so that the person being asked is comfortable and willing to listen to all the aspects of the Ask. The Ask should be an *extension of the trust and faith* the prospective giver has in your group. If you involve someone in the Ask who does not exude that feeling of confidence and trust and who is not close to the person, that prospective giver will lose interest in what the askers have to say, and the Ask will not be seriously considered.

WHAT IS THE BEST SETTING FOR THE ASK?

Now that we have some rules and guidelines on who should do the Ask, the next thing we need to turn our attention to is selecting the best setting for the Ask. The best setting entails not only the venue, but the tone, that is, the asker's body language; whether or not you should bring, exchange, or leave a paper proposal; and what you wear when you do the Ask. Orchestrating these features takes more work than you might think. The objective is to find a place that is quiet, calming, and with no distractions which matches the personality of the person being asked.

Location

The place where you select to do the Ask should be somewhere the person being asked and the asker both feel comfortable. Exhibit 4.3 lays out some characteristics to look for when selecting your venue.

EXHIBIT 4.3. *Selecting the Right Venue for Your Ask.*

1. A place that you and the person being asked have frequented during cultivation.

2. A calm, quiet, well-lit, and distraction-free setting.

3. The home or office of the person you are asking.

4. A room at the asker's organization or a private club if the environment can be controlled, preferably in a quiet office, conference room, or area within the club.

5. If the person being asked likes to meet you at a restaurant or if you prefer to do it over a meal, pick a restaurant well in advance that is as quiet as possible and as free of wait staff distraction as possible.

The ideal places are usually at the home or office of the person being asked, a private room at the organization, the CEO's or president's office, a conference room, or a private club. I say that these are usually good places to do the Ask for the following reasons. Not every person's home is a calm place, especially if she has young children, works at home, is repairing or reconstructing an area, or is taking care of an elderly parent who lives with her. You do not want these potential distracters when you ask for money. The same can be said for asking the person in an office setting. If your prior encounters at her office have been interrupted by messages from an assistant or urgent telephone calls, then her office is not a good choice.

Doing the Ask at your organization—for example, in the CEO's or president's office, a conference room, a study, or a library—may be an excellent choice, especially if the person being asked has been in these areas before and likes coming to your facilities. In that case the person and the askers will be very comfortable with these surroundings and will have a more controlled atmosphere. The askers can ensure that there are no interruptions because the organization's site is within their control.

A private room in a private club may accomplish the same goals, especially if the person has been cultivated in this atmosphere and enjoys the private club scene. It is important that the askers notify the club staff in advance that they do not want to be disturbed at a certain point in time during the meeting. For instance, if it is a meeting that involves a meal, after the plates are cleared and the coffee pouring ceases, the wait staff should disappear so that the askers can focus the person's attention on the opportunity. The other word of caution about private clubs is to make sure the person likes being taken to private clubs. Some people feel they belong in an elevated level of society and should be there. Many may belong to a club or two, and in that case you should not think twice about doing the Ask in a private club. Other people, however, may feel that a club is pretentious and that the organization should not "waste its money" on private club fees. The rule here is to know what makes the person comfortable and select that venue.

There is much discussion about whether people should be asked for money in a restaurant or café. Unless the person is available only during breakfast, lunch, or dinner or expects you to take her out to a restaurant, I would avoid doing the Ask when food is involved. It gets complicated and unpredictable for several reasons. First, even if you tell the wait staff in advance that you want some uninterrupted time, there is no guarantee they will remember and give you some time. After all, it is their job to attend to your table, and now you are asking them to leave you alone! Second, you probably cannot predict the level of conversation that will take place around you during your Ask. We all have had the experience of having a very loud and lively table next to us, and it is very distracting. You do not want to be competing for attention, and you do not want to be raising your voice over another conversation so that your potential donor can hear you. Third, you have to navigate the awkward moment when the check arrives. I have gone to a restaurant well in advance of the meeting and have given the manager explicit instructions that the wait staff give me the check. I have even supplied my credit card in advance of the meeting so that the wait staff can give me the check with my credit card and all I have to do is sign. Sometimes this works, but at other times the dreaded black leather folder containing the check is left smack in the middle of the table and the person and I end up practically arm wrestling for the check. If at all possible, spare yourself this anxiety, and select a place to do the Ask that is not a restaurant or café.

As important as it is to know some guidelines in choosing your venues it is just as important to be clear of what should not be present during the Ask. Exhibit 4.4 lists things to avoid once the setting is selected for the Ask.

EXHIBIT 4.4. *Things to Avoid Once the Setting Is Selected for the Ask.*

1. All cell telephones, pagers, and beepers (must be off or on quiet mode).
2. Glaring sunlight or overhead lighting that may distract the person being asked.
3. Computers that give a sound when new e-mail arrives.
4. Telephones that are not picked up by an outside source during the Ask.
5. Interruptions from anyone at the workplace.
6. Noise from shared printers in your office if the Ask is taking place there.
7. Background music from your computer or overhead at your office.
8. Teleconferencing equipment that goes off during the Ask in an office.
9. Venues that are in the heart of the city where traffic and sirens are most likely to be heard.
10. Even if the opportunity presents itself, do not give the details of the Ask while you are walking with the person to the venue; on an elevator; or in a public space.

Believe it or not I have had one of each element in Exhibit 4.4 happen to me during an Ask and it is not a pleasant situation. It totally distracts the asker and the person being asked, and while it is not the end of the world, asking can be a very nervous experience, so try to avoid all the elements in Exhibit 4.4. As a rule when I am driving or commuting to the Ask, I put my cellular phone on "quiet" so that I can see if any e-mail, text messages, or telephone calls came in that might affect the Ask. While I cannot control if the day I ask will be sunny or rainy, I can control where each person sits by saying, "Hi Justin, why don't we sit over here, this looks like a great seat for you," and then face him with his back to the sunlight. If the Ask is in your office or your asking partner's office or conference room, make sure all telecommunication equipment is disconnected. I have had many a stray call come in from a boomerang-shaped conference call telephone with everyone hovering over it trying to end the call—a perfect scene for a commercial but not a feature you want during your Ask. While you may not be able to control the overhead music at an office, it would be good to move your Ask meeting to someplace quieter by saying gently, "While I love music, why don't we move to this office where we don't have to compete with the music?" The last piece of equipment that you need to worry about is the shared printer. Yes, my friends, this does happen. Who could predict that your office mate or administrative assistant would choose your Ask meeting to print out all the e-mails or committee meeting notes and have them sent to your printer during the Ask? The best way to avoid this is to disconnect the printer and leave yourself a note to reconnect it after the Ask.

If you are meeting in a city-type atmosphere, whether it be a person's home, office, or restaurant, put yourself in a back room so that there is minimal street and emergency vehicle sirens and noise. Meeting at a lovely outdoor café can be relaxing and inviting but it will do you no good if it distracts your conversation. Also, you may have people that you want to ask for money who like to go to "celebrity" venues, particularly restaurants with big-name chefs. Here is my story on that one. We had a person I'll call Matt that we were going to ask for a "lead" seven-figure gift for our capital campaign. Matt loved Wolfgang Puck restaurants and when I called to set up the meeting for the Ask, he agreed as long as we met at Wolfgang's restaurant downtown. My asking partner and I thought great, we'll have the right Ask in the place Matt would feel most at ease. While we were ordering lunch, Wolfgang Puck appeared and Matt called him over to our table. While this was a memorable moment, Matt was so excited that Wolfgang spent time with us that it took a *very* long time to get him to focus on the Ask. Now, this can go either way, and if the person you are asking really has a strong preference for a particular venue you should always honor that request. Just be aware that you and your asking partner may have to be vigilant in swaying the conversation back to the Ask. Otherwise, you will have had a fabulous meal and maybe walk away with a great memory or signature picture with the celebrity, but the Ask will be postponed and you will be very unhappy on the ride back to the office.

Lastly, even if you and the person being asked get engaged in conversation about the Ask on your way to the select venue, avoid the temptation to reveal too much. It takes a lot of discipline to say, "Yes, this is exactly what we want to speak with you about but it is too important to speak more about it here, and we are just about at the conference room, so let's pick up where we left off once we get there." You will dilute the Ask if you are walking and talking on your way to your destination.

The Golf Course Ask

Now that I just said not to do an Ask in an open space on your way to your venue, we all know that many an Ask or business deal is done on a golf course, at some recreational or cultural event, and yes, I've even heard of it happening during a gym workout. Each Ask has its own place and time so if you have been cultivating people this way and you have the opportunity to make an Ask, it might be appropriate and beneficial to do so at this time. I would suggest that you limit these types of Asks to business deals, advice, recommendations, and maybe sponsorships for events but I would not recommend them for a nonprofit major, planned, capital campaign gift or a major business investment. Those types of nonprofit Asks need a secluded area, with full attention, and the person being asked needs to devote 100 percent of her time to the details of the Ask. You don't want someone swinging a golf club, happy as can be that they just might reduce their lowest handicap score, and then make your Ask. Even if you are asking for something related to business, advice, or a recommendation, make the Ask when there are the least amount of distractions, particularly noise and other people who should not be overhearing the Ask.

Positive and Professional Dress and Demeanor

During any meeting one or more persons govern the tone of the meeting. In a sales meeting, for instance, the person who reports that the team has reached or surpassed its marketing projections is filled with excitement and pride. All eyes and attention are on this one person. Ditto for meetings that involve the Ask. The person will generally mirror the energy level and level of professionalism set by the asker or askers. This is why it is so important for the asker or asking team to have high energy, be enthusiastic, be upbeat and positive, and establish strong eye contact. It starts with appearance. Even when you are asking for a gift from a studio artist, a florist, a retiree, or someone else who generally does not wear a suit or dress clothes every day, you and the others doing the Ask must look professional, crisp, and polished. This requires careful attention to hair, nails, shoes, and an appropriate handbag or briefcase. Would you want someone who looks like he slept in his clothes or who had missing buttons or stains on his clothes asking for money on behalf of your group? Wear appropriate business attire with the appropriate accessories, and you can never go wrong.

Your energy and enthusiasm should be contagious. After all, this is the big moment—the moment when the asker and asking team will be doing the final sell of a fabulous opportunity. The asker needs to be as charismatic and positive as possible so that the person will in turn be pumped up to hear the details about the gift. Mind you, it is easier said than done for each Ask to have the ideal aura. Realistically, not everyone has a good day every day, and we all have personal and professional issues that sometimes prevent us from feeling our best. When that occurs, I recommend two things to get you back on track and feeling more positive. I learned this early in my practicing attorney career, when I was scared to death to do a trial or oral argument against an experienced opposing counsel. The first tactic is to think of yourself not as you but as someone you admire. I used to imagine that I was a famous actress or politician. I focused on what that person would do and say in this moment. If you focus on someone you admire and try to adopt their star-power qualities, it will help you get out of your own head, your own funk, and be more positive and likeable. The second tactic is to do or concentrate on the things that make you happy. Put on your favorite CD, dance, sing (only if you have a good voice), buy yourself flowers, or visualize yourself as winning an Olympic competition. It just may force you to smile and, in turn, feel better for the Ask.

Positive Body Language and Tone of Voice

An asker can say all the right things but still sabotage the Ask because his body language or tone of voice is sending the wrong message. During an Ask, each person doing the Ask has to stand tall, sit upright, have his shoulders back, and his head and eyes fixed on the person being asked. The asker's body position is very important because it can send so many different signals. The asker does not want to appear nervous by looking around the room, looking past the person, reading from notes, reading the whole proposal, or rearranging the pillows on the sofa. The asker also does not want to appear overly comfortable by slouching on a chair or sofa or leaning way back with his hands folded over his head or stomach. This body positioning can be visually distracting. One of the reasons why it is always good to have two people on the Ask is to learn about one's body language. Askers may have no idea how distracting they look when they get comfortable in a cushy armchair. If only one person is doing the Ask, how can he receive feedback about his asking style and effectiveness? All askers need to be aware of their body language messages and should respond positively to feedback if improvement is needed.

Just as your body language can send a good or distracting message, your tone of voice can do the same. For instance, if an asker is nervous, she may tend to lower her voice, to cough in between sentences, or to get a dry mouth and be desperate for a glass of water. All this can be very distracting to the person being asked and can undermine the importance of the Ask. Voice and body language go hand in hand. When people lower their voices, they also generally lower their heads. Now, not only will it be hard for the person to hear what the asker is saying, but all eye contact has been lost as well. The asker's voice should be clear and convincing. It should resonate with confidence in and dedication to the mission of the organization. If it does, strong body language will follow, and then you will have the complete package for a strong Ask.

While we are discussing appearances, you should make sure that askers are not chewing gum or taking way too long with a breath mint or hard candy. It may seem silly to mention this; however, many people want to make sure their breath will not knock the person over, so right before they ring the person's doorbell they pop in a piece of gum or a mint. While you are traveling to see the person is the time to check your breath, so that by the time you arrive that activity is over. Gum chewing or positioning a mint while you are speaking is very distracting and diminishes the quality of the Ask.

Making the Call to Set the Meeting for the Ask

I am often asked the question, "Should you let the person know you are going to ask for money when you make the call to set up the appointment?" My answer is yes, but how you say it is very important. If you have done all the right cultivation moves and you have a good instinct that the person is ready to be asked, by using the tools in the readiness formula in Chapter 3 you can have the confidence that the person is ready and make the appointment. You can say, "Brandon, I'd like to meet with you in the next week or so to continue our discussion on how you can make a real difference with the organization. I have a few ideas that I'd like to share with you in person. We generally meet at your office at 8:00 A.M., so can we meet there early next week?"

Now there is no mention of the word "money" in the dialog but it is clear that you are continuing along the path to bring the person to the point of being asked. Brandon knows that you are going to be sharing ideas about what he can do. If you have previously discussed ways and amounts of support that Brandon was considering and this is the level you want him at in terms of support, then you can be more direct and state, "Brandon, I've been thinking about our past conversation and I want to share with you in person some gift (or investment) opportunities that are right in sync with what we have been discussing. How does next Tuesday work for you to meet?" Exhibit 4.5 has some suggestions when you are making the appointment for the Ask.

EXHIBIT 4.5. *Guidelines for Making the Appointment for the Ask.*

1. The asker should call the person about to be asked and make the appointment.

2. The conversation should reference whether the topic of discussion will be a new idea or continuation of a previous

(Continued)

(Continued)

discussion on how the person being asked can make a real
difference for the organization.

3. If the leadership of the organization, such as the president,
CEO, or board member, had an executive or administrative
assistant make the appointments in the past, then make sure
the assistant references the purpose of the meeting as set forth
in number 2 above.

4. If it appears that the person about to be asked keeps
postponing the meeting or is reluctant to meet, then the
person is not ready or does not want to be asked and more
cultivation, education, and involvement with the
organization is needed.

5. Always confirm the date, time, and place of the meeting a
day before the meeting.

The Ask meeting is the most important meeting you will have
so it is vitally important that the asker make the appointment. If
this is a team Ask, then select one person on the team to make the
telephone call. Notice I say telephone call and not e-mail or letter.
Asking is all about the personal relationship you have so why would
you want to distance yourself by setting the meeting through an
e-mail or letter that may take some time to read and then respond?
When the asker makes the call, as with the importance of body
language and tone of voice mentioned earlier, it is equally important
that the asker's tone of voice be upbeat, positive, and friendly. The
asker should state that the purpose of the meeting is to share an idea
or continue the discussion on how the person being asked can be of
the greatest help to the organization as referenced in the earlier
sample dialog with Brandon.

The harder issue arises when someone in a leadership role in the
organization, like the president, CEO, board member, CFO, COO,
vice chancellor, doctor, head nurse, priest, rabbi, or head of school has
in the past had someone else make the appointment during cultivation. If the person in the leadership role can make the telephone
call, that would be ideal. If not, then the assistant and, in many cases,

development staff or consultant should make sure that the purpose of the meeting is stated.

It is important to tell the person being asked the nature of the meeting because the last thing you want to do is surprise the person with the gift or investment Ask. If all the right cultivation has taken place, the person will not be put off and it will not be a surprise that they are going to be asked for money. If it appears that the person about to be asked keeps postponing the meeting or is reluctant to meet, then the person is not or does not want to be asked and more cultivation, education, and involvement with the organization is needed. This is a very different situation than the person being asked having such a busy personal and business life that it is difficult to schedule the meeting. The difference is getting a free date to meet, not a reluctance to meet.

It is highly recommended that the appointment be confirmed the day before. If the asker can do the confirmation, great; if not, an assistant or development staff person can confirm the details. Exchanging cell telephone numbers or numbers where each party will be that day would be wise in case a situation arises in which the meeting would have to be rescheduled.

Paper or No Paper Before, During, or After the Ask

The larger the amount of the Ask, the more logical it will be for you to have a written proposal. It should detail the purpose of the gift or investment; the amount; a breakdown of costs or detailed budget for the project or program; how it can be funded; how many years the payments can be made; the benefits it will bring; and in some instances how the gift or investment will be recognized and publicized.

I have a few suggestions about "paper" before, during, or after the Ask that have served me well which I hope you find beneficial as well. First, I recommend you do not send the proposal or any written document about the nature of the Ask until you actually make the Ask. If you do the likelihood is that the person will take forever to respond and generally you will walk away with much less money because the Ask was not done "live and in person." This issue usually comes up when people in leadership positions want to send something first and then meet. Don't do it! Stand firm and state that the person deserves to see the excitement, enthusiasm, and energy in the asker's face and it loses all that personal touch if it is first revealed on paper.

Second, there is a time and a place during the Ask for the proposal. If you are doing a large capital campaign Ask, or have a planned giving illustration detailing the breakdown of a gift annuity or trust, or if the details of the business investment need to be shared with much explanation, I would have the proposal ready to be shared *but only after you have made the specific Ask for the specific amount.* If you bring out the proposal while you are doing the Ask you are setting up the likelihood that the person will be distracted with illustrations, reading pages before or after you get to them, or worse, have an abundance of questions so that you never get to experience how she feels about the Ask. Make the solid Ask, be silent, listen carefully to the response, craft your answer, and then bring out the proposal, which may clarify certain points. Don't give the person the opportunity to deflect and get lost in paper before you make the Ask.

Third, and this works very well, you can always send the person a letter after the Ask meeting, detailing the Ask, the person's concerns, and the asker's responses, which can serve as a thank-you letter and codification of all the points raised during the Ask meeting. This gives you the opportunity to make it more personal because you are addressing all the questions and concerns that were raised as well as the particulars about the great gift or investment opportunity. The extra benefit of sending this after the Ask is that many times people need to share something with their spouse, personal or business partner, attorney, accountant, or financial adviser, and that person can then be brought up to date immediately if this comprehensive letter proposal is given to them to review.

CONCLUSION

The ideal asker is a person who knows the person very well, has played a substantial role in cultivation, has made a comparable size gift or investment with the organization, and is willing to follow up with the Ask, long after the Ask is made. Whenever possible two people on the Ask is better than one person to ensure that everything about the person being asked is captured, from what is being said to how it is being said. The asker should set the appointment for the Ask and it should be revealed that the purpose will be to discuss ways in which the person can make a substantial impact, now, on the organization.

When selecting the right venue for the Ask meeting, make sure it is a quiet, comfortable, and distraction-free environment and that the person being asked will feel at ease in this location. Every asker should be mindful of tone of voice and body language such that enthusiasm and energy set the tone for a positive and powerful meeting. Give careful consideration to when and if you want to share a proposal or confirming proposal letter after the Ask. It is never a good idea to send the Ask in any written form prior to asking in person because it diminishes the importance of the Ask and the need for the personal connection during the Ask. Do the Ask in person and then either at the end of the Ask meeting leave the written proposal, or a day or two later send a letter detailing the Ask and addressing the questions or concerns that were raised during the Ask. The person's close personal or business contacts may want to review the details before they can offer their advice about the Ask, and this letter will also service that purpose.

LOOKING AHEAD

The next chapter begins Part II of the book. Part II will focus on sample dialogs asking for small and large charitable gifts, for job-related causes, for creative projects, and for business investments. With each sample Ask dialog, there will be new and creative approaches, such as making the Ask good, better, and best; having two different people in two different positions make the same Ask; as well as having one person versus two people on the Ask.

The next chapter will be devoted to asking for small and large charitable gifts and will detail the ways each Ask can turn into a great Ask.

How Do I Make the Ask?

Asking for a Cause—Small and Large Charitable Gifts

T HIS CHAPTER BEGINS PART II, WHERE YOU
will find many sample dialogs on how to make a variety of Asks.
I created all the scenarios to be broad enough to apply to a variety of
situations yet specific enough to give you solid Ask language you can
adapt. This chapter focuses on asking for small and large charitable
gifts. The chapter that follows will illustrate Asks for yourself and for
your passion such as for a business, a creative project, a raise, and a
promotion. The two types of charitable Asks in this chapter will be
first asking for smaller gifts—an increased annual fund gift and an
increased gift level for an endowed gift—and then asking for a larger
capital campaign gift and a larger gift from a board member. I will
demonstrate how the *right selection of words in the right sequence* can
have a tremendous impact in making the Ask. I will also illustrate
words and phrases not to use that may weaken or dilute the importance of the Ask. There are some guidelines I will set forth that apply to
all the sample Asks that follow, which I think will be useful as you read
them and then apply them immediately to your practice. I will
conclude this chapter with some troubleshooting tips for any charitable Ask (and many apply to for-profit Asks as well) that will help you

anticipate some common occurrences that might happen prior to the Ask and how you can best be prepared.

ASKING FOR A SMALL AND SIGNIFICANT CHARITABLE GIFT

Before we jump into the dialogs for specific Asks in this chapter and the chapters that follow, it is important to have some guidelines about the sample Asks. Exhibit 5.1 sets forth those guidelines.

EXHIBIT 5.1. *Guidelines for the Sample Ask Dialogs.*

1. The amount in each Ask can be tailored to every organization's needs. Add or subtract the zeros if your "small gift" is $500, not $5,000 or your larger size gift is $1 million, not $100,000. The principles in the Ask are what matters.

2. We are at the point of the Ask where it is assumed that all or most of the elements in the readiness formula in Chapter 3 are met.

3. Since we are at the point of the Ask, there will be very little "warm-up" discussion (as discussed in Chapter 2), so the Asks will have very little dialog on the warm-up.

4. It would be impossible to cover every possible Ask scenario but these sample Asks will provide a broad spectrum of Asks for everyday success.

5. The sample dialogs will all be different, ranging from good, to better, to best; to one person versus two people on the Ask; to a person of leadership on the Ask versus a staff person on the Ask to illustrate the widest range of Ask examples.

6. The responses and follow-up to these Asks and more will be covered in Chapters 7 and 8.

7. The more practice you have with asking, the easier and better you will be in asking, so rehearse!

8. It is always a good thing when the asker is nervous, so embrace the feeling.

9. It is important that you take the sample Ask dialogs and impart your own words and language that is comfortable for you.

10. Use your own voice and you can never lose!

If you keep these guidelines in mind as you read along I think it will help you to not get caught up in some things that could distract you, such as:

- "This amount is too large for our organization."
- "This seems like you are too abrupt with the Ask—where is the warm-up?"
- "This seems awkward for me to say—can't I use these words?"
- "We are not a large educational or cultural institution so this can't possibly apply."

In fact all the sample dialogs can apply if you keep these important guidelines in mind. And with that, let's get to the Asks.

The first illustration in asking for a small and significant gift is an Ask for an increase in the annual fund. For many groups the annual giving program is the foundation of the organization's fundraising. It is where the greatest volume of people become involved with the group through either volunteering or giving. The gifts to the annual fund support the organization's general operating fund and can help it continue with its projects and programs. These unrestricted funds give the leaders the latitude and breathing space to run the organization.

The goals for the annual fund program are (1) to renew donors at a higher level than their last gift; (2) to minimize the number of lapsed donors; (3) to win back lapsed donors; (4) to acquire new prospective donors; (5) to engage donors in participating in all aspects of the organization; (6) to recognize donors for their giving, usually through gift clubs or levels; (7) to coordinate prospective givers with the major, planned, and capital campaign gift areas; and (8) to turn annual fund donors into major, planned, and capital campaign gift donors. Groups can use direct mail and phone-a-thons to achieve many of these goals, but as in the rest of this book, we focus here exclusively on fundraising in which individuals do the Ask in person. If you are serious about getting the enhanced annual fund gift, then it requires a personal Ask. It is possible to get increased annual fund gifts via mail and phone-a-thon appeals; however, the success rate is greater when the Ask is done in person. Further, the probability that high-end annual fund donors will become prospective major, planned, and capital campaign gift-givers is greater when they have been lifted out of a pool of annual fund donors, treated separately and distinctly as a special group, *and they are asked in person.*

This first Ask involves a donor named Bill who has supported a local radio station. He owns his own hardware store that has been a family business for years. Bill has made two gifts in one year. The first was a $100 gift for an on-air fundraising drive, and then later in the year $250 for another on-air fundraising drive. Both gifts were targeted for music programs. Director of Development Jacqueline acknowledged both gifts and sent a letter to Bill asking for a personal visit to discuss his interest in the station and to get to know him better. She met with him six weeks ago at his business and gave him the updates that the station was hosting their first singer-songwriter series in the summer and invited him to attend the first show in the first week of August. Bill was too busy but appreciated the offer. Bill stated that he does play the station in his store and has for years. Jacqueline said she would see him again after the first of the summer series to give him a "live update" and feedback about the concert. It is now mid-August and Jacqueline has secured another appointment with Bill.

Jacqueline: Hi Bill, it is good to see you again.

Bill: Hey Jacqueline, I'll be right with you. Please have a seat in my back office.

Jacqueline: Thank you again for your time, Bill. I promised you I would give you a personal update on our first singer-songwriter series. It was really great. We missed having you there but we hope you had the chance to tune in. There were many supporters like you as well as our "fan" listeners who came out for the concert. The weather was on our side; you know, that can always make or break an event. From a fundraising standpoint as well as marketing outreach we did really well with the event.

Bill: That's good to hear. I did have it on in the store but Saturdays are our busiest days so I caught some but not all of it.

Jacqueline: We really like to hear this and we're happy to have you as a loyal listener. Bill, we wanted to take this opportunity first to thank you again for your support and speak with you on how you can make a tremendous difference for your radio station. Bill, last year you supported our on-air fundraising campaigns and we would like to take this opportunity to ask you to increase your support. New initiatives like the singer-songwriter series can only happen with the individual support we receive from our loyal listeners like you. I am sure you are aware that corporate support has declined sharply, but we have a plan in place to make up this amount and exceed our fundraising goal from last year by personally visiting and further engaging loyal donors like you.

Bill, we turn to you now and ask you to make a gift of $1,000 in support of your radio station so that we can continue to provide you and your customers with the best quality music and programming.

Let's take a look at what was covered in this Ask. First, Jacqueline did go back to Bill as promised after the first singer-songwriter concert to give him a personal account. This is very important because often in cultivation the person or people doing the cultivation promises the potential donor that they will do certain things, mail certain pieces of information, or invite the prospective donor to an event, and it never happens. Trust me, potential givers do remember and they look forward to the person or people to do the follow-up. Second, the nature and tone of the conversation is very upbeat, positive, and since it is taking place in Bill's hardware store, it has that "down home" feel to it. Third, she did ask for a specific amount for a specific purpose and the amount was not that drastic a leap from his prior gifts. There may be occasions when you can ask a person for a substantial increase from their last gift if they have given you indications that they want to do something much more than what was given in the past, or through research or conversation it was revealed that the person had the education, involvement, inclination, and assets to substantially increase the past giving level. But in this sample dialog, Bill has only been visited once, he likes the radio station, and he is willing to listen about the new singer-songwriter series, so asking for $1,000 should be right in line for his next gift level.

Something to note in this sample dialog as well is that Jacqueline did state that corporate funding would probably decrease "but we have a plan in place to make up this amount and exceed our fundraising goal from last year by personally visiting and further engaging loyal donors like you, Bill." This would be far different from Jacqueline saying, "Bill, you probably can imagine in this economy with corporations closing, merging, or going bankrupt that we anticipate a severe shortfall and the only way we can make it up is to focus on individual giving." That might be what you say with your fundraising colleagues or it may be part of the revised fundraising plan for the year but it would *not* be something you say in that manner to a donor. The point is it is perfectly alright to share with donors the plans the organization has to hit or exceed its fundraising goal, but do not paint a negative, gloomy picture. What donor would want to give to a sinking ship?

Lastly, Jacqueline did spell out why the increase was needed, so that "we can continue to provide you and your customers with the best quality music and programming." It is always important to set forth the benefits that the donor can be proud of once the gift is made. Note throughout this sample dialog the use of the words "we" and "your radio station." While this is grammatically incorrect because the only person doing the asking is Jacqueline and therefore "I" would be more appropriate, when asking anyone for money I have always found that if you use "we" you have all the power of the organization behind you. When any fundraiser walks through the room, the donor sees and envisions the organization. Use "we" or "I" as you wish in your solo Asks because it is your comfort level with the words that matters most.

The next sample dialog involves asking for an enhanced endowed gift. I put this example here because many times donors are asked, or should be asked, for an increased gift or for an "upgraded" gift from their previous gift levels. I selected an endowed gift because many organizations need an endowment that will ensure the organization will be in existence well into the future.

An endowment is a fund that is restricted. Only the interest from the fund can be spent, not the principal that anchors the endowment. Usually, only a portion of the interest or earnings, usually 5 percent, from the endowment can be spent on an annual basis in order to assure that the original funds will grow over time.

The endowment is nothing more than what I call a stability fund. Think of it as a savings plan. Small and new nonprofits often get caught up in only planning for the current year. An endowment can diversify the organization's income and reduce dependency on year-to-year funds (Fritz). Furthermore, endowments can be very attractive to donors because their endowed gift can keep on giving well into the future by the nature of its investment.

In the next sample dialog, Rebecca has made two $2,500 gifts to the Regional Art Museum. Major gifts start at a $10,000 level at the museum. Director of Individual Giving Trevor wanted to see Rebecca personally after she made her first gift but she declined due to her schedule. He attempted to see her again before the end-of-year mailing went out the following year but she had already committed to a gift of $2,500. Both gifts were acknowledged by letters from Trevor and the museum's curator. Trevor has met with Rebecca on several occasions, mainly at the museum before or after special openings. It is year three and Trevor wants to get an appointment with Rebecca before she voluntarily sends in her gift. This is the first time he was successful in getting an appointment at her home and he intends to ask her for a $5,000 a year gift for three years to support a special fundraising effort by the museum to increase its endowment.

Trevor: Hi Rebecca, how are you today?

Rebecca: Just fine, busier than I would like but you know, that's how it goes.

Trevor: I sure do. Thanks for meeting with me today, Rebecca. As you know from our conversations and as one of our loyal patrons of the museum, we are looking to increase our endowment from $7 million to $15 million over the next few years so that we can refurbish the east wing and expand our "art after school program" for children 6–10 years old.

Rebecca: Yes, I know all about it. I saw some reference to that on the back of some mailing I received. That's a pretty big leap from $7 million to $15 million. How's the fundraising going?

Trevor: Well, Rebecca, not as well as we would like. We have several proposals into foundations and we have received a handful of $1,000–$5,000 grants. But we are really counting on our loyal supporters like you, Rebecca, to help us reach our goal.

Rebecca: Me? What did you have in mind?

Trevor: Well, Rebecca, your past support of $5,000 over the past two years has been great and we are so appreciative. We were wondering if you would be willing to support the museum with a pledge of $15,000 paid over three years. Rebecca, we really need your help and this would give us a lift to our fundraising efforts.

Let's take a look at what is OK with this Ask, and then how we can turn it into an even better Ask. First, Trevor does lay out the groundwork that the museum has a goal to increase its endowment with a specific goal of $15 million and that the endowed fund would be used to refurbish the east wing and expand the children's program. If Trevor explained the purpose of an endowment it may make the Ask a bit stronger since Rebecca may know what an endowment is, but then again she may not. It is always a good idea to spell out in easy language the nature of any charitable gift. In this instance Trevor could simply say that it will keep the museum more stable for years to come.

Where the Ask falls apart is when Rebecca asks how the fundraising is going, and Trevor responds "not as well as we would like." It is *never* a good idea to paint a negative or gloomy fundraising picture, no matter how awful the fundraising effort is going. *This is a prime example of the importance of the words the asker selects and how those words are delivered in the Ask.* It would be far better if Trevor said something along the lines of "Well, Rebecca, we certainly have our challenges as many nonprofits do when embarking on robust fundraising goals but we are confident and dedicated to reaching this goal for our museum." Now if you were in Rebecca's shoes, wouldn't you want to hear it presented this way rather than "not as well as we would like?"

The actual Ask does ask for a specific amount, $15,000 over three years, for the specific purpose of the endowment, but there are some things to examine about the amount and how it was delivered. First, I am often asked, is it better to ask for "$15,000 over three years, or $5,000 a year for the next three years?" It can be confusing to the donor so I think it is best to say, "we are asking you for a gift that *"would total $15,000 and it can be paid over three years if you wish."* My real preference is to ask for the amount outright, in this case $15,000. If the donor has to think about it, give her a day or so and if she comes back and says that it is absolutely too high, then offer to pledge it out over a few years.

Second, Trevor then says we "really need your help and this would give us a lift to our fundraising efforts." Stating that you really need a donor's help has an edge of desperation to it and I would steer any asker away from using this language. It almost makes the donor feel guilty if she does not make the gift, and you never want to place your donor in that type of awkward position.

Third, is going from a $2,500-a-year gift to a $15,000 gift too much of a leap for Rebecca, even though in essence she is really going from $2,500 to $5,000 each year? This is where donors can really get confused and I guarantee you the only thing the donor hears is the bottom line: "Someone is asking me for $15,000." When presented in this light, then yes, it is probably a stretch when asked for in this way. If you think the donor can make that increased gift, then by all means ask for it but always be prepared that the donor may be a bit surprised that you are asking for such a large increased amount. There is no hard and fast rule on this but if your prospect research reveals the donor can make this size gift, or if in conversations the donor intimated that she has the capacity to give this amount or has supported other organizations at this level, then ask. If you think spreading the $15,000 over three years will be much more doable for the person, then go with that strategy.

ASKING FOR A LARGE AND TRANSFORMATIONAL CHARITABLE GIFT

There is no doubt that large gifts can transform an organization into a powerful and transformational position. It signifies that the organization has strong leadership, vision, and ethics and that it carries out its mission every day so that many people and causes can receive the money and services they deserve.

Each organization has their own definition of what constitutes a "high-end" Ask. For a smaller grassroots organization that may be in the range of $5,000; for a medium organization it may be in the range of $100,000; and for larger organizations, it may be in the range of $1,000,000. All high-end Asks should have someone in a leadership position either making the Ask or present for the Ask, *provided that person was part of the cultivation.*

---

10 Things to Know About Any Ask—#5

Top-level gifts require that someone in a leadership position do the Ask or be present for the Ask *if* they were part of the cultivation process.

This just makes good sense. If you are asking someone, a couple, or a group of people to make one of the largest gifts to the organization, the person or people being asked are going to logically expect that the leadership wants them to make this level gift and therefore they must do the Ask or at the very least be present for the Ask. It is imperative that the leadership knows the person or people being asked and has taken part in some significant cultivation. Can you imagine if the person being asked never met the leadership and now she is asking for a seven-figure gift? I assure you there will be a whole lot of surprise on that donor's face!

Please note that I did phrase this as "leadership does the Ask or is present for the Ask." There are plenty of people in leadership positions in the organization who would rather forgo their summer vacations than actually say the well-scripted words of the Ask. If they are this uncomfortable, then the top development person or volunteer donor who has made as close to a similar gift as the person being asked should be present and they can do the Ask. The person of leadership can do the warm-up and follow-up and the development person or volunteer can do the Ask. Let's see how this can work in the next example.

In this example, a university is in the silent phase of a $100,000,000 capital campaign. Each of the trustees will be asked to make a "stretch" gift towards the campaign before any outside donor will be asked so that the university can say they have "100 percent" participation from the leadership of the university. The campaign has already raised

$18,000,000 from several trustees. President Miller to date has been present for all the Asks but prefers that Vice President for Advancement Lynn actually do the Ask. Trustee Bridget has been a loyal board member for six years and has served on many committees. Both President Miller and VP Lynn know Bridget very well and have brought her to special events and visited her at her home in Chicago. She has generously given over $250,000 towards her named scholarship and just recently formed her own very successful executive recruiting business. She is going to be asked for a $1,000,000 gift and has agreed to come back to campus to meet with President Miller and VP Lynn.

> *President Miller:* Bridget, thanks so much for coming in to meet with us today. I hope it was not too inconvenient for you to come crosstown.

> *Bridget:* Oh, no problem. I have a lunch appointment close by so it all worked out fine.

> *VP Lynn:* We are so glad you could make it. Bridget, when we last met with you, you were launching your own executive recruiting business. How is it going?

> *Bridget:* Surprisingly well. We may be able to expand to the east coast sooner than we had planned. Strong CEOs and executive leadership are in high demand. President Miller, I bet you receive telephone calls all the time.

> *President Miller:* Occasionally I receive a call but I am very satisfied here at the university.

> *Bridget:* Oh, I had no doubts about that and we really need you here.

> *President Miller:* Thank you. That is always nice to hear from a trustee. Bridget, as I stated in my letter setting up this appointment, we wanted to first and foremost thank you for all you have done for the university. Your work on the board, the committees, and our strategic plan has been a key to our success. As you know we are in the silent phase of a seven-year capital campaign and we have secured seven gifts from our board members, totaling $18,000,000.

> *Bridget:* You are making good progress.

> *President Miller:* Yes, we are. And it is so important as you have heard me say that we receive 100 percent participation from all our board members. It shows strength and confidence to our constituency and outside funders that our board is behind this campaign 100 percent.

Bridget, we are here today to discuss your participation in the campaign and, Lynn, why don't you take it from here?

VP Lynn: Bridget, as President Miller stated, we are very proud of our fundraising efforts to date and we are very optimistic that together we can provide our students and faculty with the best education and university experience they deserve. Your past support, largely your endowed named scholarship fund, has made a dramatic impact on many students and we thank you for your tremendous generosity.

Bridget: Yes, I really do like attending the yearly scholarship reception and meeting the students and hearing their stories.

President Miller: Yes, that is one of the university's highlight events and it is such a pleasure to match the students with generous donors like you.

VP Lynn: Bridget, the success of this initial phase of our campaign rests with full participation from our board. We are asking every board member for a "stretch" gift because this is a transformational moment for the university. We turn to you now and ask you for a $1,000,000 gift towards the campaign. You can spread the pledge payments over a number of years and we have several charitable gift vehicles, outright and planned, that you can use to make your gift. We thought you may wish to enhance your existing scholarship fund with part or all of your new commitment toward the campaign. Bridget, as a trusted and loyal trustee, how do you feel about this transformational gift opportunity?

The purpose of this illustration is to take a close look at what effect the Ask has on the person when the head of the organization asks versus someone else. Let us start with the positive points to this Ask. First, there is a nice flow to the dialog and President Miller and VP Lynn have an even exchange of conversation with Bridget. During the Ask it is very easy for one of the askers to "monopolize" the entire conversation, which is why scripting the Ask as set forth in Chapter 2 is so important.

Second, the dialog weaves in important features to the Ask:

1. Recognition of Bridget's new job.
2. Her prominence as a dedicated and generous trustee.
3. The importance of the campaign.

4. The importance of 100 percent participation from all trustees.

5. That all trustees are being asked for a "stretch" gift.

6. Bridget's primary area of interest, supporting scholarships.

7. The Ask was for a specific amount for a specific purpose.

8. The $1,000,000 Ask was not an "outrageous" amount because she could pay it in pledges over time.

9. She could do a "blend" gift, by paying some of the amount outright as well as incorporating a planned gift.

10. She was asked "how she felt about the *transformational gift opportunity.*"

All these elements are essential to the Ask. This Ask could have had a larger impact if President Miller did the actual Ask. Put yourself in Bridget's shoes. Let us see and feel how this slight difference of President Miller doing the Ask, not VP Lynn, would sound. We will pick up in the above dialog after the warm-up of discussing Bridget's new job and make some changes:

President Miller: Thank you. That is always nice to hear from a trustee. Bridget, as I stated in my letter setting up this appointment, we wanted to first and foremost thank you for all you have done for the university. Your work on the board, the committees, and our strategic plan has been a key to our success.

Bridget: You are most welcome. I'm happy to work with you and the board to get the university in a more competitive position.

President Miller: Yes, you're right. We cannot afford to let our enrollment slip in order to continue to attract the best and most deserving students. Bridget, the reason we wanted to speak with you in person is to bring you up to date on the capital campaign. As you have heard me say, it is essential that we receive 100 percent participation from all our board members. It shows strength and confidence to our constituency and outside funders that our board is behind this campaign 100 percent.

Bridget: That makes sense.

President Miller: Bridget, VP Lynn can bring you up to date on the success of the campaign.

VP Lynn: Bridget, as President Miller stated, we are very proud of our fundraising efforts to date and we are very optimistic that together we can provide our students and faculty with the best education and university experience they deserve. As you know, we are in the silent phase of a seven-year capital campaign and we have secured seven gifts from our board members, totaling $18,000,000.

Bridget: Wow, that is pretty impressive.

President Miller: Yes, we are very pleased. Bridget, your past support, largely to your endowed named scholarship fund, has made a dramatic impact on many students and we thank you for your tremendous generosity.

Bridget: Yes, I really do like attending the yearly scholarship reception and meeting the students and hearing their stories.

VP Lynn: Yes, that is one of the university's highlight events and it is such a pleasure to match the students with generous donors like you.

President Miller: Bridget, the success of this initial phase of our campaign rests with full participation from our board. We are asking every board member for a "stretch" gift, a gift that may be a bit larger than what each board member intended to give. This is a transformational moment for the university, and we need transformational gifts to make that happen. We turn to you now and ask you for a $1,000,000 gift towards the campaign. You can spread the pledge payments over a number of years and we have several charitable gift vehicles, outright and planned, that you can use to make your gift. VP Lynn would be happy to work with you and your financial advisor or attorney to make sure you select the most beneficial gift plan for you. We thought you may wish to enhance your existing scholarship fund with part or all of your new commitment toward the campaign.

Bridget, as a trusted and loyal trustee, how do you feel about this transformational gift opportunity?

Can you feel the difference between this Ask and the previous one? This Ask has the biggest "plus" going for it—President Miller did the Ask. As stated before, top Asks really require the top person such as the CEO, president, chair of the board, or top donor to make the Ask. It is only logical that when the head of the organization asks, the person being asked feels the importance of the moment because their prospective gift will have a tremendous impact on the organization. Additionally, when the top person asks, there is a sense of security that the gift will be used wisely, that it will be "taken care of" because the head of the organization asked and surely this person in a leadership role will do everything in his power to make the organization strong, vibrant, and secure well into the future.

This Ask also has some "enhanced features" that you can incorporate into your large Asks:

1. There is an even exchange of information between President Miller and VP Lynn on updating Bridget on the campaign.
2. President Miller is the one to emphasize the importance of 100 percent board participation.
3. President Miller defined "stretch" gifts to set Bridget's sights a bit higher.
4. The word "transformational" was used several times to let Bridget know this is a very special and extraordinary time for the university.
5. The final paragraph, the Ask by President Miller, has breaks in it signifying that each component is important and cannot be blurred together.
6. President Miller offered the services of VP Lynn to work with Bridget's financial advisor or attorney to select the best gift vehicle for Bridget.

Again, this Ask emphasizes the importance of having a script. When you see the physical breaks in the paragraph of the actual Ask by President Miller, it causes you to read it more slowly so that the Ask will be delivered slowly and not all jumbled together. There are simply too many important parts in that last paragraph: definition of a stretch gift; amount of the Ask; amount can be paid over years; gift can be outright or planned; VP Lynn can work with anyone Bridget wishes so that it is the most beneficial for her; the gift can enhance Bridget's existing scholarship; and the question on how Bridget feels about the "transformational gift opportunity."

Whenever possible, convince your leadership that their voice in making the Ask can be the difference between getting the large Ask amount versus a much smaller amount. If need be, hire a professional consultant or coach to practice with them to the point where they feel comfortable in making the Ask. It is an investment in the organization's financial future.

> Exercise #5: Assess whether your CEO, president, or board chair could use some training or coaching in making the Ask and share with them "enhanced features" in the sample dialog when the leadership makes the Ask.

TROUBLESHOOTING TIPS TO APPLY PRIOR TO THE ASK

As I am writing these sample dialogs I can hear the questions you are raising as well as different scenarios that you have encountered and where you may need some advice. I thought I would create this section so that I could share with you my thoughts on some questions I have been asked over the years about asking for charitable gifts. I have a hunch these are the questions on your mind. Many of these questions also apply to for-profit Asks, which we will explore in Chapter 6.

1. *What if the person about to be asked constantly cancels the appointment when we were going to make the Ask?*

Unfortunately, this happens more often than we would like. The reality is that some people are just that busy. The issue here is to find out if this is truly a scheduling problem or if the person is really not ready to be asked. The way you can do this is to say:

> "I know how enormously busy you must be. We never seem to have enough time to get it all done. Mark, it is very important to the future of the organization that we take just a bit of your time to meet with you in person to discuss your prospective gift. Is there any date or time that would be best for your schedule?"

I think you need to put it out there that you will be discussing a prospective gift and if the person cannot commit to a date to meet or is avoiding your telephone calls, then that may be a really good sign that they need more involvement or education about your organization before they can be asked. There is a definite lack of engagement, otherwise the person would not be trying to avoid the Ask.

2. What if your boss is the one who has a habit of cancelling the appointment when she is needed to do or be present for the Ask?

We just established in this chapter that high-end Asks really require that someone in a leadership role do the Ask or at the very least be present. It can be extremely frustrating to any development officer or development senior staff when the person is ready to be asked but it is the organization's leadership who cancels.

I think it is up to the development professional to have an open and honest discussion with the leadership on the importance of his role in the Ask. No doubt things do come up and there are numerous pressing needs that occur day to day in any nonprofit. That said, it simply sends out the wrong message to the potential donors that the leadership is more important than they are or that the needs of the organization constantly take precedence over potential gifts. In this time when every gift counts it would be imperative for everyone in a leadership role to embrace their importance in raising money for the organization. The longer the Ask is postponed, the more likely the person being asked will need to be "re-cultivated" due to the lapse in time and this is not where you want top Asks to go—back in the recycle bin for more cultivation!

3. What if your boss wants to do the Ask by putting it in writing and sending it to the person about to be asked?

I cringe when I hear this. Asking is all about the personal relationship and when you put paper between you and the person being asked and it arrives in the mail, the personal relationship and all the work done in cultivation has just evaporated. I realize that it can be a real timesaver to put Asks in writing and send it in the mail and that more details can be shared thoroughly and accurately when it is in writing. I have heard more arguments in favor of doing the Ask this way, including that "this will ensure we don't forget any detail and the person can take their time to think it over."

The best you can do here is hopefully draw upon a past experience where asking in person went well, or if you can, ask a donor who made a gift and was asked by someone in a leadership role how important it was that the leadership asked in person. Make sure that your boss' time is being used wisely and that perhaps smaller Asks can be done by the development staff and/or with a volunteer. The best resort is to "ask" your boss why she prefers writing and sending the Ask when all along she enjoyed assisting in the cultivation activities. Furthermore, emphasize that the person being asked would find it strange and impersonal at this point in time if those personal meetings discontinued at the point of the Ask.

4. What if you have been with your boss before and you know she does not like asking and you have to do the Ask?

The good news is if your boss does not mind you doing the Ask, then do it. Not everyone has the skill set, the mindset, or the comfort level to actually make the Ask. If you know this ahead of time, then in your script and your rehearsal of the Ask do not make any pretenses. Simply state: "Your presence and time devoted to asking our top people for money is so appreciated. If you like, as we discussed earlier, I have no problem with asking for the specific amount and the specific purpose." It is always best to get it out in the open, utilize the strengths and talents where you find them, and focus on capturing the most gifts for your organization.

5. What if you are the boss and you have experienced in the past that you are not as up to speed with all the information on the person you need to ask for money?

This is a very easy one for me to share my advice. As the "boss" you need to sit down with your co-asker well before the Ask and request that you be briefed in person as well as in writing on all the activity and conversation that has occurred with anyone associated with the organization and the person being asked. Oftentimes people in development may "assume" that you know but if you make it quite clear that you want all communication, and you should prior to the Ask, then you and your co-asker will always be prepared. If that person is not forthcoming with the information, then as a boss, I think you know you may have to discuss the severity and damaging consequences this may have, but ultimately, this is not fair to the person being asked. That person *deserves* to have each asker be fully knowledgeable about him.

6. *What if someone in a leadership role prefers to do the Ask alone but has a history of not revealing all the important details that were discussed during the Ask?*

First, let us be happy that the leadership wants to do the Ask in person. The issue here is that the leadership does not embrace the theory that "four eyes and ears are better than two," meaning it is always a plus if two people can do the Ask especially if someone in a leadership role is part of the Ask. The reality is much of the follow-up work will be done by the development person and if that person is not there during the Ask, they spend wasted time trying to hunt down the leadership to extract every word and sentiment that occurred in the Ask meeting.

Try to discuss with the leadership that their job will be so much easier following up with each Ask if the development person is present. Also, remember that people feel strength in numbers, so two people would always be ideal, as long as both have cultivated the person being asked and are liked by the person being asked. Explain that you may be spending way too much time hunting down the leadership to get the details of the Ask before you can move forward. Try to establish a pattern that if the leadership does do Asks alone, perhaps he can have a standing weekly meeting with the development person or send an e-mail or memo very soon after the Ask with the details. This way at least the person being asked will not feel that too much time has passed before they are followed up with by the organization.

7. *What if I think we are going to ask for too much?*

If you have done your homework and researched the person you are about to ask, cultivated this person and know her, and had the pre-Ask conversation, and they fit most of the elements of the readiness formula, then you should by now have a very good idea of the amount you want to ask. It is very normal and can be expected that many people second-guess themselves, get nervous, and " assume" that they are about to ask for too much. Deep breath. If you have done all the steps in all the chapters leading up to now, you will know the "right amount to ask for" and stick to this amount.

8. *What if I think we are going to ask for too little?*

This is a harder question because we can all get in a room and at the last moment prior to the Ask, be tempted by how much we really have to raise, and suddenly, all the work we put into strategizing on how much we should ask for goes flying out the window. Be careful on this because if you thought long and hard on crafting the right Ask amount for the right purpose, then stick to it.

I have heard of incidences where in a dual Ask, the person more senior tells his co-asker that even though they planned and rehearsed for *x* amount, the more senior person thought about this all night and re-lived several conversations he had with the person about to be asked and stated that he wanted to ask for double of *x*. Can you imagine? The worst that can happen is that you receive the first gift on the spot, then go back and do an Ask at the right time for additional funding.

9. *What if my boss/volunteer has all the top people to ask but never gets to the Ask and will not give the development staff the chance to do the Ask?*

This is a hard situation. You do not want to go over your boss' head, and in the meantime you are being extremely diligent by keeping focused on the top people that need to be asked. First, you can give your superior weekly charts and updates on who your boss needs to see and ask. Always state that you are free at any time to discuss strategies on each Ask. Second, set up meetings so that both of you can prepare for the Asks. Third, offer to set the appointments with the people who need to be asked. Many times this is just an administrative task that gets put to the bottom of your boss' to-do list. Fourth, work with your boss' executive or administrative assistant. Give him or her strong guidance on how and when you can reach the person who needs to be asked. Again, the point is to make this as seamless and effortless as possible so that your boss does not have to do all the work and the person who needs to be asked will be asked in a timely manner.

10. *What if we have many divisions, alumni relations, development, planned giving, the annual fund, external affairs, and marketing and communication and we are all in silos and I want to ask someone for money but I don't know if another division has other ideas?*

Welcome to "dysfunctional organizations." This is way too common, much to my regret. The only way—and I do say the *only* way—there can be cross-communication is for all units to have a standing meeting with all or have representatives from each group meet on a regular basis and discuss individuals they want to work with and, more important, what the strategy is for each person. It is a tremendous setback to any organization's constituency that those people are cultivated with inconsistency and with too many voices and self-serving purposes. It generally takes the head of the organization, whether that be the CEO, president, vice chancellor, or board chair, to realize that this is so detrimental to the organization and actually stymies gift giving on all levels.

To the person seeing this who is not in a leadership role but may head one of these conflicting units, I say, be the trailblazer and bring to many people's attention professionally and ethically that all units need to work together and have a joint prospect management meeting for the betterment of the organization. If you love where you work you can make this happen and your donors and prospective donors deserve this coordinated attention.

CONCLUSION

In this chapter we have illustrated asking for small and large charitable gifts. Hopefully, through the sample dialogs and the mixing of voices and word selection, it is abundantly clear that a well-thought-out script for any size Ask is your road to a successful Ask. Please keep in mind that the higher the Ask amount, the more imperative it is that someone in a leadership role from the organization do the Ask or be part of the Ask, as long as she hopefully participated in a meaningful way in cultivating the person to be asked.

The troubleshooting tips should help prevent or forestall any anxiety moment before the Ask and I trust will help you be very well prepared prior to any Ask. Just keep in mind, with each Ask there may be the element of surprise that you cannot anticipate but if you are as prepared as you can be, the Ask will always go well due to your confidence.

Looking Ahead

The next chapter will illustrate Asks that involve asking for oneself—for a job, a promotion/title change, a raise, money for a creative project, or investment for a business venture. All the principles thus far apply but with the help of some sample dialogs to use in asking for oneself, you will be well prepared and well positioned to ask for anything you want.

CHAPTER

Asking for Yourself

THIS CHAPTER DISTINGUISHES ITSELF FROM traditional fundraising books on how to ask for charitable gifts for nonprofits because it takes the steps and methods detailed in all the previous chapters on how to "ask" and applies them to "asking" for things in our everyday living. So often we separate our professional lives from our personal lives and forget to use the skills we have in the fundraising profession for things we want for ourselves. This is extremely prevalent when asking for things that are important to us, such as a job, a new job title, or a raise; money for a creative project; or funds for a business venture. While there are numerous other Asks in everyday living, this chapter will illustrate how to ask for job-related causes and for creative projects and business ventures. Remember, all the material in this chapter can apply when asking for a loan; medical advice; time off from work; job relocation or time to work from home; or feedback on a project that you want to develop. In short, the principles apply to anything you want and desire; now all you have to do is make the right Ask!

It would be a good exercise to go back to Chapter 2 and review the section "Three-Step Method Prior to Any Ask," particularly "What are the top three reasons you think the person you are about to ask will hesitate or say no to the Ask?" and "How can you turn around these three reasons to make a positive and passionate statement about your Ask?" The reason I suggest this is that if you can predict why someone like your supervisor would hesitate or not give you a promotion or a raise, and then have all your persuasive reasons that would possibly change her mind lined up, you will be very prepared and confident to make your Ask. You will be in a much better position of getting what you want if you anticipate, prepare, and deliver your persuasive case for what you deserve.

While there are numerous books, Web sites, and seminars on finding the right job or launching a new business, this chapter is not meant to be a self-help, comprehensive overview of those areas. Rather, it is meant for you to see the strong parallels of the principles in raising money that can apply to things you want in your everyday life.

ASKING FOR A JOB-RELATED CAUSE

Asking for a new job is like preparing and asking for a major gift. You should know your prospective employer inside and out by doing the research you would do on a person you would like to ask for money. During the interview, it is much like cultivating a new prospective donor: you share your background, and you ask open-ended questions about the job, the prospective employer's management style, and expectations for the position. You make the similar type of Ask. When asking for a gift, it is for a specific amount for a specific purpose. When asking for a job, you are asking for a specific position and detail the reasons why you are best suited for the position and what unique skills you can offer the organization.

Exhibit 6.1 describes the preparation you should do prior to asking for a new job that is parallel to the preparation you need to do when asking for money.

EXHIBIT 6.1.   *Guidelines in Asking for a New Job.*

1. Research the organization inside and out.
2. Research the background of the interviewer and department staff.

3. Use your network of colleagues, friends, and professional organizations to find out their views about the organization, its leadership, and its challenges.

4. Dress for success and maintain good eye contact and body language.

5. Rehearse the questions you want to ask and the main points you want to make.

6. Ask specific questions that show you have done your research on the organization.

7. Ask for the job with convincing clarity and highlight a few points why you are a good match for the position.

8. Listen to every word the interviewer uses and be able to use key phrases and important points that were emphasized.

9. Discuss how you will follow up once the interview is concluded.

10. Stay positive as if you are going to get the job.

Taking these one by one will illustrate the similarities. First, you should do as much research as you can about the organization. Pore over their Web site and read their annual report or Form 990 if they are a nonprofit. You want to know the history of the organization; who is on the board; the state of their finances; revenue streams; where they do business; the names of their departments; their mission; case statement; business plan; and goals.

The same holds true for researching the interviewer or interviewers and the members of the staff of the department that you are applying to for a position. In addition to the Web site, annual report, and Form 990, use the Internet social networking sites such as www.google.com; www.facebook.com; www.linkedin.com; www.zoominfo.com; and www.whoswhoonline.com. You want as much information as you can find to be able to draw common bonds in your personal or professional backgrounds. For example, you may have attended the same school, lived in the same geographic location; or worked previously at similar institutions. This is just like doing prospect research, detailed in Chapter 3, about the people that you want to ask for money.

Next, use your network to determine what people and other organizations think about the organization where you want to work. Call colleagues, advisors, friends, and members of professional organizations that may be linked to this prospective employer. This is very similar to "peer screenings," discussed in Chapter 3, when asking board and committee people if they know anything about or have any personal connection to the people you would like to cultivate and ask for money. It is very important to get the feedback on what people from outside the organization think about your prospective employer.

It should be beyond obvious, but look well dressed for the interview and pay close attention to establishing eye contact and maintaining good body language. This was emphasized in Chapter 4 in preparing for the Ask. I have interviewed many people in my career as I am sure most of you have and there are horror stories about what people wear for a professional interview. Dress professionally and be aware if you have the tendency to look down, read too much from your notes, or if you are hunched over in your seat. It says volumes about your self-confidence, and employers will take notice of these details.

It is so common to be nervous for the interview; however, if you practice with a friend or relative or write down the points you want to make and the questions you will want to ask, then you will be less nervous and more confident. This is exactly like "scripting" out the Ask for yourself and/or the person who is accompanying you on the Ask, as covered in Chapter 2. Writing it all out, while it may appear to be time consuming, will most likely set you above the other candidates because you'll have a well-thought-out script that includes highlighting your achievements, matching them to the job description, as well as asking salient questions of the interviewer that demonstrates your organizational skills and strong desire to get this job. Suggested questions you can ask are

- "In six months from now, if I am hired what would you want me to have accomplished?"
- "Tell me how I will be evaluated, by whom, how often, and how we prioritize my job responsibilities."
- "How will I be trained and by whom so I can be up to speed to perform the tasks detailed in the job description?"

- "Does this organization have a track record of promoting its current staff at the appropriate time so that there is room for advancement at the company?"

I like these types of questions because it shows that the job applicant wants to succeed and there are no surprises when and if the job is offered on how the person will learn the nuances of the job, be evaluated, have job duties prioritized, and can advance so there is room to grow and learn new skills.

Listening to the words, phrases, and jargon of the industry is very important. It is equivalent to being "silent" after the Ask (see Chapter 4). It is so essential that you be a very good listener and not interrupt or be too eager to show off your skills and past accomplishments. Often interviewers are giving you signals of what skill sets are needed; how the department operates; the degree of interaction the department has with the leadership; and whether the staff is harmonious or fractious. As the rule in Chapter 2 states, if you speak next after the Ask it will result in no gift; so too if you jump in too soon when the interviewer is explaining the position or interrupt to make the point that you have those skills. If you do you will most likely not get the job.

When the interview comes to its natural close, take the last few minutes to discuss how you can find out when a decision has been made about the position. This is the same as not leaving the Ask meeting without a date and time when you will follow up with the person you just asked for money (see Chapter 2). This follow-up step is important because many organizations vary on how they notify the candidates and some only notify the person selected and let the other candidates assume that the passage of time means they did not get the job, which is terrible. Some interviewers will not mind if you call or e-mail within a reasonable amount of time after the interview; others will be specific that there is no need to contact the interviewer or organization because the human resources department will handle the communication. It is always best to get those details resolved before you leave the interview; otherwise, you are "chasing" after the interviewer to find out about the position, much like "chasing" after the person you have asked for money to see if she has made a decision.

The last point really can separate you from the other candidates. No matter how the interview goes, or even if your instincts tell you that you may not be the person selected for the job because the interview did not go the way you planned, always *stay positive and act as if you are going to be selected.* This is exactly like staying optimistic after each Ask and speaking with the person you just asked for money as if he is going to say "yes" very soon (see Chapter 2). You have nothing to lose and everything to gain with a pleasant demeanor and a winning personality. This may be the very trait that the interviewer is looking for—someone who can be cheerful during hard, challenging times. When in doubt, smile—it is free!

So now you can see how any Ask for any purpose, whether it be for a nonprofit or for yourself and your career, uses the same principles and techniques. In the section that follows we are going to explore some sample dialogs on asking for a job, asking for a new job title, and asking for a raise (I'm sure this will be quite popular). As in Chapter 5, we will assume that there has been a warm-up period between the parties and we are now at the logical point of making the career-related Ask.

Asking for a Job

This example can apply to someone who just graduated for whom this would be the first major job or for those people who may have switched careers and this would be their first job in the new industry. Here, Sasha has written for several local newspapers and has applied for a newswriter position at a local television station, WMBC. She has never had a job with the television industry, but her writings in the newspaper of course are online and have been on the newspapers' Web sites. Evan is head of the news desk at WMBC and would be Sasha's immediate supervisor.

> *Sasha:* Thank you for going over with me the history of the station and most importantly for giving me the opportunity to interview. I did do my research on the station and I have a few questions. Would this be a good time to ask them?
>
> *Evan:* Sure, what's on your mind?
>
> *Sasha:* I read some articles where your general manager wanted to attract the 20- to 28-year-old market audience. Are there any plans in place to make that happen and a time frame to achieve that goal?

Evan: Good question. Yes, we have done some focus groups and the feedback is we need to make our online news more interactive. We plan to roll out in a few months a new segment with a reporter in that age group who will do a sort of "what are you doing now," much like Facebook, but it will be on travel, finding a job, trying to buy tickets for a nearly sold-out concert, along those lines.

Sasha: That would be pretty interesting and fun to watch. Evan, I am being conscientious of our time since you said on the telephone we only had 45 minutes. Is there anything I did not cover that you would like to know about me?

Evan: No, I think we covered it all. If I think of anything I'll give you a call.

Sasha: Sure, anytime. I just want to thank you once again for giving me the opportunity to interview for this position. While I'm sure you have many candidates, there are three things that I feel I can bring to this job that would be beneficial for you and for the station. First, I'm from the area as you know and I can be a real resource for making the connections or getting the people we need to interview for the stories. Second, while this would be my first job in television, and you did say that you needed a quick but accurate writer, many times we were under newsbreaking deadlines at the newspapers so I have the experience of writing under pressure but delivering each story with accuracy. Lastly, WMBC is important to me. We all grew up watching this news station and this is where I want to learn and grow my writing career.

Evan: Those are all good qualities that we will take into consideration. There is a lot of competition out there as you know and many have prior television experience.

Sasha: I'm sure there are many good candidates and again, thank you for considering me. Evan, do you have a time frame of when you are going to make your decision?

Evan: I'd say within the month.

Sasha: Would it be alright if I called you or sent you an e-mail to check on the position?

Evan: I would say send an e-mail, but I'm hardly ever at my desk. Don't worry, someone will call you either way. We are not one of these companies that let people hang or call them well after we made our decision.

Sasha: That is refreshing and very ethical of you. It speaks to the integrity of the station.

Evan: Good luck, thanks for coming in, and we'll be in touch.

In this sample dialog, Sasha hits almost all the points for a really good job Ask. She did her research on the station and asked a good question about expanding the audience to reach 20- to 28-year-olds. What is missing is a question directed for Evan or something to indicate that she researched him. She could have added:

Sasha: Evan, I see you have been with the station for three years and that your previous job was in Chicago at WCBA. In addition to a promotion, what attracted you to WMBC?

This one sentence will get Evan closer to Sasha because now he is speaking about himself, much like we want people to share their experiences about the organization and their motivation to give when we ask them for money. It will lead to much more of an exchange of experiences, which is exactly what you want in an interview.

Another way this could be improved is if Sasha had her own ideas on how the station could draw in the targeted 20- to 28-year-olds. I always think it is a good idea to be proactive by bringing new ideas and creative approaches to help the prospective employer with any of the challenges the organization is facing. It shows that you did your homework and that you know the organization inside and out.

Sasha does state three reasons why her skills and background are well suited for the position, and by stating that there are "three reasons," she makes a solid case as a strong candidate. This would have been even more powerful if she added the following:

Sasha: Lastly, we all grew up watching this news station and this is where I want to learn and grow my writing career. Evan, WMBC is important to me and that is why I am asking for this job.

Now I know the common term is to say "I hope you will consider me for the position" but if you do not find it too abrasive, and if it fits your personality, I would highly recommend that you be crystal clear in what you want—you want this job so *ask for this job.* It does not mean that you will get the job on the spot, but if you use the right tone of voice and are positive, enthusiastic, sincere, and honest about your qualifications and your personal interest to get the job and grow with the company, then asking for the job and using those words will flow naturally.

The follow-up in this dialog was handled nicely. Sasha was direct in asking if she could call or e-mail Evan to check on the status of the position. If you notice, she even got one last plug in for the station by stating that it was "refreshing" and "ethical" that someone from the station would notify all the candidates once the decision was made. It can never hurt to close your Ask with a compliment for the organization or the person you just asked because you will be leaving on a positive note that may sway the decision to get what you asked for—the job.

Asking for a New Job Title

I specifically wanted to cover this type of Ask because many organizations due to budget reductions, downturn economy, or revenue shortfalls, often give current employees more job responsibilities without the title that reflects all this additional work. Does this sound familiar? The first place to start is defining why a job title is important. Exhibit 6.2 sets forth some of these reasons.

EXHIBIT 6.2.   *Importance of a Job Title.*

1. Reflects your current professional identity within the organization.
2. Describes the quantity and scope of the work you do every day.
3. Signals loyalty to the company that you want to advance and make a significant contribution.
4. Shows your authority and rank within the organization internally as well as to external constituents, clients, supporters, foundations, corporations, and competitors.
5. Carries weight and prestige and will be of great importance in securing money or raising money for the organization.

I am sure there are many other reasons you can add to this list but the point is that job titles do matter, but if you don't have the one that reflects your work, then you need to ask for the title you want. In the following sample dialog, Shaun is a sales representative for certain regions within Southeast Asia. His immediate supervisor, the sales manager who oversees the four sales representatives in this area, leaves, and Vice President of International Markets, Tina, promotes Shaun to his boss' job without giving him the "manager" title because she wants to give him a six-month trial run to see if he can handle this managerial position. It is now month 7 and Shaun has yet to get the title change. He has been told over this period of time that Tina is pleased with his work, so he translated that to mean the change in title would follow. No such luck, so now Shaun has to "ask" for the title.

Shaun: Tina, I greatly appreciate your vote of confidence for me to step into the sales manager role several months ago.

Tina: That was a good decision for us and our revenues are up and our clients seem to be pleased with how things turned out.

Shaun: That's wonderful to hear and thank you too for your positive feedback and suggestions you gave me, especially in the first few months. Tina, thank you for agreeing to meet with me today because I want to discuss with you something that is very important to me. I love my new role and adding the management skills to my portfolio in the company. The only thing that is missing is the title change.

Tina: I thought that it was taken care of a few weeks ago.

Shaun: Unfortunately, it hasn't happened. Was there some paperwork I needed to fill out? This may be my oversight but I thought when I accepted the new responsibilities that if you were pleased with my work the title change would happen automatically within six months.

Tina: Shaun, you should know nothing happens here automatically. Let me look into this.

Shaun: I greatly appreciate it. It is important for me to share why the title is as important as learning new skills and being promoted. I have found that a more senior position gives me more leverage and I have been able to close more sales deals quicker because of my rank in the company. My co-workers also need to know that the company promoted me and this is my new title within our division. Lastly, the title allows me to do my job with continued excellence because I know the company wanted my title to reflect accurately the scope of sales and now management that I do each day. So Tina, I am asking you to give me the title that reflects my work and please let me know if you need me to do anything to make that happen.

Tina: I hear what you are saying and give me a little time to get this resolved.

Let us see what we liked in this Ask and how we could improve it. Shaun was direct, not overbearing, and very complimentary, especially for the feedback he received, and focused the meeting on the job title. Right here I think instead of saying "the only thing that is missing is the title change," Shaun could have said "and I believe we agreed that if you were pleased with my work my title would change to sales manager in six months." That would be less harsh, flip, and also would remind Tina what the title should be. Supervisors are very busy and one should not assume that she would remember what the title was supposed to be, so make the request easier and be direct: "I'm asking for my title to be sales manager as we agreed when I was promoted."

The other elements in this dialog that are very helpful is when Tina agreed to look into why the title had not been changed, Shaun still let her know why the title was important to him. He could have let it go right there and been happy that Tina agreed to take action. I firmly believe that in any work situation you will do well if your supervisor knows your motivation, values, and beliefs that reflect who you are, what matters to you, and how you see your role within the organization. Shaun lays that out nicely here because he touches on how it is important to his clients; his ability to close deals quicker with his new authority; his co-workers who need to know the hierarchy within the organization; and for his own self worth that his job responsibilities match his job title.

I know it may sound like "overkill" but even though Tina agreed to look into changing the title, Shaun still said "So Tina I am asking you to give me the title that reflects my work and please let me know if you need me to do anything to make that happen." If you feel comfortable with delivering this straightforward Ask, I think you will feel how powerful it can be to articulate with clear words exactly what you want, *and* offer to help in any way to get what you want. It also serves to close the meeting on a positive note and there can be no misunderstanding or confusion as to what the person is to do after you made your solid Ask.

Asking for a Raise

This is the part in the book that I think will have a wide appeal! Asking for a raise can be very emotional because you are evaluating your contribution to the organization, assessing your worth, guessing and second-guessing whether your boss will agree or disagree with your request. And then what will you do if she says no to your Ask for the raise?

Quite simply, everyone deserves to get paid for the value of their work. This is very similar to asking for a new job title. The raise reflects the true value of the work you are performing and by industry standards, or company policies, you should receive the requested level of compensation. I think it would be valuable to look at the common reasons why we do *not* ask for a raise, as put forth in Exhibit 6.3.

EXHIBIT 6.3.   *Reasons Why We Don't Ask for a Raise.*

1. It is a challenging economy and now is not the time to ask.

2. If I ask then everyone else in the department will want a raise.

3. It may signal that if I don't receive the raise I will leave and then I am a less valuable employee.

4. I was hired at a higher rate than they wanted to offer me so maybe I should wait.

5. The raise will put me above others in my department that may cause bad feelings internally.

It is very hard not to hear these voices in your head or other reasons when you want to muster all the confidence you have and ask for extra money in your salary. Once you go through the exercise in turning negative thoughts about your Ask into positive, passionate statements as outlined in Chapter 2, you will be in the position of asking from strength, not self-doubt. Remember, when you ask for a raise you are not asking for a "favor," you are asking for the fair value of your work performance.

---

10 Things to Know About Any Ask—#6

Asking for yourself is not asking for a favor—it is asking for what you believe you deserve.

I have heard so many Asks sound like "favors" rather than the direct words of what the person wants. A "favor" is someone performing an act of kindness, doing a good deed. An "Ask" is making a request for someone to give or to contribute something specific. An Ask is much more proactive, inviting, and engaging. Let's explore an example of asking for a raise.

Melissa is the office manager for a family-owned construction company and reports to both of the owners, who are brothers, Roger and Richard. She has been with the company for two and one-half years. When she was hired the company was doing well; however, over the past two years, her responsibilities have increased greatly due to the growth in the company. The number of construction projects increased by 37 percent and the company hired two new subcontractors to keep up with the volume of new work. This is great for the company but now Melissa has to do over one-third more scheduling appointments, meeting reminders, client and vendor calls, invoicing, paychecks, and accounting than she did when she started. She did receive a small raise after her first year, but Roger and Richard have not given her a second raise yet. As with small businesses there is no formal policy on when or how raises are given. Melissa has held out asking for a raise until now because she is finding herself working way too many hours overtime to keep up with the work, which is taking away all her personal time. She tried to meet with both Roger and Richard at the same time to discuss her raise, but only Roger was available.

Roger: Melissa, you wanted to meet about something? Richard is out on the project and I don't expect him to be back before 7:00. What's up?

Melissa: I mentioned last week when we set this up that I hoped the both of you could be here but I totally understand. It is about the amount of work I have been doing lately. We have two new subcontractors who I've tried to train in our procedures for invoicing our clients and how we need all the documentation in during the projects, but that has been a challenge. What I really want to talk about is giving me a raise for all the extra work and hours I have been doing for a very long time.

Roger: I'll talk to the contractors if you like but I thought all that was working out just fine. A raise, hmmm, what did you have in mind?

Melissa: Well, it has been about a year and a half since my pay was increased and with all the extra work I have been doing and the extra hours I have been putting in, I was thinking that my salary should increase by 15 percent.

Roger: That's quite a big jump, don't you think?

Melissa: Roger, I think that is pretty fair considering I received a 6 percent raise after my first year, and no raise after that. Essentially, I have had no increase for one and a half years. If I had gotten a raise in my second year I hope I would have received at least the same 6 percent but considering all the extra work with the increase in projects, asking for 15 percent seems very reasonable to me.

Analyzing this dialog, there are many ways we could make this a much better Ask. First, if the decision of the raise will be made by two people, have both decision makers in the room at the same time. Both need to hear what you are asking for and *how* you are asking for it at the same time. It is the same thing when you are asking for a charitable gift and you know it will be a joint decision by both spouses or partners, but only one is present during the Ask. You have no control how the person you just asked is going to *translate* your Ask; what they will say; what they will leave out; and most importantly, how passionately or non-passionately they will relay what you asked. Sometimes it is unavoidable that only one decision maker will be there, but do make the best effort you can to have both decision makers present during the Ask.

Second, make sure the person you are asking for a raise knows the purpose of the meeting. It is the same as when you are setting up the meeting to ask a person for a charitable gift; the person has to know this is the purpose of the meeting, not just another cultivation meeting. In this dialog, Melissa could handle this meeting setup the following way:

> *Melissa:* Roger and Richard, I would like to set aside some time soon, so that the three of us can discuss the wonderful growth of our company and how I can be further compensated for the increase in my responsibilities. I'm sure you agree this extra effort by me has helped the company to keep up with our current success and our future growth.

This is a *very positive invitation* for all three to have a conversation and reflect on why the company is so successful. It implies that Melissa has had a strong role in keeping the company together, and without her managerial details the company would have been backlogged in paperwork, with probably some very unhappy clients, vendors, and subcontractors.

Third, always begin the conversation on an up note, not how much you are swamped with work. Here Melissa says, the purpose of the meeting "is about the amount of work I have been doing lately. We have two new subcontractors who I've tried to train in our procedures for invoicing our clients and how we need all the documentation in during the projects, but that has been a challenge." A better way to start the meeting would be:

> *Melissa:* Roger, I appreciate that you are taking the time to meet with me and I understand that Richard is unavailable. I have been so happy to be a part of the success and growth of the company. Thinking over my past two and a half years, we have really increased the number of clients by word of mouth on your reputation as the best and most reliable, local, and family-owned construction company.
>
> Roger, as you know, my work has increased exponentially to keep up with the company's growth and I would like to discuss with you now my request to increase my salary by 15 percent. Let me explain.

I think you will agree that this is a much softer, gentler, inviting way to begin the conversation on asking for a raise. Never paint an overwhelming picture of the work you do. It is the same as approaching a person for a charitable gift by stating that the charity "could be doing better," or "is not in the greatest financial shape right now," or "gifts are down but we are counting on your support." The person considering the gift is almost "guilty" if he does not give. No one wants to give to a struggling institution where their gift may just be going to alleviate a deficit (see Chapter 1). The same applies here. No employer wants to feel "guilted" into giving a raise to a person who is desperate, tired every day, and overwhelmed with work. Show yourself to be a positive, contributing member of the team no matter what the size of the office, and you will have a much better chance of getting the raise you want.

Lastly, Melissa does a pretty good job justifying the request for a 15 percent increase when she states: "That is pretty fair considering I received a 6 percent raise after my first year, and no raise after that. Essentially, I have had no increase for one and a half years. If I had gotten a raise in my second year I hope I would have received at least the same 6 percent but considering all the extra work with the increase in projects, asking for 15 percent seems very reasonable to me." I think if she said the following it would be more persuasive:

> *Melissa:* Roger, at first it may appear as rather a large increase but let me explain. A year and a half ago I received my first and only raise to date, and that was very generous of the company to give me a 6 percent increase. Believe me, that really helped. I think with us being so focused on the volume of business we overlooked a salary increase in my second year. So when you think about it, the 15 percent is really fair because it reflects the additional work I have done to keep up with the business' 37 percent growth, with no additional administrative personnel, and it has been one and a half years since my salary was increased.

Nothing speaks more loudly than using numbers, dates, years, and the employee's willingness with a positive attitude to do the extra work when needed. This dialog lays out those facts so that Roger can actually see a timeline in front of him and has a crystal clear picture of the extra work Melissa has performed, how that added to the success of the business, and how she has not been compensated for one and a half years.

In asking for a raise, picture yourself making your favorite sandwich. You first select your favorite bread. That is the warm-up, when you compliment your boss and the company on its achievements and how you enjoy being an integral part of the team towards that success. Next, you select the meat or vegetarian items you want as the core of your sandwich. That is the Ask, when you state clearly and positively exactly the amount of raise you want and why you deserve to have this raise now. Finally, you put your next piece of bread on top of your sandwich. That is the "close" when you thank your employer for her time; for listening to you; for considering the raise you asked for; and state that you look forward to hearing her decision soon. If you bring up a graphic illustration you will not miss a step in making your Ask for a raise, and above all else, stay positive throughout the course of your conversation and speak as if the answer will be "yes." But be careful, you may get hungry when you try this exercise!

> Exercise #6: Script the dialog you will have with your boss asking for your next raise. Use the example of making a sandwich so that you do not miss any positive steps in asking for the raise.

ASKING FOR A CREATIVE PROJECT

There is so much talent in this world that goes unnoticed because in many instances the creative projects never come to fruition because they needed money to create, produce, show, or display to the public and no one asked for it. I have been asked so often, "How do I ask for money when the person has to believe in my work before it is created?" or "I have a great independent film, art show, new play, concert I want to take on tour. How do I 'find' the money?" The answer, surprise, surprise is . . . you ask for it.

Let us walk through this next example of Tamara, a new young playwright, who has written a powerful story of a woman's journey through Asia and Australia and the cultural and political awakenings she experienced that shaped her future acting career. Tamara has written a few plays before, and has had success with a few theaters hosting staged readings for her work, but to date her plays have not been produced.

She learns that a small, local theater, Great Horizons, has a "Celebrate Female Playwrights" series but they do not take unsolicited material. Lucky for Tamara, she has a friend who knows the artistic director at the theater, Annika, and Annika agrees to review her play. While Annika is moved by the script, unfortunately, the plays have already been selected for the series. Annika tells Tamara that she could do the play in the studio, not the main stage, the last week of the series but that Tamara would have to find funding for the production costs, which would be around $20,000. Tamara's father's childhood friend, Justin, is a business entrepreneur and is extremely supportive of the arts, particularly organizations that showcase new work. Justin knows that Tamara has been trying to get her work produced but Tamara has never asked him to help her or to provide financial support. Justin knows that Tamara's family does not have the means to put their money behind Tamara's work. Tamara wants this so badly that she decides she is going to ask him to be the sole "investor" in her new play. Tamara discusses this with her father to make sure he would not feel uncomfortable if she asked Justin and her father has no problems with her asking.

> *Tamara:* Justin, thank you so much for meeting me in your office. I know how busy you are and I will not take up too much of your time.
>
> *Justin:* Don't be silly, how's your dad?
>
> *Tamara:* Busier than ever. In fact, I think he is working more than ever since he retired. He says "hello" and I want you to know he knows we are meeting today.
>
> *Justin:* He mentioned something like that when we last spoke. So what is this about your new play?
>
> *Tamara:* Yes, Great Horizons has a "Celebrate Female Playwrights" series.
>
> *Justin:* I never heard of that.

Tamara: It is only for a few weeks and they produce the shows on the main stage. I met with their artistic director, Annika, and she really liked the script but the plays were already selected.

Justin: Well, that's bad timing.

Tamara: No, lucky for me she offered to produce my play in their smaller performance space, the studio, during the series so that my play could be part of this powerful series.

Justin: This one must be good. What is it about?

Tamara: It is a story about a woman's journey through Asia and Australia, the unlikely people she meets, the unusual jobs she takes, and the discovery of how narrow and, at points, prejudicial her upbringing has been and how these new awakenings shape her acting career in a dimension she never expected.

Justin: That sounds pretty powerful.

Tamara: Oh, Justin, it is, and the theater will do the work in the studio if I come up with $20,000.

Justin: Wow, how are you going to do that?

Tamara: Well Justin, I feel a bit awkward asking you since you have been a friend of my dad's and our family for so long, but I know how much you like the performing arts, and new works, and this would be right in line with supporting your interest.

We can give Tamara credit for asking for a specific amount for a specific purpose but I think you know that this Ask can be made even more effective with a few changes. It was good that Tamara thanked Justin for his time and tried to keep the meeting brief, being conscientious of his time at work. It is unclear from the dialog if Justin really knew of the purpose of the meeting. He knows it has something to do with her new play, but remember, like asking for a charitable gift, the person you are asking should know the purpose of the meeting. Tamara could have said when she set up the meeting: "Justin, I've written a fabulous new play that a theater wants to produce and I want to meet with you to talk about possible investment opportunities." Then Justin knows exactly the purpose of the meeting.

Tamara does do a nice job of explaining that her play was not originally selected but that it has the opportunity to be produced with the series but in a small space, the studio. These facts are important because she is painting the entire picture for Justin. She could have just stated that she has the chance to get her play produced in the studio and left out the part that others are being produced on the main stage but that would have lessened the excitement and grand scale of the "Celebrating Female Playwrights" series.

She also explains the essence of the play, which got Justin involved, but she could have fleshed out more of the details, such as where the idea came from to write this play, when she wrote it, what other theaters did a staged reading, and more of the "behind the scenes" details that any potential investor would want to know. I specifically mention this here, even though it may seem beyond obvious, because I have coached people through these types of Asks and have found that these important background facts are left out. People get so quickly to the Ask amount and what benefits that will bring to the potential investor that they do not walk through the whole process. The more details the person knows, the more quickly he will reach his decision.

Where this Ask could use the most improvement is in the Ask. Tamara says, "The theater will do the work in the studio if I come up with $20,000." "If I come up with $20,000" is *not* asking for $20,000. It leaves Justin thinking what his ideas are to raise this amount, not whether he would consider giving the $20,000. Make the Ask to the point and specific. Tamara could say:

> *Tamara:* Justin, you have been a long-time friend of my dad's and the family. This may be a bit awkward but I firmly believe that producing this play will give me that first chance I need to be recognized as a new playwright. You love and support the arts that produce "new work" and this is right in line with your passion. Justin, I am asking you to be the sole investor in my work by investing $20,000 so that my play can be showcased in the Great Horizons' studio.

First, she acknowledges that this may be an awkward moment. When asking colleagues, friends, and family, it is always a good idea to be forthright and honest that it may be uncomfortable but that this is extremely important and you want the person to have every opportunity to invest with you (see Chapter 3). Second, the Ask is specific. This is much more direct, and it ties Justin's main interest with an investment opportunity. In other words, Tamara made *"the match"*—

an investment opportunity with a key interest of the investor. Also, note that Tamara got it out in the open that "it may be awkward" since she was asking a friend of the family's for money.

All the rules and tips we have been discussing when asking for a creative project can be applied when looking for investors for an independent film that has a large production budget; to help a private collector purchase exquisite pieces of art that she cannot initially afford so when the pieces are sold, everyone shares in the profit; or for a local theater that can no longer afford its rent or to cover unforeseen deficits. If you have a creative project that you need to get money to support, apply the elements above and be persistent and positive. Good results will follow.

ASKING FOR A BUSINESS VENTURE

It seems that every day, someone, somewhere, is either launching a new business, expanding a new business, consolidating or merging an existing business, or closing one business and opening another. No matter what stage you are in with your business, at some point in time you or you and your partners or sales team will need to ask for money. That can be in the form of asking a bank loan officer, a venture capitalist, an entrepreneurial investor, or just someone you found through a professional network. It could even be a very close friend or colleague.

I thought it would be useful to give you a sample dialog in asking for a business venture that is broad enough to cover all these possibilities while at the same time would give you the opportunity to "tweak" it to meet your individual situation. So on that note, let us take the example of David, who is a small business owner of Research and Results, a company that has to date specialized in pharmaceutical market research. Research and Results' clients have been the pharmaceutical companies and doctors who need specific research before drug patents expire while a new drug is seeking Federal Drug Administration approval and to test-market the colors, designs, and words that would appeal the most to prospective patients for new drugs. The company prides itself on having the best market research software that is based on years of experience with personal interviews and quantifiable data analysis. David developed this software with the goal that it could have a wider application beyond the health care field.

Research and Results is so confident in their research techniques and this software that David wants to "apply" these research methods to the real estate market. In the scenario that follows David is asking a potential "new" client, Marcela, who is a real estate developer in Miami, Florida, and whom David met at a business networking event, if she would hire Research and Results to do the market research analysis in the South Beach area before the developer converts two existing hotels into condominium units. This Ask is not about asking for specific money at this stage, because that will come later. *This Ask will illustrate how to "sell," "pitch," and "open the door to new business opportunities."*

David: Marcela, it was good to see you last week at the cocktail reception at the new W Hotel.

Marcela: Yes, David, I'm glad we had a chance to meet there.

David: South Beach seems to be doing well with hotel construction despite the slump in the residential housing industry.

Marcela: Well, it is hard to say how long this will last but in South Beach with all the trade shows and conventions that are booked here each weekend, hotels are doing well.

David: I have been to a few conferences here and, yes, it is pretty exciting. Especially the art industry that has really taken hold of the Miami area.

Marcela: Yes, our Art World Exhibition has turned into a week-long event with every hotel converted into gallery space and has spread throughout the Miami area. You literally have to book a year in advance if you plan to come and get tickets to an art opening and a hotel room.

David: That's good to know. Thanks for the advice. Marcela, thank you, for meeting me today. I wanted to spend a little more time speaking with you about how I think my company can help your company make some of the critical decisions you mentioned last night that you need to make in the very near future.

Marcela: Yeah, there are some big ones. Tell me again, what exactly does your company do in real estate market research?

David: My company, Research and Results, has been in existence for over 16 years. I am the owner and founder and we have a staff of 15.

The home office is in Philadelphia but our client base is national and international. We originally began as the premier market research and data analysis company for drug companies, doctors, and hospitals that needed the research before launching a new drug; before a patent expired; and to test-market the words, color, and design for new drugs and their containers. Our approach was innovative because my team has the expertise to conduct interviews and focus groups and to produce the quantitative analysis hand-tailored to meet every client's individual needs.

Marcela: That sounds fine but have you done this in the real estate business?

David: That is exactly what I wanted to speak to you about today. Three years ago we developed the software called "Research and Results for Any Industry." We took our years of marketing practices and data analysis matrixes that we applied primarily in the health care field and created the software that could take those proven practices and apply them to any industry. I have an abbreviated version of the software as well as some "preliminary" market research I did in preparation for today's meeting, to give your company an idea of the market research we could do for your company to help you decide about the possible hotel condominium conversion you are contemplating.

Let us take a look at this scenario again for what we like and how perhaps we can make it better. I will then give you some tips that hopefully you can use for any new business venture.

First, it is very good that David followed up very quickly with Marcela after their business networking evening. How often do we go to one of these "networking events" with a handful of business cards or texted telephone numbers and do not contact these new business connections for weeks, or sometimes not at all? This is exactly the same as the follow-up with an Ask that is described in Chapter 3 and detailed further in Chapter 8.

Second, David is careful to weave into the conversation very quickly the important topical information that applies to Marcela's business, the growth of the hotel industry, with this piece of dialog:

David: South Beach seems to be doing well with hotel construction despite the slump in the residential housing industry.

Marcela: Well, it is hard to say how long this will last but in South Beach with all the trade shows and conventions that are booked here each weekend, hotels are doing well.

David: I have been to a few conferences here and, yes, it is pretty exciting. Especially the art industry that has really taken hold of the Miami area.

It is always a good idea to know exactly what is important to the business person you are meeting and engaging especially if you are not in the same geographic location. In this example, David's home office is in Philadelphia but he is speaking with Marcela about her business in Miami, Florida. Try to be "in the business moment" of the person you are meeting. Knowing the local community and the topical issues that may affect that person's business is essential.

Next, David brings up the most important part of the previous discussion they had at the networking event:

David: That's good to know. Thanks for the advice. Marcela, thank you for meeting me today. I wanted to spend a little more time speaking with you about how I think my company can help your company make some of the critical decisions you mentioned last night that you need to make in the very near future.

Marcela: Yeah, there are some big ones. Tell me again, what exactly does your company do in real estate market research?

David remembered that Marcela said her company needed to make some critical decisions soon that would impact her company's decision whether to convert hotel space into condominium space. It shows that the person who wants the business can zoom in on the heart of the prospective client's business issue and be of service. Whenever you're looking to forage into a new business arena, positioning your talents and your company's talents as a form of "help," "guidance," and a "relief of pressure" will keep the conversation alive and I guarantee the prospective client will want to know specific ways and within what time frame your company can help.

The last part of this dialog is the hardest because David must anticipate that at some point Marcela is going to jump in and ask:

Marcela: Tell me again, what exactly does your company do in real estate market research?

This is where asking for new business can all fall apart. If the person who wants the new business, David in our example, goes on and on about how fabulous the company has been for decades, the stellar clients he has, and the waiting list of clients who are dying to have his business, the prospective client, Marcela in this example, will gloss over everything he has said and will silently convince herself that David's proposition is too risky. What you are asking for here and what you are selling is your proven success in one area and how you have or *will transition that success to make the prospective client's business successful and profitable.*

In this example, it is right at this point where we could make David's pitch, his Ask for new business, a bit better. Notice how he falls into the trap of "selling" the past successes of his business as the first response to Marcela's question of how this applies to real estate:

> *David:* My company, Research and Results, has been in existence for over 16 years. I am the owner and founder and we have a staff of 15. The home office is in Philadelphia but our client base is national and international. We originally began as the premier market research and data analysis company for drug companies, doctors, and hospitals that needed the research before launching a new drug before a patent expired; and to test-market the words, color, and design for new drugs and their containers. Our approach was innovative because my team has the expertise to conduct interviews and focus groups and to produce the quantitative analysis hand-tailored to meet every client's individual needs.

Then we have Marcela asking again:

> *Marcela:* That sounds fine, but have you done this in the real estate business?

What we want to avoid is having the prospective client ask twice how your current business can help the client. So in this example, instead of David saying four long sentences about the history of his company, perhaps he could have said the following:

> *David:* That is exactly where we are headed. Three years ago we developed the software called "Research and Results for Any Industry." We took our years of marketing practices and data analysis matrixes that we applied in the health care field and created the software that could take those proven practices and

apply them to any industry. Over the past year and a half, our company has been approached by several real estate companies, especially with the current state of the real estate market, to do some critical research on the changing demographics in certain cities to help with their growth and revenue projections. With the help of some of my technology colleagues, I developed the software that can do expert market and data analysis for any market, but it grew out of my company expanding from primarily health care to real estate.

Bingo! Now this will most certainly keep Marcela's interest piqued and the conversation will be 100 percent focused on how David's new software can help her company with the possible condominium conversion. See how this dialog can really steer the conversation so it has the spotlight on helping Marcela's business, not immediately leading in with the past successes of David's company. Later on in the conversation David can bring her up to speed on the company's history, or even leave some brochures or lead her to the Web site. If you do the exercise of "scripting" your Ask, as detailed in Chapter 2, then you will be more than prepared when a potential client jumps in in the middle of the conversation and wants to know on the spot what your business can do for their current business. Now you see how this all fits together and how important it is not to miss any of the steps and suggestions in Chapters 1–4 that will guide you and prepare you for any Ask.

The next and best thing we can add to the sample dialog is the following:

> *David:* Marcela, now that you have the facts on how my market research and data analysis has and can work for the real estate industry, I am asking you to let me show you a demonstration on how this can help you make the decision you are facing now as well as those you may have to make in the future. I truly believe my company can be of great service to you and your company.

There you have it—the Ask for potential business. The specific Ask is to show how David's company can help her reach her decision now and for later decisions. It is always a good idea to project your company as helping an immediate problem as well as ones that will surely arise in the future.

To recap what has been illustrated above, Exhibit 6.4 contains some tips you can use for any business venture Ask.

EXHIBIT 6.4. *Tips for Any Business Venture Ask.*

1. If you meet a potential client, investor, or anyone who you think can be helpful for your business, *follow up* right away and get an appointment with that person.

2. Do all the research ahead of time on the prospective client, investor, and her company and speak with the person as though you are knowledgeable about her company.

3. If you did meet a potential client or investor at a networking event or through a colleague, make sure you weave in the conversation you had at the networking event or similarities between your work or the people you know in the industry.

4. Avoid giving too much past history and a litany about the success and greatness of your business in the beginning of the conversation.

5. Anticipate that your prospective client or investor will want to know very quickly what you and your business can do for them, particularly if the person told you of a pressing business issue.

6. Make sure you state the "match" between your prospective client or investor's immediate and future business needs and the opportunities you and your company can bring to meet those needs.

7. Ask for the business.

Asking for prospective business is no different from asking for money as you can see from this sample dialog and the suggestions in Exhibit 6.4. You have to do your research; you need to get the appointment quickly; you have to find the "match" between what is important to your prospective client and investor and the business opportunity you and your company can offer; and you need to speak "with" your prospective client or investor, not "at" them. Lastly and most importantly, ask for the business. I believe that if you do all the exercises detailed in Chapters 1–4 you will be well prepared to get all the prospective business you need.

CONCLUSION

This chapter laid out the steps you need to take and guidelines you need to follow when asking for a job-related cause, a creative project, or a business venture. The steps and guidelines are parallel to asking for a charitable gift, so if you work or volunteer for a nonprofit and you want to ask for a job-related cause or launch a side business, do not forget all the knowledge you have about asking for a gift because it all applies in asking for a job or for a business investment. The same holds true if you are in business and now you want to help raise money for a local charity.

With each Ask for yourself or your creative or business venture, believe in what you are asking for; describe in detail why you and your company are the best fit for what you are asking for; lay out all the facts with a positive demeanor for the person being asked; and state that you are "asking" for this money; "asking" for this job, position, or title; or asking for this prospective business because this is extremely important to you and/or your company and it will fulfill you personally and professionally.

LOOKING AHEAD

Now that we know the preparation we need for any Ask and how to make the right Ask, it is time to focus on the array of responses to the Ask you will get. The next chapter will illustrate the most popular responses to the Ask there are. It will also showcase some unusual responses to demonstrate that even if you do prepare for and anticipate the various responses you may receive, there are those instances where you will be surprised with what you hear. The point of this is to be flexible, a good listener, and to keep the Ask on track while you hear and address the response.

Handling the Responses to the Ask

OING THE ASK MAY BE THE MOST "nervous" part of making the Ask. The second most "nervous" part is waiting to hear the response to the Ask. It is so common and so typical for the asker to assume the person being asked will say "no" or may need so much time before she decides. The key to dispelling these preconceived ideas is to anticipate the response as best you can and prepare solid answers to the anticipated response or responses. If there is one thing this chapter will emphasize and re-emphasize is that handling any response is all about preparing for the response. Think about everything that was done and said during the cultivation period and/or during the conversation you had leading up to and during the Ask. All the signals, signs, and warnings were right there *if* you paid attention to them and were not distracted by trying to "convince" the person being asked that they *should* do what you asked.

Only through preparation and anticipation of the person's response can any asker feel fully confident about answering the response. This chapter also suggests ways to best prepare for the person's response, so that the conversation remains upbeat, the dialog flows smoothly, and there are few surprises or unanticipated responses. Naturally, there will be the occasion where one could not possibly have predicted the response but in my experience this is the exception, not the rule. That said, this chapter does give examples of some of those "rare unexpected" responses and ways to address them so that you can anticipate some of the unexpected reactions you may receive. Keep in mind the responses and suggestions in this chapter *apply to any Ask;* you just need to adjust some of the words to fit your particular situation.

PREPARING FOR THE RESPONSE

By now the asker or the asking team should know the person who was asked inside and out and therefore should be able to anticipate the person's response. For instance, if the person being asked shared with you information about recent family illnesses, that the economic recession caused his portfolio to decrease by more than one half, that his company may be moving to a new location, that his brother was just laid off and the family is pitching in to help him find another job and to make ends meet, or that his children are considering very expensive private universities, you should be alerted that these issues may come up when you ask for money. This is anticipating the person's response. *It should not prevent or postpone the Ask* you were planning, but it should guide you in the overall preparation that needs to be done. Sit down and make a list of what you (and anyone who is participating in the Ask with you) think the person will say to the Ask. This is not to suggest that you will correctly guess the specific response all the time, but it is a powerful exercise for not getting caught completely off guard by the person's response. Exhibit 7.1 lists several items to consider in preparing for the response.

EXHIBIT 7.1. *To-Do List in Preparing for the Response.*

1. Recall in your mind the conversations you had with the person being asked, and anyone else who was part of any communication with her.

2. Go over your contact reports or notes that you made during cultivation, when you were getting to know the person being asked and engaging and educating her about the organization, your project, your proposal, and your request.

3. Write down the hints or direct points the person being asked made about challenges she was encountering personally or professionally or things that were worrying her about the organization where you work or that you want to create.

4. List every possible response you think she may give to your request.

5. Script out in detail how you will calmly and positively address each and every point she made in her response.

6. Practice your listening skills.

7. Pay close attention to your body language and tone of voice and that of your co-asker.

8. Memorize the body language and tone of voice of the person you are asking.

9. Avoid the temptation to argue, be overly aggressive, or overly enthusiastic in addressing the responses.

10. Know that patience, passion, and practice will bring the Ask to a "yes."

This may seem a bit time-consuming but it is well worth it in the end. Keep in mind, especially if you are fundraising for a nonprofit organization, that you will be working with many people in many stages of cultivation—asking, following up, stewarding—and it is very hard to remember every detail about the person you are about to ask for money. Similarly, if you had conversations with your boss about budgets and hires and you are asking for a raise, most assuredly these issues will arise when you ask for a raise but now you will be prepared to address them and not let them overpower the importance of your Ask.

One point that I must emphasize here is that in numbers 3 and 4 in Exhibit 7.1, writing down the challenges the person you are about to ask has stated and then listing the possible responses you may get in light of these challenges *is by no means a way for you to postpone your Ask.* If you feel it is the right time, knowing that these issues will come up, then you should still do your Ask, with sensitivity and acknowledgment of these issues. We will see concrete examples of this later in this chapter but for now, if you know the person you are about to ask has had some financial hardship with the family or the person has referred to how hard this economic climate has been on her industry, if you feel it is the right time to ask, then do so. *How* you do it and *what* you say can make all the difference in the world. You could say:

> *"Brooke, I know that the economic climate has not been the best for your business and if there is anything we can do, please let me know. Thank you for sharing those thoughts with me. Brooke, I by no means want to sound insensitive to your concerns or that I have not heard your concerns. You and I have been discussing for quite some time your investment in this new company. While this may not be the ideal time, let us talk about how together we can make that happen either right now or in the very near future. Let me explain about the ideas I have."*

This is how you take what the person you are about to ask has told you and use those concerns during your Ask. This serves many purposes. First, it shows the person you are asking that they have been heard and that you have not forgotten the past conversations and what is pressing on the person's mind. Second, it is an "inclusive" conversation. You know that the person you are asking would like to invest in your opportunity, and that there are some things that may or could get in the way but if you acknowledge them right away, you both are working toward a solution to make the investment happen. Third, you have smoothed your way over the response because now the person is more focused on hearing your suggestions and you are on your way to "yes," not "I really don't think so."

---

10 Things to Know About Any Ask—#7

The anticipated responses you may receive should not prevent you from asking if you feel the time is right, provided the Ask is done with sensitivity and understanding.

Perhaps the fourth and most persuasive reason why you should still do the Ask if you feel it is the right time despite knowing the person may have some personal or professional reasons is "competition." With the overwhelming number of nonprofits nationally and internally, chances are the person you want to ask *will* be asked by another nonprofit and now you have dropped down on the priority list. This happened to me when I was working as a major gift officer at a hospital. The woman I wanted to ask for a first-time major gift of $20,000 told me she was helping her sister with her estate and she was traveling a great deal to help her sister. I postponed visiting her until I thought things would settle down for her. While I was waiting, her church met with her and asked her for a major gift to support the renovation of the church's roof. She said yes. When I met with her a few weeks later she said, "Oh, I would have considered that but now I am committed for the next few years to make these gifts to my church." You can imagine how I regretted that decision for years. However, one learns from each mistake so that is why I encourage you to not put off the Ask if you feel it is the right time despite an issue or two that the person tells you about.

Similarly, creative and business opportunities are countless. Chances are if you do not make the timely Ask, the person you want to ask *will* be asked by others to invest in them or their company. The bottom line is do not let negative discussions drive your decision to postpone the Ask. If a person tells you that due to their concerns, they are not going to make any investments or gifts whatsoever, tell him you understand and that you want to be the one group, the one artist, the one business venture that they consider backing at the moment he is ready.

What the person says right after the Ask will guide you on how you need to follow up and keep the Ask "alive" until you have a "yes." This is why it is *so crucial* that every asker listen to the person's concerns and pay strict attention to the person's tone of voice and body language. Yes, you will anticipate what the person's response will be but you must be flexible because the person may say something that even with all the preparation in the world you could not have anticipated. People live very complicated lives that change daily if not a few times a day and things may arise that you could not possibly know.

This is why *listening* is so important. If you do not hear what the person says right after the Ask, how will you know what to say next? The asker needs to let the person talk as long as she wants to, because then the asker will have the total picture of what is going on in the person's mind, and what concerns her the most. As the asker is listening, she should be careful not to interrupt the person, which is so hard to do because you want to win them over. This is not a win-lose situation. This is giving someone the opportunity to invest with your cause, your company, or you, period. Please do not lose sight of this fact because if you do, you will not get what you asked for.

Body language is extremely important for the asker. Really practice keeping upright shoulders, head straight up, eyes focused, feet squarely on the ground with knees in a slightly loose position. Do not lean your elbows on your knees, or lean so far into the personal space of the person being asked that they feel uncomfortable. These details really are important no matter how well you know the person being asked. Remember, you are the organization, the company, the promise of big returns when you do the Ask. If you are focused, the person being asked is focused. That should motivate you to be ultra-observant of your body language.

The same applies for your tone of voice. It should be natural, not a pitch the person is not used to hearing, and make sure it is clear and can be heard. I have been on many Asks where people had no idea how low their voice was; how outside noises, especially restaurant sounds, drowned out their conversations; and how after the Ask the person being asked really had no idea what was said. Make your voice upbeat, strong, and convincing, and practice being the voice of someone you admire if you have a hard time "pushing" your voice to sound more convincing or persuasive.

It is equally important that you take note of the body language and tone of voice of the person you are asking. Make a good observation of their body language, tone, and pitch of voice when they make their response. What does it say or sound like to you? Are they nervous; anxious; matter-of-fact; pensive; clearing their throat; tapping their foot; and are their eyes roaming, focused, or looking down? All these are indicators of how you will have to handle their verbal and nonverbal communication. To ignore or be unaware of these neon signs would be tragic to your Ask.

Lastly, being overly aggressive, argumentative, or overly enthusiastic has not gotten anyone too far in an Ask. All too often people doing the Ask are so wrapped up in the mechanics and script of the Ask that they oversell the Ask. Speak clearly, naturally, and with pride, passion, and purpose in your voice. That is truly the best you can do. Closing Asks takes time, and it is highly unlikely that the person's first words after the Ask will be, "All right," "OK," or, "Where do I sign?" Remember, these are people who have a genuine interest in you, your organization, the concept, the idea, the project, and what this will bring to your beneficiaries, and in all likelihood have demonstrated loyalty and commitment. They deserve to have the asker or asking team be 100 percent focused on their needs in a professional, polished, and passionate manner.

Addressing the Person's Response

There are many, many possible responses you will get to your various Asks so the best way to coach you in addressing the responses is to share with you the most popular ones I have received and the ones I am asked about when I speak on this topic. I tried to put the most common ones first but in your new-found career in asking for what you want, you will probably encounter all of them. Each one has a short evaluation in assessing what was said in the response and provides concrete suggestions on how you can address the response.

"I HAVE TO THINK ABOUT IT." This is perhaps the most popular response you will receive. Think about it—no one likes to make a split-second decision on the spot and naturally, the person you just asked will need to think things over. There is a floodgate of questions they ask in their minds after the Ask:

- How much money do they have to do this?
- Where will the money come from?
- When is the best time to do it?
- Is this in their or their organization's best interest?
- What will their family, financial planner, attorney, business partner, or community say if they do or don't do what you asked?
- Does your past performance really merit a raise, promotion, new job title?

- Will the creative project you want to launch really happen?
- Will the business you want to create have a solid financial foundation?
- Can the business you want to expand really be successful in other markets?
- Will this mean I cannot do that other thing I had planned?

This is why it is very important to give them the breathing room they need when they are discussing what is on their minds after the Ask. The best response you can give someone when they say they need more time to think about it is:

"IS IT THE AMOUNT, OR THE TIMING?" I love this question because with each response the key is to know *exactly* why they cannot decide now and to avoid "fill in the blank" fundraising by guessing the reasons and concerns that are on their minds. They may not be able to decide because perhaps they thought about making a much smaller gift or supporting your project or raise with a much smaller number. They may not be able to decide because of personal or professional things right now going on in their lives. For instance, there may be an illness in the family; they may need to do major repairs at home or at work; or they are focused on saving much of their resources for a future need. This is why it is so important to ask this *very open-ended question* to clarify exactly what is on their mind so that you can address their response. Let's show some ways to answer when it is the timing versus the amount.

- When They Need More Time
  - "Important decisions take time, and we are very happy to hear that you will give this opportunity/request serious consideration."
  - "How can we help you while you make this important decision? Do you need any additional information from us?"
  - "Right now, tell us how you feel about the gift opportunity we just described?"
  - "We would like to contact you in two weeks. If you need more time that is perfectly understandable, but we would

like to listen to your thoughts and answer your questions as you reflect on this important and exciting business venture."

- When It Is the Amount
  - "We understand perfectly, and we are sure there are many factors you will want to consider. But right now, how do you feel about the gift opportunity we just described?"
  - "We are not surprised at all that you need some time, because this may be a larger amount than you might have anticipated at this time. As you know, this is an extraordinary time for our organization, and we need to rely on a handful of treasured families/business colleagues, like you, to make this happen now."
  - We know this may be a very large investment but this project is so important that we hope you will give this Ask your full consideration.
  - We are asking our closest friends like you to stretch their giving a bit because we feel you share the dream that together we can accomplish great things for our beneficiaries."

"WITH THIS ECONOMY I THINK IT IS BEST TO WAIT AND SEE WHEN THINGS GET BETTER." No doubt in tough economic times when asking for money people are going to reflect on the economy and how that can help or hinder their personal and professional finances. As I am writing this book in 2009, there are numerous seminars and conferences worldwide on how to raise money in an uncertain economy. As was put forth throughout this book, one cannot postpone the Ask if the person is ready to be asked because the asker or the asker's boss or board feels it is insensitive to ask now. The question for people who may be thinking this very same thought is "Can anyone know with certainty when the economy will improve nationally and internationally?" I venture to say the answer is "no" so you may be waiting a very, very long time before the economy improves, and your charitable beneficiaries will be the ones who suffer the most, as will the creative projects and business ventures that do not get produced or launched.

Most certainly the economy will be on people's minds when you ask them for money; however, re-read the response in this chapter when the asker addresses Brooke's concern about the economy. It just takes sensitivity, understanding, and creativity in your answer to the person's concern about the economy. The key goals are to:

- Keep the Ask alive for the person's consideration when the person feels more comfortable giving.
- If at all possible, have the person give something now to the overall Ask amount, like a down payment, and revisit periodically the possibility of the person making payments towards the Ask so at least your Ask remains a priority.

As you will see later in this chapter, I am a strong advocate that you do not come off the Ask "price" during the Ask and that you stick with the Ask amount for a little bit of time. The rationale is that you thought long and hard about the amount you wanted to ask for so that if you lower the "Ask price" during the initial Ask, it makes the person being asked feel that you really didn't think this through and you are willing to "bargain" or take any "negotiated" amount. If you are a nonprofit then your beneficiaries as well as your life-saving, cutting-edge projects and programs are worthy of this size gift together with other gifts of this exact size that you are going to attract very soon. If you are a business you know the exact costs of what it takes to run the business and make a profit and you need this amount invested to stay on track. If you are asking for a raise and you instantly take a lesser amount, you have now diminished all the strong reasons you just put forth quantifying and qualifying why you are worthy of the asked raise amount. Only when the person being asked states *strongly, clearly, and emphatically* that they cannot give you the amount you asked because the economy has diminished their assets do I suggest either: a) you thank them for their honesty and meet with them in a month or two to see if they can reconsider the amount, or b) if they want to do something now with the promise of giving the full amount at a later time, at least you have their commitment to revisit the full amount in the future. To the extent you can stay flexible with how they wish to give you the full amount without it impeding on your pressing cash flow, then this has every promise of your getting what you asked for.

Here are some additional ways to handle the response about the economy:

- "We understand and thank you so much for your honesty. It is really affecting a lot of people but we at the organization are optimistic that our loyal supporters/new investors will appreciate that we are dedicated to and focused on accomplishing the goals we just discussed that can have an impact as small and as important as one life, and as global and transformational as one country. Together we will get there, so let's brainstorm some things you may be able to do/afford now and revisit the larger picture very soon."

- "We have had a few people with similar concerns and let us share with you how we worked with them so that they were comfortable in their current level of giving and the quarterly pledge agreement that alleviated their worries about giving too much of the amount up front."

- "We know this amount is a large Ask considering the economy that no one can control or predict. We think you share our vision and know the importance of maintaining a stable and secure community for yourself, your family, your loved ones, and your neighbors as well as a financially vibrant community for our school, hospitals, arts centers, and merchants. We have been discussing this size giving/investment opportunity for quite some time, and we would be very grateful if you give this very important Ask your total consideration. The needs of our community are real and with your generous help, we can maintain the quality of life we all want to enjoy, today and well into the future."

- We absolutely understand, and hopefully the economy will be on an upswing very soon. And some people might question why we are asking our good supporters like you for a gift now. That's easy—because the needs of our beneficiaries don't go away, regardless of the economy. We think you share our vision that this is a special time for our organization, and we have but a handful of strong leaders like you to help us make this happen."

"THE ASK IS TOO HIGH." Everyone second-guesses themselves when the person they just asked for money wants to give a little or a lot less than what was just proposed. First, don't back down from the Ask, and recall all the reasons why you thought this person would be a perfect person for this size gift or this size investment. Remember, people need a road map, they need to know where you want them and at what level you want them in your Ask. Second, if you immediately back down, that signals to them that they really aren't that important and that you do these types of Asks at least three times a day so what difference does it make if they give you less? Answer: it makes a great deal of difference so acknowledge that yes, this is a high/generous/stretch/very large Ask and get back to why the money you are asking for is so important. What will it do? How will it make the person feel after she gives/invests it? If he is a person who loves recognition, how many accolades (within *all* the bounds of ethics) can you give him? Lastly, do not throw away all the research, thought process, and cultivation that led you to make the best Ask amount at this moment because you hear this response. Here are some suggested ways you can address this response:

- "We understand perfectly that this might be a very large amount, and believe us, we do not ask for this every day."
- "You are but one of a handful of people we can turn to and ask for this very important gift."
- "As a top supporter of the organization, you are one of the few people we can turn to for this extraordinary gift opportunity."
- "We hope you take this as a compliment. Our intent was to make sure that you were among the first families to be offered this exciting and transformational opportunity."
- "We realize that our campaign goal is very ambitious, but we are asking our closest family members to consider a 'stretch gift' at this time. We would be happy to talk about the ways you can fund your gift as well as the timing of your prospective gift."
- "No one can know with certainty how much a person will give/invest. Based on everything we have discussed over the past few months, your ideas and your past support/involvement with our group, we wanted to ask you for this amount so that we could fulfill your desire to bring our group to new heights."

- "We have no idea if you are willing to make this type of leadership gift, but as you are one of our top visionary leaders and long-standing volunteers, it was important that we come to you first."

Honesty always wins out when someone appears to think or flat out tells you that what you asked for is higher than what they had in mind. Thank them, and thank them again for their honesty, and adapt some of the above suggested ways to address this response. I think you will be well on your way to getting the exact Ask amount.

"I NEED TO DISCUSS THIS WITH OTHER PEOPLE." Naturally, if you ask one person in a couple they may need to discuss this with the other person, or others will want to consult financial advisors, attorneys, business partners, and believe it or not, psychics. No joke, but some people need to know the stars are aligned for them to make this "dramatic move." Regardless of who needs to be consulted your response should always be to:

- Offer to speak with the other decision maker.
- Offer to send additional information to the other decision maker.
- Offer to send the person you just asked an exact account of the Ask.

I've found in my experience if you don't do the third bullet above, it turns into the very old "telephone game"—what one person heard is not what is being conveyed to the second person, and on, and on. Your Ask is far too important to have it translated and diluted to another person, and you and you alone know all the specifics, the background, the research, the cultivation, the conversation, and the e-mails that transpired up to now, and to have someone else crystallize the conversation would be extremely disappointing. Try to do all three above and if all else fails, you will have to do the due diligence outlined in the next chapter, because now you will have to get the information from the person you asked on how their discussion went with the other decision maker went, as well as how the person being asked feels now.

Did the other person talk them out of it? Did they have so many questions and concerns that the Ask is history? It is amazing where your mind will go with very bad negative thoughts, whereas if you do the follow-up, you'll know exactly what was said and how you will have to proceed. Here are some ways to address when someone else needs to be consulted:

- "Absolutely, we want you to discuss this with important people in your life. We would be delighted to help you and your spouse/partner/business associate make this important decision. Would our meeting with you two together be beneficial to reaching a joint decision?"

- "Before I made my gift I felt exactly like you that I needed to discuss this with my partner. Please take some time, and I would be delighted to be present or to answer any questions that you have in person or by telephone or e-mail."

- "That's terrific that you want to discuss this with your accountant/financial advisor/attorney. We are very fortunate to ask you for this amazing investment just when you planned to have a meeting with your accountant/financial advisor/attorney. We would welcome the opportunity to be a part of that meeting if you wish, or to answer any questions."

- "I realize that you may have to discuss my raise/job title/promotion with the executive director/vice president/CEO. If I have not fully and completely shared and documented with you why I strongly believe this raise/job title/promotion is right for the organization and the future contributions I can make with the team, please let me know.

- "Naturally, you need to discuss this with others and that is one of the reasons why we came to you. You are organized, a strategic thinker and planner, and you make decisions that work best for you and your company/interests. We know and *respect* that you will not make a move until you know it is best for you."

This is a very good sign that the person wants to discuss with and seek advice from others about your Ask. It means that the person is going to give it the careful consideration it deserves. Do not view this as being "blown off" or "shelved" with no decision date in sight. Stay positive and remember to make yourself available to meet the other decision makers and to offer any additional information in person, by e-mail, or snail mail that would be helpful to all involved with the decision making process.

"I GIVE OR INVEST WITH NUMEROUS ORGANIZATIONS/BUSINESSES." In many instances, people who make charitable gifts give to more than one nonprofit. Similarly, business investors and backers for creative projects generally do spread their investments over many places. So it would not be an uncommon response to your Ask that they either just made a gift or investment with another nonprofit or business or that they don't want to give you the amount you asked for because they know they want to give to other places and need to hold back or save some money for that. This can also apply when you ask for a raise or a promotion. Your boss may be thinking that they only have x amount in the budget and they would rather spread it around than give it to you in a larger portion, or that if you ask for a promotion everyone else will ask for one and it would be better to see how things play out in the office before giving one person a higher status or more money. When you hear these responses you can be prepared by saying:

- "We understand perfectly. Many of our top supporters give to more than one organization."
- "There are so many great groups to support. I have felt the way you do now, but after giving it much consideration, I simply had to make giving this larger gift a priority. We hope that you will think about this a bit and make it your priority as well."
- "Our purpose here today is to introduce you to this exciting opportunity and to hear your thoughts about it. Obviously, you have interests with other businesses, but right now, how do you feel about the investment we just described?"
- "This request is really for our future needs and for the community. We welcome your annual support, but let's keep talking about the campaign. Gifts at this level will ensure the success of our organization for years to come."

- "We are asking everyone to consider what their combined extraordinary support can do for the organization. Right now, if what we have described for you is exciting and you want to join with others to make this happen, then let us keep the discussion going and find some creative ways that we can make this happen."

- "I realize that others from the office may want to ask for a raise once they find out that I just asked for one but that may or may not happen. What is important here and I believe worthy of your full consideration is one question only—whether you feel, and I hope you do, that my past performance together with the new assignments and new managerial responsibilities has demonstrated to you and the company that I am a valuable employee, worthy of a salary increase."

- "Please know that I do not take asking for a job promotion lightly and I have given great thought as to when it would be the best time to ask you for this promotion. My Ask demonstrates my desire to stay with the organization, to contribute at a higher level, and to have the opportunity to learn more skills."

The point here is to make sure the person you are asking stays focused on your Ask, instead of "projecting what may happen in the future." You want to avoid as best you can leaving the person thinking about other organizations and the way that you do this is by reiterating why your organization should continue to be a priority for the person you are asking. Likewise, if you are asking for a job-related request and the person comments about what limited resources there are to give you more salary or whether the whole organizational chart will turn upside down when everyone in the office asks for a new title or promotion, keep the person you are asking focused on you and your request in this moment in time because you simply cannot predict or second-guess what might or might not happen in the future.

Exercise #7: Write out the anticipated responses you may get to something you want to ask for, and then use some of the scripted suggestions here so that you can be prepared to address any and all responses you may get to your Ask.

"I'M NOT INTERESTED IN SUPPORTING THAT PROJECT/MAKING THIS INVESTMENT." Sometimes, although not too often, you are 100 percent certain that you have an exact match—the perfect gift/ investment opportunity that matches a key and important interest of the person you want to ask. You make the Ask and the person, somewhat out of the blue, says to you, "I'm not interested in that." There is no way you could have predicted it; in fact, throughout your cultivation you probably were having some serious discussions about the person prospectively supporting this particular project. Well, life is a constant revolving door and sometimes a person simply changes her mind and what was appealing a few weeks ago has no appeal today. So what should you do? Here are some suggestions:

- "Thank you for being so candid and honest with us today. Please know that we did think long and hard about the right gift opportunity for you. From our previous conversations we thought this gift opportunity would match your key interests."
- "Can you tell us where your key interest lies within the organization? We want to hear more from you."
- "Now that we know that you would rather make an un-restricted gift for the overall good work of our organization, we would be happy to share with you how unrestricted gifts benefit the entire organization."
- "We understand that our donors choose to support things that interest them the most, and we are here to honor your philanthropic wishes and desires. Please know that many donors do like to support our endowment because it allows our organization to continue its good work well into the future and provides the financial backing for us to provide the very best services for our beneficiaries."
- "Our discussions led us to believe that your key interest was to take the production on tour, but now that you shared with us that you think it can generate more revenue by keeping the show here for the next year and then spin off for the tour, we'd be happy to walk through our projected budget for the year."

- "Thank you for sharing with us your exact ideas for growing our foreign markets. Our product line is stronger in the United States but we would be happy to discuss with you the plan to increase our product line abroad over the next five years. Let's talk about this more and ways you can make a major investment."

What wins the day here is: 1) acknowledging the person's honesty; 2) not arguing with the person or trying to convince the person they really want to stick with the initial investment idea you have been discussing all along (surely you will lose that argument); 3) staying flexible and really listening to the "new" concept that excites them even more than what you originally planned; 4) being good on your feet and able to explain some of the ideas and benefits of giving the same amount you asked for but now in this new direction that is of key interest to the person; and 5) letting go of the original Ask purpose when the person told you they are no longer interested. This last one is hard because it means relinquishing control of something you so desperately want to contain. A gift, an opportunity, an investment has to tug on the heartstrings and hit a homerun on the excitement meter in order for someone to give what you are asking. If they are not interested or are no longer interested in the gift and investment idea, have them tell you what the key interest is and fly with it!

"THE CHANGE IN LEADERSHIP/THE ORGANIZATION HAD SOME BAD PUBLICITY." Turnover in leadership for business and nonprofits is very common but can cause potential donors and investors to take a "wait and see" attitude out of fear that the successor may not be as productive, visionary, likeable, or charismatic as the former leader. Many of your discussions during cultivation would have included why the organization was so successful, including that the leader (CEO, president, executive director, artistic director) demonstrated strong leadership skills and vision and instilled confidence and a winning direction for the organization. Take her or him away and what will happen to the future of the organization? It is difficult to ask for money when there is a change in leadership because of the uncertainty of how the new leaders will perform. This same "wait and see" can occur if the organization has had some bad press, such as a donor going public that his money was not being used for the purpose he was promised and wants it back; someone in a leadership role having an extramarital affair; rumblings that the company may merge or move out of its central headquarters; or the entity is being sued for false advertisement or harm done by its products. There are many more reasons for bad publicity but when you want to ask someone for money or right after you asked for money and one of these situations occurs, it can be very hard to persuade the person you asked to still give the Ask great consideration "despite" the fact that this unfortunate event occurred. Here are some ways you can address these types of situations:

- "Yes, we do have a new president who will continue the important work of our organization. We ask you to think about the thousands of people we serve. We think you share our vision that they deserve continuous support from our loyal supporters like you."

- "We think you will be most pleased with the new director. Already she has had a tremendous impact with our beneficiaries and in our community. Here is some information on her, and we would love to have you meet with her sometime very soon."

- "We are here to listen to your views and to share with you the facts about the organization you have so generously supported over the years."

- "We take your views very seriously and we would like to have our president (or CEO) personally contact you."

- "A few investors shared your views, and in a short span of time we regained their trust. We are here to regain your trust and respect. We know that may take some time, but you are very important to us."

- "It is most unfortunate that this is getting blown up in the press but as you have heard in our statement, we stand behind the company and we hope you will stay a loyal business partner with us. Your support and trust right now is the most important thing to us and we know it is challenges like this one that will make the company stronger."

Change in leadership can be pull-back time, a time to wait and see, so the best thing you can do is first and foremost thank them for their honesty and second, get the new leaders to meet with the hesitant person and win them over. This may seem like a lot of work and I'm sure the new leader will have many things on her plate in the new position; however, important and large gifts as well as major investments are well worth the new leader's time in getting to know her "new best friends"—your large givers.

Bad publicity can be a delicate and often tense time so the best thing you can do is acknowledge that the unfortunate and unpleasant publicity is hard on everyone and get the person focused on all the good things he liked about the organization or company before the incident occurred. This may not always be possible and indeed some people may really want to wait it out and see what happens before they will make a commitment. To the extent you can reorient the conversation to the continuing needs of your beneficiaries, their past loyalty and trust with the organization, and the need to have that support now more than ever, you may indeed be able to have that person be a champion for your cause who will stand by your side and continue to be a top supporter.

"THE ENVELOPE ON THE TABLE HAS THE AMOUNT I WANT TO GIVE." I saved the best for last. I have had the experience where people knew I was coming to ask them for money as we had discussed previously and they knew I was going to ask them for something much larger than they had given previously, and as I walked in the door, there was an envelope with my name on it on their desk or dining room table. Could I make this up? There are a few ways to go with this one but in any case *I always still make my Ask for the amount I originally was going to ask.* It can be an awkward moment, especially if everyone is staring at the envelope and not saying anything. Suddenly, you feel like you are in a silent movie and you have no idea when it will end. If after I made the Ask the person said to me "well I had this in mind and here it is" and points to the envelope, this is what I would say:

- "This is so wonderful that you thought ahead of time to make a wonderful gift and investment with us. Your past support has helped us attract so many new supporters and we are so appreciative. What is important right now is, how do you feel about the opportunity I just described?"

- "Thank you so much for being so thoughtful and generous by thinking ahead of time to further your magnificent support. *I have no idea what is in the envelope that you so generously gave me but it is so important to us that we know how you feel about this unique investment. I assure you whatever amount you so carefully placed here can and will be used towards this new opportunity.*"

- "Great minds think alike and I am so happy that we are both on the same wavelength to discuss today your continued support. How does it feel to know that your prospective new support, combined with others, will help us serve 1,700 more under-privileged youths? If this something that is very important to you and your family as you have shared with us many times, then I'm most certain that together, combining this gift with future gifts, we can make that dream happen."

What is important here is that you go back to some of the fundamentals mentioned earlier in this chapter in dealing with some of the responses, and focus the person on how they feel about the Ask you just made to ensure you have the right match and to really hear their enthusiasm and joy that this prospective investment will make. Regardless of what is in the envelope, stick to having the person being jazzed up about the prospect of delivering more services to your beneficiaries, helping the organization fulfill its mission and vision, and being part of a vibrant, stable, and healthy community.

I like the second bullet point above because it is true, you can always have the person "apply" that amount towards the Ask amount. It can be like a "pledge" towards the new, higher amount. It can lessen the awkwardness of the envelope versus the new Ask because now you are on the same sheet of music with the focus on making the gift happen with the amount you have right there in the envelope as a "down payment" for the investment.

Now, we have been speaking all along with the understanding that the amount in the envelope is *less than* the amount you asked for. What if the amount in the envelope is *more* than what you asked for? Isn't it amazing that our minds always go to the lesser amount or that the person will always want to give less than what we are about to ask? The best thing you can do is be ecstatic about the amount and make sure the person still wants to put it towards the program, project, area, or general investment, unrestricted gift that you had been discussing. Then go home and be happy, not depressed that you should have asked for even more, as I am sure some of you will do. You just received a great, large investment. Be happy and celebrate with your office mates!

CONCLUSION

Anticipation and preparation to the person's response to your Ask are the two most important ways you will be able to address any response. With a careful review of the conversations you have had prior to the Ask, and writing down what you think the person will say based on these previous conversations, you will have a really good idea how the person will react. Nothing is guaranteed but in your mind you have done all the necessary preparation. By paying close attention to your body language and their body language, being an avid listener and staying extremely flexible to what they are saying, yet focused on how you can keep the Ask alive by addressing their concerns, you will be confident to handle whatever is said once you make your Ask.

LOOKING AHEAD

We are at the point that in my experience is the most neglected part of the Ask—the follow-up. So many times we leave the decision in the hands of the person being asked, then days, months, and sadly years go by with no definitive answer to the Ask. It then becomes assumed that with so much passage of time, the answer assuredly must be "no" and we drop these people and focus on others who may be interested in what we need. This next chapter (and one of my favorites, so hang in for this one!) will lay out all the steps you and others need to take to *close* each and every Ask.

8

Following Up with Each and Every Ask

WHILE IT MAY BE TIME-CONSUMING, FOLLOWING UP WITH each and every Ask is a *must*. It does not matter if you ask once in a while or many times each week. Our natural tendency and comfort zone at times is to let the person have their space, let them think it over, and perhaps they will appreciate that you don't bother them with constant telephone calls, e-mails, or personal notes so that eventually, and on their timeline, they will contact you with their answer. I assure you this is *not* the approach or mindset you want. There is a system, a timeline, and some solid steps you can take after each Ask that will ensure you receive the answer to your Ask, allowing a reasonable time for the person to make her decision, while at the same time you have courteously driven the process.

NEXT STEPS AFTER EACH ASK

Important steps need to be taken after each Ask to keep the Ask in the forefront of the person's mind and ensure that questions are answered and additional material or expertise is provided. Because each person being asked will respond in a unique way, it is important that you have planned a series of solid next steps you can do after each Ask. This chapter describes these steps. It also explores how to juggle and balance your time so that you can make several Asks while following up on each and every one. The reality is always that after one Ask is made, many more Asks and many important follow-ups to previous Asks have to be made. Without an organized system to manage the asker's time, things can slip through the cracks, resulting in too much time elapsing between the Ask and the follow-through. The more time that transpires between the Ask and the follow-through, the harder it will be to refocus the person on your original Ask.

Exhibit 8.1 details all the important next steps you can take (and it is highly recommended you *should* take) after each Ask.

EXHIBIT 8.1.   *Solid Next Steps After Each Ask.*

1. Thank the person immediately after you have discussed and addressed his response (Chapter 7).

2. Convey to the person asked the importance of her decision, the impact it will have, and the *reason why it is important to make the gift or investment or decision now* as opposed to later.

3. **Set a time and date when you are going to follow up with the Ask.**

4. Send a handwritten note, a formal letter on company stationery, or an e-mail when appropriate thanking the person for meeting with you and taking the time to seriously consider your Ask.

5. Call the person the next day and thank them for meeting with you and for their time while they are making this very important decision. Ask again if they need additional information or if meeting with anyone else in the organization would be helpful in making the decision.

6. Send immediately any additional information requested by the person or data, budgets, or testimonials that you think may be helpful to close the gift.

7. *Mix up the communication and the communicator*—vary who contacts the person and what you say.

8. Tell the person about any new gifts or investments that have occurred while he is deciding—it conveys strength in numbers.

9. Try to get the person to come to the organization so you can showcase any new project, program, development, or to have him meet with your beneficiaries so he can experience how he will feel once he decides to give or invest.

10. Stay positive throughout the entire follow-up process and treat the person as if she is going to say "yes."

These solid next steps should be completed after each and every Ask. What good would an Ask be if no one followed up? This is not the time when you want to leave the ball in the person's court. Out of sight is out of mind and that is not where the asker wants to be. Even though people may well need time to consider a variety of things and to reflect on the relationships they have had with people in the organization, the asker who follows the steps listed in Exhibit 8.1 will ensure that the Ask remains a high priority for each person.

Immediately at the close of the Ask meeting, the asker or asking team needs to look the person directly in the eyes, and with all the warmth and sincerity possible, thank her for her time, for her past support and volunteerism, and most important, for giving the Ask and all the opportunities it will bring serious consideration. You cannot thank a person enough for their time, and this particular thank you should not be taken for granted.

Right after this thank you the asker or asking team needs to convey the importance and the impact this prospective gift or investment will have for the organization, beneficiaries, and the growth and future of the company. The person should not feel that if he says "no" it's no big deal because there are plenty of other potential supporters who can do what was asked. You need to use your own words and your own situation to tell the person calmly and with conviction *why you need this amount now.* The way you can craft this message is to ask yourself:

"What will not happen if we do not receive the money now as opposed to months or a long time later?"

"What benefits are there to saying "yes" to the request now as opposed to months or a long time later?

Once you answer these questions you then turn it around to something positive, visionary, and inspirational that will be enormously attractive to the person being asked. For example, if you work for a hospital and you know the patient numbers are escalating but the paying patients versus indigent care are disproportional, you can say:

"We all know the importance of the hospital in this community and our mission to serve the community and beyond. Right now with this economy, the number of patients whose insurance cannot cover their life-saving care has increased by 460 just in this quarter. These people deserve the care as so many deserving patients do, which is why with your help and with support from others, we can fill this gap in patient care needs."

For a company that just developed a new product that will be patented in the near future and has the promise to increase revenues, you can say:

"We are on the cutting edge to have this technology patented. Once that happens we have a whole marketing plan, as you know, to roll this out to every supermarket chain in the Midwest. With investors like you, we can get ahead of the curve and market the software now. If we wait until next quarter to get our investors on board, our profits for the projected revenue is anticipated to decrease by 10 percent. However, with the right investors now we are looking at a 20 percent increase immediately."

I think you get the point. No matter what you are asking for, you need to think strategically about *what it is that you and the organization wants to achieve, quantify it, and then in positive terms* state "we have every aspiration of achieving the 'joint goal' we have been talking about and right now we are on track *and*, with your gift or investment, we will get there."

I like this exercise because it forces you to quantify the numbers of people affected; the months of steady positive momentum for your volunteers, progress, projects, and programs that will experience a setback; the services that will not be performed; and the basic health and mission of the organization that is such an important part of the community that will have a severe negative impact. For instance, if your company wants to expand to two larger cities in the next six months and your company needs x amount to make that happen, chances are competitors will penetrate those markets first, which will be a financial setback. Hence, there is *urgency*. If you work for a social service agency and due to hard economic times unemployment rates increased to 9 percent and your agency now has to provide triple the amount to food banks, there is *urgency*. If the Ask is for a fundraising event such as a community block event or for a campaign gift, then urgency is easy to convey because the organization needs to raise a precise amount within a tightly defined time. It is harder to convey urgency when the Ask is for a yearly gift without a specific campaign or fund drive and you must be creative about doing it. Put yourself in the person's shoes. He could be thinking, "It's not a big deal whether I make the gift now, in a few months, or a few years; the organization will receive it eventually." This is why it is very important with any Ask that a sense of urgency for the gift be clearly spelled out for the person.

This can apply to job-related requests as well. Anyone with a new title, promotion, or raise is ready to hit the decks running, putting more energy and creativity into the company, which can only boost morale and make the organization more productive and successful. There is *urgency*. If the decision is postponed, the person waiting will probably not be as beneficial to the organization as if she had the answer to the question much sooner. There is resolution and not a limbo time that makes everyone uncomfortable.

Notice I use the word "urgency," not "desperation." You want to avoid making people feel guilty that there is so much need and that they are really bad people if they don't act now (see Chapter 1). Rather than sounding desperate, you just need to lay out the facts of the gap between where you are and where you need to be, convey that with their help you can get there, and that they will be the ones who will be remembered for helping your organization get there—*now*.

Number 3 in Exhibit 8.1 is a *must*. You have to get a time and date when you are going to communicate, hopefully in person, with the person you just asked. I guarantee if you don't, it will take weeks before you are able to reach the person to follow up. Think about it— you ask on a Tuesday; you call the person to thank them Wednesday and you get their voicemail; you e-mail or text them on Thursday and you get no reply; you give them Friday and the weekend and try again on Monday. All this is wasted effort. Instead, you could have simply asked:

> *"Can I call you on Thursday at 10:00 A.M. to follow up with our conversation?*

Then the person will say:

> *"Oh, Thursday is not good, and I won't be back in town until next Tuesday."*

Then you can say:

> *"Great, how about I call you on Tuesday afternoon? Just let me know the time that works best and the number where you can be reached."*

All that was done in a matter of a few short minutes and you have your next contact step to discuss the Ask.

This thank-you needs to be followed up with a formal letter or personal note no less than 24 hours after the person has been asked. The letter or note should include more than a thank-you for his time; it should trickle in something important or even humorous that was discussed at the meeting. For instance, if the person just returned from a fabulous vacation, then start the letter or note with, "It was so good to see you yesterday and to hear about your very adventurous vacation. I will have to keep that in mind for future vacation destinations." If the person revealed some personal discussion about family or business, then start the letter or note with, "It was great to see you yesterday, and congratulations on your new grandson," or, "Please keep us apprised of your company's prospective acquisition of a new line of semi-conductors." It keeps the Ask personal and important, and it shows that the asker or asking team really listened and focused on the person throughout the entire course of the meeting.

While you are doing your thank-you note, pick up the telephone the next day, or send an e-mail or text when appropriate and thank the person for her time. It is perfectly alright that you leave voicemail if you do not reach her; the point is to be very conscious of using precious time right after the Ask to follow up. This is also another opportunity to ask the person the next day if she thought over the Ask and if she needs any additional information or needs to speak with someone else to help her make the decision.

There are many instances when during the Ask it is very clear that the person being asked needs additional information. This is very often the case when the Ask has multiple components, such as asking for a capital campaign gift when the donor may be interested in supporting a new project but she needs more information on the timeline and current support for the project; or in asking for a creative project, the prospective investor wants to see a track record of past successful money-making films to be assured that this new film will make money. The point is that people being asked like to have as much information provided as possible and if this is the case, then the asker or asking team needs to get this information to them right away by either dropping it off at the person's home or office, or putting it in the mail right away. This type of immediate follow-up conveys to the person being asked that you are very serious about this Ask and if you follow this up diligently, then you are organized, dedicated, and very serious about this Ask.

This next point I guarantee will make your follow-up easy and enjoyable—*varying the communication and the communicator.* Think about it, would you want just one person with the same voice saying the same thing? "Hi, it is Laura, just checking to see if you reached this very important decision we discussed." After a few times the person being asked will be totally bored and will avoid your telephone call, e-mails, and text messages. You can spare yourself this misery by planning three simple things:

- Who else should be involved with the follow-up?
- What should they be saying?
- What medium should they be using?

The first one is simple. Think of everyone involved in the cultivation process—they can help you now in the follow-up. This includes the head of the organization or company, leadership, staff, volunteers, beneficiaries, and other donors, if they had at any point any communication or encounter with the person being asked. This flows into the second question. The president or CEO can state why it is important to have this person's gift or investment and what it will mean for the future growth and stability of the organization; a beneficiary can detail how past support transformed his life and the lives of his family; a past donor can state how she hesitated at first but now having made the gift, she feels so good about her contribution to a worthy organization. Then all you need to do is find the right medium for these people to feel comfortable in conveying this information. Some may like to make telephone calls, some may want you to draft the letter, while others will want to speak at a special event where the person will be and publicly announce the importance of this type of support right now.

In the follow-up it is important to use your existing resources to help you convince the person you just asked that their gift or investment will be joining existing money, and even if it is the "initial" money that will launch the new business, that this investment will kick off the most spectacular project. For instance, nonprofits can use their newsletters, Web sites, brochures, and special events internally, as well as external media to highlight and brag, if you will, about any recent new gifts. People like to give where others have given; there is strength in numbers. It is never the situation where people think "Gee, this organization just got a large gift so they don't need my money." In fact, the exact opposite happens. People get more attracted to that organization because it is doing "all the right things" and it is "managed well" and "my money will be invested safely with others." That said, do not be deterred if this Ask was for start-up money or seed money to start a new company, launch a new project, or an initial gift for a nonprofit that was just formed. Here the sell is that this person will be the first or among the first to launch something exciting. You can still use the internal and external media if they are available to talk about all the great benefits of upcoming support as well as the number of other people you are approaching for support. Remember, strength in numbers is always flypaper for new investments.

It will also enhance your follow-up activities if you can get the person you asked to your site, your plant, your office, or your institution because it is a visual reminder of all the wonderful things that are taking place and will continue to take place with his gift or investment. Nothing is more powerful than giving a prospective donor to a hospital the chance to see grateful patients receiving expert care; volunteers guiding the public to the right area of the hospital; doctors, nurses, and medical staff in the cafeteria eating and discussing the day's activities—you get the point. The person can "feel" the power of giving. The same holds true if you bring a person to the studio, theater, gallery, plant, or prospective site where the new construction will begin; they are all visual capsules of what "can be" with the person's help.

Lastly, you have a choice as you go through your follow-up activities. You can be pessimistic and guess that too much time has gone by and the person probably is not interested in what you asked, or you can be optimistic that what you asked for will be given. It costs you nothing to be optimistic so I encourage you to stay positive throughout all the follow-up process, and believe that it will happen. Positive energy is what the person being asked needs, not someone who is filled with doubt or negative vibes. Treat this entire process as if the person is going to say "yes."

JUGGLING YOUR TIME TO DO ALL THE FOLLOW-UP

One of the hardest things for anyone who wants to raise money or ask for something for himself is learning how to strike the right balance between organizing time to ask and then staying on track with all the steps after the Ask. We have just explored the essential next steps that need to be done after each Ask to ensure that too much time does not elapse between the Ask and the resolution to the Ask. Time and balance are essential components of the Ask. This brings us to the next essential thing to know about any Ask.

---

10 Things to Know About Any Ask—# 8

The Ask is 25 percent of your time—the follow-up is 75 percent.

It takes a great deal of time following up with each Ask. Chances are you have many Asks that you are doing in the same time period, which is a blessing. However, do you (or do you and the person who asked with you) have the weeks, months, and sometimes year or two to do all the follow-up steps detailed in Exhibit 8.1 and more? *So much money is left on the proverbial table because people have been asked, and then the follow-up was never completed.* Think this over: you just spent much time identifying, cultivating, educating, and involving this person; you asked her; a small effort is made to follow up to guide her to decide; and then the asker or asking team moves on to another person to identify, cultivate, and/or Ask. This would be a colossal waste of precious time and fundraising effort.

There is no formula that applies uniformly to all fundraisers for determining the appropriate number of Asks per month or year in relation to the number of outstanding Asks that need follow-ups. However, in Chapter 2 the section titled "Prioritizing Your Top People to Ask" did provide some guidelines for gauging how many people you should be working with *comfortably and evenly* to ensure that you have the time to identify, cultivate, ask, follow through, and steward each person, with considerations for the size of your organization and the amount of other responsibilities you have in addition to this work such as meetings, travel, reports, managing, and board and committee work.

Exhibit 8.2 is a pipeline tracking chart I created that may help you see where a person is on a timeline to ask, follow up, and steward for the next gift or investment opportunity.

This has been a great resource to me over the years and I sincerely hope it helps you. Naturally, your columns will be a great deal larger and longer as you fill each in so this is a model you can use and adapt. I am not an advocate of "shadow databases" and yes, all the information in this chart should be in your database. However, I think it would really help you if you have this chart in hard copy on your desk each day so that you can visualize what stage each person is at and what you need to do to ensure each person keeps moving *to the right of the columns.*

I guarantee that as you fill in the chart as I will guide you next, *a majority of people will be stuck in column 3—the cultivation cave!* I say

EXHIBIT 8.2. *Pipeline Tracking Chart.*

1. Name	2. Research	3. Cultivation	4. Pre-Ask Conversation	5. Ask Response	6. Follow-Up	7. Steward-ship

this from experience as I have been guilty of this as well. It is so comfortable and enjoyable to cultivate someone, take them to lunch, meet them at special events, bring them to the organization, and everything is flowing nicely, *except* you are not getting to the pre-Ask conversation, as detailed in Chapter 2. *("Laura, when and if you were ready to do something that was meaningful and significant with our group/business, what would that look like?")* This is why this chart is so important.

The same holds true with having many people stuck in column 6, the follow-up. If 75 percent of your time is needed to do the follow-up then that column should be filled with activities done and activities to do to ensure the Ask comes to a close. This is why column 6 should be much larger! Let's see how we fill out each column.

In the first column place the names of all the people you want to ask. Remember in Chapter 3 we called that your Top List and Next List. Then in the second column list the topical research points you need, address, giving history, and employment, as detailed in Chapter 3 in the section titled "Research Can Help to Prioritize Who to Ask." Specifically, Exhibit 3.2 lists many details you want in the person's profile, but for this chart's purpose, just list the key things you want to know that will be helpful in cultivation.

In column 3 list all your cultivation activities that you have done or plan to do. As stated above, be mindful and gauge if you are doing too little or too much with cultivation. The goal is to get to column 4 and have the pre-Ask conversation. If the person has no idea what they might do and your instincts tell you they need more education and involvement (remember the readiness formula in Chapter 3), then you need to re-examine your cultivation efforts to make sure the person can be brought to the point of being asked.

In column 5, list the specific amount and the specific purpose of your Ask with the response you received. That will be your gateway to all the follow-up steps you need to take in column 6. Once you receive a positive response, then you will list the stewardship activities you plan to do to ensure this person continues to give at enhanced levels. We will fully explore what to do when you receive a "no" to your Ask as well as a "yes" and what you can do to steward that person in Chapter 9, but I thought it was important in dealing with the follow-up now that you create a chart like the one in Exhibit 8.2 to stress that follow-up will take time. This chart will also help you juggle your time so that each person is worked with evenly and that people are asked and followed up with for each Ask. If you find that you cannot get to all this activity, then that is a really good sign that you simply are working with too many people. It is better to work with fewer and do it in an even and balanced way, than to work with so many that each person is not being moved to the right of the chart!

There is an important part that needs to be emphasized about the time to ask and follow through. Everyone involved in the Ask needs to have the time to follow up. This was discussed in Chapter 4, but it is so important it needs to be repeated. Unfortunately, this happens particularly when it involves someone in a leadership role. The president, CEO, board member, prominent volunteer, or investor may be available to do "some" cultivation and be there for the actual Ask. Chances are she will have time to call or send a thank-you letter but then she vanishes. Nothing can turn off a person being asked more than not to have all the time and attention after the Ask that he had before the Ask. Trust me, people being asked are very sensitive; if it appears they are being "handed off" to someone else in the organization to follow through they will feel neglected.

These are suggestions and guidelines on how to follow up with each and every Ask as well as how to juggle and organize time before and after the Ask. Again, it is one of the hardest tasks to get right on a consistent basis because even though the asker or asking team may be able to control the course of the Ask meeting and the setting and tone of the Ask, from that moment on it is the person being asked who can require anything from a little of your time to all of your time. Some people are low maintenance but others are very high maintenance. Plot your time as best you can, and stay flexible. If you find that you are overwhelmed and things are getting way out of control, then you need to cut back on the number of people you want to ask and concentrate on the people who have been asked and execute the follow-up steps. Stay positive, learn from your mistakes, communicate constantly with everyone involved with the Ask and the follow-through, and you will have learned the fine art, the dance, of how to juggle it all.

Exercise #8: Use the chart in Exhibit 8.2 to fill in the activities you have done and plan to do with your universe of people you want to ask. Gauge the number of people you are working with as well as *where* they fall in the chart and make adjustments based on the guidelines and suggestions in this chapter.

TROUBLESHOOTING TIPS FOR THE FOLLOW-UP

The follow-up is so important that I thought it would be helpful to go over some questions you may have and situations that you have had or anticipate having with the follow-up.

1. *What if it is impossible to reach the person you asked—how can you follow up?*

The first thing to remember is the Ask is on our minds 24 hours a day, seven days a week but that is not always the case with the person being asked. They return to the business world and their personal lives and, in short, they are just very busy people. Try not to take it personally or internalize it as a "no," which is difficult to do because we all are looking for a quick and positive "yes."

I would still leave voicemail stating that you do not want to intrude in their personal or professional life but the issues you discussed are important. Let the person know that you are there and stand ready to address any issue that might have come up after the Ask. This is another reason why it is so important to mix up the communication and the communicator so that the person being asked does not hear from just one voice.

2. *How long do you hang in with the person you asked before you get an answer?*

This question comes up quite frequently, and I have a very simple answer. *You hang in until you have an answer.* Remember, these are your top or next tier people. I have hung in and worked with people over a period of years, particularly with planned gifts such as bequests and trusts, because some people just take that long to decide.

In one of my past jobs, I asked a gentleman to increase his annual gift from $1,000 to $5,000. At that time and for this organization, $5,000 was a very large gift. After the Ask he said he was most certain he could do it and it was just a matter of when during the year he could make this outright gift in one payment. I did all the steps in Exhibit 8.1 and thought I was sailing my way to capture this new major gift. Wrong. When I tried to follow up on the telephone (and he was elderly with no e-mail or text message capabilities) I could not reach him for over a year. I left messages every three weeks and had some of our beneficiaries write personal notes to him stating how important his prospective gift to the organization would be and detailing the nature of those benefits. I heard nothing. Then after a year and a half, he called me. His sister died and he had to go to Florida to settle her estate. It was very complicated and it took him a very long time to settle every detail. He did receive all my calls and was grateful for my effort to reach him and did not think it was "pestering" him at all. He soon sent his check and thereafter became a very strong major donor. The point here is you can be persistent, not pestering, and if a person really does not want to hear from you they will be the first to let you know.

3. What if the person you asked with is no longer with the organization and the person asked feels less confident to give now that the co-asker is gone?

We cannot control who goes and who stays with the organization and there is turnover in staff with any job. I think the best you can do is instill as much confidence as you can about the solid and fiscally sound organization, and that while it is unfortunate your co-asker left, there are plenty of good leaders, staff, volunteers, beneficiaries, and happy customers that make up the organization and they are there to help in any way possible the person being asked. Reiterate that their prospective gift or investment will be joined by present and future gifts and investments. If the co-asker went to a new job that was a step up from the current position, let the person know this fact. Certainly, anyone will applaud job advancement.

If this is a high-end Ask and it is very important for the organization to have the person being asked associated with the organization, then it would be advisable to have someone in a leadership role contact the person being asked and reassure her that this is an important and pivotal time for the organization. This type of high-end attention usually helps the person being asked to feel more "secure" that the organization is worthy of a "yes" to the Ask because the leadership took the time to reach out individually to her.

4. What if during the follow-up the person asked wants something more than what was discussed before and during the Ask?

This can certainly arise. In business someone may want more of an investment share; may want more advertisement or name/company recognition than what was proposed; or may want to have her equipment, employees, or advisors play an even greater role than what was previously discussed. When asking for a promotion or raise, the employer could ask that the employee take on even more assignments, be relocated to another physical office, or supervise more people. In nonprofits, the prospective donor may want to be on the board, may want certain board members removed, or want more or larger name recognition. The bottom line is that things may come up that you now have to address that were never on your radar screen before.

First, use your all-important listening skills and have the person spell out everything she wants. No matter what position you are in, let the person know you will get back to her. It is never a wise thing to agree or disagree on the spot because there is a very good chance that what is asked for additionally may require more approval; may stray ever so slightly or greatly from current policies, or worse, your mission/business plan; and you may be setting a bad precedent to open the door for future people to want much more than you can offer.

In one story I heard a planned giving officer in a nonprofit was working with a donor to secure a large charitable gift annuity. Throughout the course of the cultivation and Ask, it was clear to the prospective donor that according to the American Council on Gift Annuities, at age 64 she would receive a 5.4 percent return on her gift annuity. She thought about it and would do the gift annuity only if she could get a 6 percent return. The nonprofit followed the rules strictly and had to let the prospective gift go. This is just an illustration of what can happen after the Ask and how it is so important that you stay focused and listen, but know the boundaries of what your organization can and cannot do.

Second, as in the paragraph above, you have to be honest and sensitive and explain that this is something that goes against company or organizational policy, by-laws, business plan, or gift acceptance policy and that regrettably, you cannot do what they asked. While it is disappointing not to get what you wanted, in the long run they may have done you a favor. I come back to an old adage that has served me well:

"How the person asked treats the process of deciding on the Ask is how he will behave for the duration of the relationship."

By this I mean if a person is very difficult after the Ask, if it feels that he wants your organization to bend or break some current rules or policies, and he is only thinking about the benefits to himself, and not to the organization, then this is what you are going to get long after your agree to his first "change" to what you have been discussing for a very long time. In many instances, you can work it out and move on. In others, just be aware that these people do not automatically change once they get the extra thing they asked for. This is who they are and this is how they stay. This is just a cautionary note.

Third, be very careful that if you do it for one person and you stray a little from your mission, business plan, or policies, word travels faster than you think and you will most certainly have to do it for other people who make similar requests. I was in a situation where a donor was about to make a large endowed gift. He was in the finance industry. He was all set to go when he at the last minute wanted to decide how his endowed gift would be invested. At the time the institution had equities, real estate, and bonds. He wanted more of his gift in the equities pool. It was decided to agree to his terms. Guess what? Very soon after, we had many more donors requesting that their gift have a different investment mix than the organization's. This is an example of how this can snowball out of control because "one time only" rarely translates into one time.

5. What if the person wants the gift now to be a "challenge gift" or for businesses wants us to find three more investors before they will commit?"

This actually is not a bad situation and can work in your favor if you have the pool of potential people who can and want to add to this initial gift or investment. For nonprofits, challenge gifts are when a person is about to make a gift and wants her gift—for this example, say $100,000 for a specific program—to be matched by new gifts to the organization. With creativity this is actually a very good leverage point for the nonprofit. Find out if there are restrictions to the challenged gift. Does it have to be for the specific program that will receive her gift or can the challenge be used to raise money for the annual fund (unrestricted money is always a plus for a nonprofit!). If she only wants it to match gifts to her program then before you agree *make sure you have the donor base that may be willing to match this particular program.* I have had the situation where someone wanted to "start" a program and the organization knew it would require funds much larger than the initial gift but the person said "don't worry, my friends, colleagues, and network will come through." Then you ask these people for money and only a trickling comes in and now you promised this new donor this program would happen, with the matched money, but the matched money does not come in. The result? A major loss for the organization or damage control because now you have to go back to the person and say, "We cannot do the program because we have not raised the funds to cover all expenses." Not a good moment for the organization.

For businesses, it is standard practice that most investors and buyers will try to negotiate as much as they can and most people are prepared. It should be mentioned, however, that if you are on the Ask, you need to know your company's policies and how much authority you have and in what areas to make this decision by yourself or with an asking partner. Again you don't want to offer one special thing for one customer or investor that you do not want to offer or agree to with others.

In the area of job-related Asks the employee *really* needs to be prepared for the extra things an employer may request. Think of all the things you think the employer could ask for in exchange for what you asked. This is an "extension" of the exercise in Chapter 2 in the section titled "Three-Step Method Prior to Any Ask," which now includes "what are the things that may be asked for you to do in response to your Ask?" In this example of a job-related request it may be to relocate, take on more responsibilities, or manage more people. If you are prepared for this to occur in your follow-up and have thought through whether or not you will take on more responsibilities or relocate, then with everything we have said in this book you will be prepared and that will win the day! You may have to forgo the promotion or the raise but at least you know you are unwilling to relocate or take on more. The bottom line is, be prepared to address additional conditions on your Ask.

6. *In our industry waiting for an answer a few months is a long time. Waiting a year is unreasonable.*

Every industry and organization is different. If one year plus time to work on the follow-up is too long, then move on. I only caution you that these people were selected to have the most potential to give money. Of course, with job-related requests if your supervisor will not address your request in a "reasonable time," and that would be far less than one year, then they are signaling to you a "no" response without getting those words out.

I merely suggest that you gauge this within your industry standards and give it a little extra time and effort in the follow-up. This person may not give a solid answer either way but you owe it to yourself and your job to find out why the person cannot decide and in my experience this can vary as far as the Grand Canyon is deep. Once you know the why you will then have the personal satisfaction that it was not you or your technique; something set them off with something someone said or a particular person in your organization. Trust me, if you begin a habit of not following through with people who are asked, you will fall into the dangerous pattern of quitting on your Ask too soon.

7. *The person asked has left it in the hands of the family/financial advisor/attorney to decide and you have never met these people or have had limited contact with them.*

This is very similar to handling one of the responses in Chapter 7 (*"I need to discuss this with other people"*). Do all the steps that were set forth in that section and remember this is a good thing because the person being asked wants to make sure that the people who are closest to her personally, financially, and professionally are lending their expertise to make the "right choice." The goal here is to get the contact information for this third-party advisor and to see or speak with him together with person being asked or just with you so that you can brief him on all the details and provide backup information. It is your opportunity to promote all the benefits of the Ask and what that will mean to the future of your organization as well as the people who benefit from the organization's good work.

Also, think of it as expanding your network, your donor base, and your circle of influence. You now have the opportunity to meet more people who are close and very important to the person you asked. Stay optimistic because that good energy will be inviting and appealing to these third-party advisors. You do not know who else they know and by speaking with them and involving them any way you can, you may well be "expanding" your circle of people who may in the near future want to support your organization and your cause.

8. *What if during the follow-up period something tragically happens to the person asked, such as an illness or death?*

This is a rare situation but it is worth strategizing on possible solutions. People can become ill, or even worse, it may result in their death. It is a very delicate situation because many times you are only dealing with one person. You've been cultivating *that person*, you know *that person* very well and hopefully you know some or at least a few of the names of people who are close to them, such as business partners, family members, colleagues, or people in their social and business circles. In the case of illness, if the person is capable of speaking with you, I would state that their health matters most and if they cannot or do not want to continue your discussions of what you asked that you will be back in touch when their health is better. Showing sensitivity and caring is always a priority, especially when the person's health is in jeopardy.

That said, if the person wants you to speak with other people as in the example of #7, then do so, again with all the sensitivity and honesty you can muster. Spell out to these people what you have asked for, what the person was considering, and ask "What do you think I should do?" If you have been reading this book all along, you know I am a big fan of *open-ended, honest questions* with any person when you truly do not have the answers you need and you are seeking advice or help on how to proceed next with closing your Ask. You may get some terrific advice and at least the people closest to the person being asked will be aware of what is going on and they may be able to steer you in the right direction to help you get to the right people to act on the behalf of the person you asked. Conversely, you may not be able to reach these people or they may not know what to do. In either case you have done everything possible to see the Ask through and you should be very happy that you took these very important steps. It also illustrates how important the person asked is to you and the organization. Many people may think that this is "ambulance chasing" or "showing insensitivity" to the family and friends because all you are thinking about is getting money or whatever you asked for. Steer away from these negative projections because if you use honesty and sensitivity and show a genuine sense of caring for the person you asked, no one is going to think you are selfishly doing something for your own personal gain.

Issues arise if you have no contact information whatsoever on these people. At the very least you can send a letter to the address of the person you asked or leave voicemail stating that you were in the midst of discussing something that was very important to the person you asked and she suggested that you contact them. Then ask them to call, write, or e-mail you and provide them with your contact information.

In the situation where the person dies, this calls for even more sensitivity. First, you have to decide whether what you asked for is truly important enough to involve the person's family and business partners. That is your call and only you will know if it was important to the person asked that it be discussed and resolved after the person's death. If it was, then you should reach out to these close family members and business partners but with extreme sensitivity. Second, you could drop the whole thing and move on to other people you need to follow up with or cultivate and ask. If this is what you select I would then consider if it is appropriate to write to the family members and business partners, expressing your condolences and in the gentlest way saying that you regret not being able to fulfill a dream, plan, investment that was very important to the person you asked and *if* the family or business partners want to know more about it to contact you. At that point you have covered your bases. And you never know to what extent the person you asked had discussed your Ask with these people. They may just want to carry out the wishes of the person you asked.

   9. *What if during the follow-up the person says "no."*

We are going to cover that at length in the next chapter. Deep breath because "no now may not be no later!"

   10. *What if the person during the follow-up says "yes."*

First, you do a "happy dance," beam from ear to ear, and congratulate yourself and your team. Honestly, we do not celebrate ourselves enough when we have worked so hard to ask and then we actually get what we asked for. We are going to cover this as well in the next chapter, because now you will need to acknowledge, recognize, and in some instances honor the person who just said "yes" and, as important, *steward* her to the next gift or investment.

CONCLUSION

The follow-up to each and every Ask is your true success to closing each and every Ask. Why do all the work finding the right people; mapping out the right cultivation strategies for each person; finding the right match between their interest in you, your cause, your passion, and an opportunity you can present; and making the right Ask that matches their interest and your opportunity, only to leave it up to them on their timeline to decide? The answer is that is not an effective way to keep each Ask on track. By using the pipeline tracking chart shown in Exhibit 8.2, you will ensure that each Ask will be followed up to each answer. Be careful not to have your pipeline of people you want to ask or have asked stuck in the "cultivation" box or the "follow-up" box. When these boxes get top-heavy, meaning most of your potential supporters are in these categories, it is a red flag that you need to do extra activities to get them to the Ask and then get them to decide.

As with anticipating the response to each Ask as set forth in Chapter 7, it is equally important that you think out any problems that may occur during your follow-up. The troubleshooting tips in this chapter should provide you with the framework you need to avoid being stuck in the follow-up stage to your Asks and should give you solid suggestions on how you can get the answers to your Asks in the quickest time possible.

Looking Ahead

Now comes the fun part—learning how to deal with a "no" and a "yes" to your Asks. There are next steps that need to be done with each response. With a "no" answer the rule is "no now does not mean no later, so it is not a time to be discouraged. It is in fact a time to think of when and how you will approach this person at a later time. With a "yes" answer, we are not home free yet. There are some vital steps that need to be done to ensure that the person is properly thanked, acknowledged, recognized, and "not dropped" from your or the organization's attention because the person said "yes." The next chapter will detail the "stewardship" steps that need to be taken after the "yes" so that this is not a one-time "yes," but in fact will be the stepping stone for future "yeses" from the same person.

When the Answer Is "No" and When the Answer Is "Yes"

W E ARE IN THE HOME STRETCH NOW IN
this chapter. We have already explored in Chapters 7
and 8 all the things you need to do when you get the answer that
the person asked needs time to decide, so we are at the point when the
person you have asked has made a decision. You have done all the right
steps to follow up with the Ask and it comes down to one of two
answers: either a "no" or a "yes." In this chapter we are going to
address first the more unpleasant response—the "no." But I think you
will be surprised and less "deflated" when this chapter illustrates how
"no now does not mean no later," because with the right next steps
you can pave your way to return at a later time and revisit your Ask.
On a much more pleasant note, when the answer is "yes" it is a time to
feel *really* good about yourself, your organization, and the people who
will benefit from your hard and persistent work. However, there is
more work to be done after that wonderful, positive answer, which we
call "stewardship," and if you follow these stewardship techniques as
this chapter will outline, there will be a *very strong* probability that the
person or persons who gave you a "yes" answer will want to do more

for you, your organization, and business, and you will have a very loyal giver and investor.

A "No" Answer

Getting a "no" answer can be very discouraging at first. You put all this time and effort into finding the right people to ask; cultivating them; finding the opportunity for them so that you maximize their key interests. You make the right Ask at the right time and then you wait patiently while they decide, being persistent but not pushy. And then they say:

- "Sorry, but I can't."
- "No, I don't think I can or want to do this."
- "Even though this sounds like a great idea, it is out of the question right now."
- "I want to limit my giving this year so, unfortunately, I'm not making a gift this year."
- "I would love to give you and others a raise this year but our budget just won't allow it."
- "I know job titles are very important and they can and should reflect the quantity and quality of your work but I cannot make the change at this time."
- "I cannot give you the amount you asked for."
- "I know we discussed this for awhile but I talked it over with others and it is not something we want to do."
- "Your project sounds great but I've got others asking me to back their projects and they are much further along than you are."
- "When your start-up business shows more profit, give me a call. Your revenue projections are idealistic, especially with today's market."

These are just some of the types of "no" answers you may receive. I have never had someone just say "no" and nothing else when I have made an Ask. That would be a rarity. These are people you know very well and they are not going to leave you hanging or guessing why they decided not to do what you asked. If they did just say "no" and nothing else, remember to use open-ended questions when you need more information and simply ask "why?" Then use all your wonderful listening skills to hear the key factors in their decision. Once you know why the person decided "no" first, you will learn from the experience and second, know what you need to do in the future to have this person give your Ask another consideration.

For instance, let us look at the types of "no's" and see how you can respond to gather more information:

- **"Sorry, but I can't."** There is no explanation as to why the person "can't" in this statement. That is your cue to ask "Why?" or "Can you tell me a little bit more about why you can't?" What usually happens in this situation is you hear the word "can't" and that can be tough but if you can ask "why" it will be so beneficial to know the real reason why the person "can't." It is beneficial because if it was something in the course of your Ask that the person did not like, then you will know that perhaps you may not try that technique, language, or situation the next time. "No's" are teachable moments and learning from each of them is invaluable.

- **" No, I don't think I can or want to do this."** There are two things going on at once in this answer. First, "don't think I can" means there is an obstacle to their decision; usually this means lack of funds, not good for the business, does not fit in my priority list, or the person's boss will not let it happen. When you hear this type of response, ask, "Can you tell me more about why you don't think you can do this?" There are so many factors it could be and you do not want to guess what they are. If the person is reluctant to let you know, tell her, "It would be helpful for me to know so that I can learn from this experience." With this type of statement the person may be more willing to explain if they think it will help you and your organization or business in the future. Second, "I don't want to do this" signals that what you asked for is not their key interest or is not a priority. This statement clearly tells you that there are other things that interest the person more and right now the person has no burning desire to do what you asked. When this happens say, "Can you share with me the reason or reasons why this is not something you want to do?" Let the person explain that it is not a priority or that she is half interested but not enough to say "yes." The more information you can gather the better.

- *"Even though this sounds like a great idea, it is out of the question right now."*
- *"I want to limit my giving this year so, unfortunately, I'm not making a gift this year."*
- *"I would love to give you and others a raise this year but our budget just won't allow it."*
- *"I know job titles are very important and they can and should reflect the quantity and quality of your work but I cannot make the change at this time."*

I put these together because while each of them is referencing a different Ask (giving, raise, and title), they all are saying the same thing. That is, the person you asked cannot do it *now*.

This falls right in line with the saying I created: "No now does not mean no later." These examples illustrate how the person being asked is simply saying:

- "I love your idea but the timing is bad."
- "I like your organization but money is tight so we cannot support you for now."
- "We see the merits of your raise but with the budget the way it is, we really cannot explore this issue."
- "Job titles are significant but this is not the right time."

With all these examples it just boils down to the wrong time for the Ask. Notice the person's response did not say, "No, you don't deserve the raise," "No, you cannot have the job title," or "No, I will not give to your organization again." These are the things we *think we hear* when we do not get a "yes" answer but actually these responses are great news. The door is open for you to come back later and revisit what you asked. The key here is to find out *what is meant by "right now."* Does it mean this month, this quarter, this year? Ask the person, "By 'right now,' what time frame do you mean?" Once you have your answer, then you will know when you can go back and possibly have that person reconsider your Ask. This response also keeps the discussion alive and you may be able to glean a little more information about how the person really feels about what you asked. For instance, he may say, "While you are more than qualified and deserving of a raise, we don't have the funds to cover it now," or "I have a few more pledge payments to my other nonprofit that I support and with money being tight this year, I could not make any other commitment." Get as much information as you can, which will help you abundantly in the future.

- *"I cannot give you the amount you asked for."* The good thing is that you did not come off of the Ask amount until after the follow-up, as recommended in Chapter 7. In Chapter 7, it was highly suggested that you give the person some time to consider the amount you requested and then let the person decide. We are at the point now when they have decided—it simply was too much. You have some options right now. First and foremost, please *do not* say, "What did you have in mind?" You are in the driver's seat and the asker should be the one who determines what amount, if any, should be considered next. If your Ask was a large one, one that would be used for an important new project, program, creative venture, or business, the question you must ask yourself is, "Do I have other people who could support this as well so that the project, program, creative venture, or business could start with this person's smaller gift or investment?" This is a very important question. I have seen many nonprofits and businesses use this "initial amount" to "get going" on their plans, only to realize there is not enough money or funding to sustain the program, project, or business. It is far better to wait and to raise the money you need *before* anything new is implemented; otherwise, you run the embarrassing risk of beginning and then being forced to halt production because the funding ran out.

If the Ask does not have any contingencies (for instance, it will be used to sustain an existing project, program, creative venture, or business), then you have to make a choice. Would you be better off waiting a bit until the person can give you the amount you initially asked for or should you ask for a lesser amount now and consider it a down payment or pledge toward the initial amount? There are pros and cons to either decision. If you wait, then you run the risk that the person will keep postponing the commitment for the full initial amount. If you ask for the lesser amount and the person agrees, then she may only give you that lesser amount and maybe never the larger amount that you originally asked for. The only way you can make this type of decision is by reviewing everything you learned in cultivation and making your best and wisest determination. There is no right or wrong choice here. You and only you will know the best route to take, because each person is different and each circumstance is different.

- **"I know we discussed this for awhile but I talked it over with others and it is not something we want to do."** The good news is the person thought enough about your Ask that it merited discussion and input from others. The bad news is that outside persons steered the person you asked to give a "no" response. It will be very helpful for you to know if you can gather this information and find out exactly who the person spoke to or met with—was it a relative, business partner, financial advisor, attorney, or friend? Try saying, "If you don't mind it would be so helpful to me to know who you talked this over with. You do not need to give me names. It is just important for me as I go forward to know who most people entrust in helping them make these important decisions." You can get a sense from all my suggested open-ended questions and requests for more information that this is for your growth, your success, and turning what could be a 100 percent negative situation into a 100 percent positive learning experience. This information will help you for your future Asks. For instance, if you find that most people consult their attorneys and when they do so, if you are not part of those discussions, the person comes back and says "no," then you need to make every effort to be part of those discussions in the future. Otherwise, you are going to receive a consistent "no" to your Asks. As much as you can, keep a written or mental record of the types of people the person you ask consults with in deciding the Ask. Certain patterns may appear and then you will know what you have to do to the best of your ability to ensure that you are part of those dialogs.

- *"Your project sounds great but I've got others asking me to back their projects and they are much further along than you are."* This statement clearly lets you know that the person you are asking does not invest unless the project is at a certain stage. Unfortunately, your project was not at that part of the developmental stage when the person would have made the investment. Now you know some of your future investors will want to see how the proposed project pans out before they decide to invest. This may not be the course for everyone but you have a green light to ask the person if you can come back once your project is at that stage to update her on the progress. You have nothing to lose and everything to gain by keeping her apprised of your progress. It just might lead to getting the backing for your project at a later stage, or backing for your next project. At least you know the "timing" of when this person likes to be asked.

- *"When your start-up business shows more profit, give me a call. Your revenue projections are idealistic, especially with today's market."* This is an example of a person who wants more assurance that what they will give will be a wise investment. Up until now they could have given you every signal that they liked your new business, that it had great potential, and that they had genuine interest, but when it came to the actual investment, the person just wanted more proof of the business' future success. I would suggest if you get an answer like this that you take careful note of exact wording. In this example, you could ask, "How much more profit would you need to see?" or "Can you tell me in your opinion why you think this may be idealistic for today's stock market?" Everyone is entitled to their opinion but in this example the more concrete you can get the better. You may be thinking the person wants to see one solid year's worth of steady revenues or that they will not reconsider the investment until the start-up business does well despite the current stock market. Let the person quantify "more profit" and share with you why she thinks it is now "idealistic." Only when you have this information can you know the timing of when you can re-ask.

As you can see, a "no" answer is much like doing all the next steps to the follow-up detailed in Chapter 8. By using open-ended questions and asking the right type of simple, nonthreatening questions so that you are crystal clear as to why the person said "no," you will know what you can do and when you can do it. This leads us to the ninth principle to any Ask:

---

10 Things to Know About Any Ask—# 9

"No" now does not mean "no" later.

It will be an absolute rarity that someone will say:

- *"No, and I never want you to ask me again."*
- *"No, and do not ever call me or send me any mailings."*
- *"I would never support you or this project."*

These are some of the fears to asking we explored in Chapter 1; however, if you did all the steps from Chapters 2–8, you would have weeded out anyone who came close to giving you this response. Now you see why it is so important to take the time to find the right people to ask; have the right business plan and case statement; carefully cultivate each person so that they know you and you know them; have the match of their interest and your opportunity; and deliver the pre-Ask conversation. It is in the pre-Ask conversation that if the person were going to give you a hard, closed door, never-contact-me-again answer, it would have been said right there at that stage. If that were the case, then you would not have asked and you would have moved on to other people who had better potential to support you and your cause.

Exhibit 9.1 details what you need to do when you receive a "no" answer.

EXHIBIT 9.1. *Next Steps to a "No" Answer.*

1. Thank the person for their time and for carefully thinking over the Ask.

2. Ask simple, open-ended questions to clarify the reason or reasons for the "no."

3. If at all possible, have the person "quantify" the reason or reasons for the "no" response.

4. Determine at what point in time can you re-visit the Ask or do a new Ask.

5. Determine if you are willing to take a lesser amount than the original Ask amount or whether it would be more advantageous to stick with the original Ask and re-visit it at a later time.

All of these points in Exhibit 9.1 have been discussed above in this chapter, and this exhibit should serve as a checklist of what to do when you get a "no" answer. The critical thing about the "no" response is to bear in mind that in all likelihood you will be able to re-visit your Ask in some later point in time, or do a new Ask based on the information you received when you got your "no" answer. This is all great information, and you can learn from each "no" experience if you keep an open mind; listen attentively; ask gentle, easy questions; and move forward. Always keep in mind, "no" is not a steel door slamming in your face. It is a wonderful opportunity to become even better at making your next Ask.

Exercise #9: Challenge yourself and think about or anticipate a "no" response and apply the steps in Exhibit 9.1.

A "YES" ANSWER

Well this certainly calls for a celebration! All your hard work and preparation really paid off and now you got what you asked for—amen! It would be logical to most people that your work is done, short of "collecting" the money you asked for or learning the details of when your promotion/job title is effective. We are not quite home free yet. There are some next steps that I highly recommend you take because if you do, you have an amazing chance of getting future gifts, investments, promotions, and creative projects from the very same person who just said "yes" to your initial Ask. In nonprofit fundraising there are some expressions we use to emphasize the importance of not dropping the person who just said "yes" to your Ask:

- "Your next gift will come from your last donor."
- "Steward your first gift and it will be the first of many."
- "This gift is a down payment for future gifts."
- "Out of sight is out of mind, and if you do not pay attention, this will be a one-time donor."
- "People who are stewarded will give and give again."
- "There are plenty of organizations a person can support. If you do not make the person feel appreciated and involved, he will find another organization."

What is meant here is that if you "steward" the person well who just said "yes" to your Ask, he will be very happy and connected with you and your organization or business and will be more willing to help you again. We all know the importance of having "every customer a happy customer" because happy customers are loyal and will continue to buy your product. The same applies here. It is simply human nature that if you go out of your way to let the person know how appreciative you are and how meaningful it is, and quantify the impact of the gift or investment, there will be every likelihood that he will repeat his support and loyalty to you and what you represent.

Stewardship is the continuous personal interaction, consistent progress reporting, and constant exchange of information right after the person said "yes" to your Ask (Fredricks 2001, 177). This sounds exactly like cultivation as defined in Chapter 1. Think of this as a timeline. Everything you do up to the answer to your Ask is cultivation. Everything you do after you receive a "yes" to your Ask is stewardship. It is the same types of activities with some extra important steps to ensure the person is informed and involved.

Here is an impressive study that will emphasize why stewardship is so important to steady, future support. In a March 2009 study by Bank of America, *2008 Bank of America Study of High Net-Worth Philanthropy*, with 700 respondents with household incomes greater than $200,000 and/or net worth of at least $1 million, the number one reason why 40 percent of these respondents stopped supporting a particular charity was because they were "No longer feeling connected to the organization." (*Advancing Philanthropy*, May/June 2009, 6) There are a lot of wealthy people an organization can lose by neglecting to take care of their top givers. This is why it is so important that you do the necessary stewardship steps and create a stewardship plan for each person who supports you and your organization in the very near future. Exhibit 9.2 details the stewardship techniques that comprise a stewardship plan to apply to all the "yeses" to your Asks, namely for a charitable gift, business investment, creative project, or job-related request.

EXHIBIT 9.2. *Stewardship Techniques.*

1. Have as many people as possible thank the person in writing and in person.

2. With permission, publicly acknowledge the gift or investment.

3. If appropriate, honor the person or give them special treatment, such as VIP seats, invitations to select events, or tickets to their favorite events or sports.

4. Provide quarterly or yearly updates to the person, the person's family, or business colleagues of the progress and impact of the person's gift or investment.

5. Demonstrate that the gift or investment has been wisely invested, the money is being properly managed, the leadership is strong and ethical, and that the person's support has enhanced the mission and purpose of the organization or business.

6. Bring the person to the organization or business to let them "experience" the joys and benefits of their gift or investment.

7. If appropriate, appoint them to a board, advisory board, auxiliary board, or committee position.

8. Periodically call the person "just to say hello" and to maintain a steady stream of communication.

9. Quantify the added benefits you have brought to the organization or business since your raise, promotion, or new job title.

10. Create individual strategies for each person to give or support you or the organization or business in the *very near future*.

Let us go through each of these strategies one by one. First, it may be beyond obvious, but at the moment you receive a "yes" answer, thank the person right on the spot whether you are in person or on the telephone. If you receive this response via e-mail, text message, or snail mail, then pick up the telephone and call the person immediately to thank her. The next thank-you should come in the form of a written letter. In very hectic and chaotic times, one can forget to send the very important thank-you letter since after all, you already thanked her in person. Your written thank you can be a handwritten note or on letterhead stationery, but it is a must. Even if this is a relative, your best friend, or business partner that you have known for ages, send it. You can keep it short and sweet but the most important features are to include *how important this is to you, the organization, its beneficiaries, and the industry*, and that you will *keep the person apprised of all the progress* and *future growth* of the organization and business that was made possible by this person's support. Regardless of the size of the gift or investment, every person wants to know that what they gave will have an impact. For a job-related thank-you, it is important to state that you *appreciate your boss' and the organization's faith in and support of you* and that your *goal is to be a major contributor to the success* of the organization.

Many nonprofits have or should have a written policy for acknowledging gifts of certain levels. Depending on the size of the organization and the level of gifts, a plan can be created so that there is uniformity in acknowledging gifts that reach a certain level.

For instance, if this is a small organization whose top gifts would be in the range of $1,000–$5,000, then perhaps gifts up to $500 are acknowledged by the head of the development office while gifts of $500 and above are acknowledged by the head of the development office, the president/CEO, and a board member. It is always a good idea regardless of the gift size to have a beneficiary or volunteer send a thank-you note because the person selected your group to support, and this type of thank-you makes the gift "come alive" because it touches the life or lives of the volunteers and beneficiaries. If the organization is larger, then up the scale and have gifts of $10,000 or more acknowledged by the leadership. The bottom line is that one cannot be thanked enough from as many people as possible from the organization. You can have deans, faculty, doctors, nurses, patients, park rangers, docents, performers, artists, priests, and rabbis acknowledge gifts to the organization, which is incredibly meaningful to your donors.

It is a wonderful thing when you can publicly announce and show your appreciation for your recently received large gifts and investments. A strong word of caution here is to make sure and *check again if the person will agree to have this form of publicity*. Many givers to nonprofit organizations wish to remain anonymous. In May 2009, the *Chronicle of Philanthropy* reported that in the past 10 months when the stock market took a steep plunge, gifts of $1 million or more hit an unprecedented high level. "Eighty gifts worth $1 million or more were made anonymously from June 2008 to April 2009, nearly 19 percent of the 422 total during that period." (*Chronicle of Philanthropy*, May 7, 2009, 10). In tough economic times, it can be undesirable for people to stand out and be recognized for their gifts when many people are dealing with unemployment and loss of investments. Furthermore, many people choose to be anonymous because they do not want to be asked by other charities, and some may not want their families or business associates to know about their wealth and the amount they select to donate.

In international fundraising there may be cultures that have to be anonymous because of their beliefs. Many feel it is "bad manners to draw attention" to the fact that a family may have money; it would appear as the "height of arrogance to seek or bask in the spotlight that will obviously fall on a large gift," or "may fear kidnapping or personal harm to themselves or their families" (Kirkwood 2009, 15). Know the culture in which you are raising money and be extremely sensitive that many people may not want anyone to know of their wealth or generosity.

Make triple sure you have the person's permission to announce the gift or investment in your newsletter, brochure, Web site, annual report, and advertisements. If you have someone who is unsure whether it would be wise to let out her name, business, or amount of the gift or investment, I always tell the person that their generosity or wise business investment is so important because it is like "fly-paper"—it will attract more money. People can be persuaded and convinced to give when they know their money is being joined and invested with other monies. *If* you have this person's permission, it will have a ripple effect to attract new monies. Another tactic you can try is to have someone, or even yourself, interview the person for one of your upcoming publications and have them talk about the process they went through in making the decision and how they feel now that they decided "yes." These heartfelt and business-wise stories can be very powerful magnets to attract more money.

Depending on the level of the gift or investment and if the person would appreciate it, you can offer to honor that person at a gala or special event recognizing their philanthropy or investment in the business. You can also think back over your cultivation period and recall the person's interests and hobbies and give them tickets to their favorite cultural or sporting events. A few caveats here. First, make sure this activity is within the bounds of the ethical practices and procedures in your organization and industry. For instance, many non-profits have a policy that they cannot accept holiday gifts or tickets from vendors because it has the appearance that the vendor will be favored when the contract is up for renewal. In business it is very common for salespeople to take out new or loyal customers, suppliers, and manufacturers to benefit the business; however, many businesses also set limits on how much and what types of things and activities they can offer customers, suppliers, and manufacturers. Second, notice in the first sentence of this paragraph I say *if the person would appreciate it.* There are many people, especially in nonprofits, that feel you are wasting their gift money if you buy them lunch or dinner and they would rather you use 100 percent of the gift on the beneficiaries. In business there are many people who just want to do business with you without the rituals of wining and dining them or taking them to a ball game or a show. The bottom line is "know thy giver inside and out" and follow her comfort zone and your ethical boundaries.

It is imperative, and not an option, to give the person, and the person's family or business associates where appropriate, timely reports on how the gift is being used and invested. The three questions you need to answer through your reports since the time you received the money are

1. How has the money been invested?
2. What benefits (new program was launched or profit shares are up) did the money bring to the organization?
3. How many people have benefited and in what ways?

Your progress report to the person who supported you should contain the answers to these questions or at the very least the progress you are making towards these goals. Every giver wants to hear that the money they entrusted with your organization and its leadership is having an immediate positive effect and that but for this investment and the investment of others, none of this would have happened. It really hits home if you can quantify the benefits, such as:

- *"In just six months we were able to train three new volunteers for our literacy program."*
- *"With this new infusion of money, we were able over the past nine months to win over two of our 'borderline investors' so that now we are ready to expand production."*

Progress reports can be the standardized annual reports and growth charts. To the extent you can, send something more personalized in addition. You may want to send photographs of the people who have benefited from the person's generosity; outings and special events where people are smiling and feeling proud to be a part of the organization; and outside media publicity your organization might have received to make the person feel very good that your group is recognized by a larger community or by an industry leader or professional association. You will bring that person much closer to supporting you again because they are engaged, educated, and feel that they are a significant part of a positive and successful organization—a real winner!

Another great personal touch is when you bring the person to the organization or in some manner physically show the person what their gift or investment has produced. Site visits are like action films in the person's mind. These tangible visual images show that your organization is moving forward, helping people and worthy causes, and it is all possible because of this person's generosity. Always try to have the person meet the beneficiaries, the leadership, or any person within the organization that is important to your supporter. For instance, when I was working at a hospital, we had one donor who supported our department of nursing and he had a favorite nurse who gave him a private tour well before he made his major gift. We made sure that every time that donor came to the hospital that nurse was there to spend some time with him. It is just that simple, and very enjoyable. Now you see how cultivation activities are sometimes exactly the same as stewardship. During cultivation you identified people who are close to the people you are cultivating (in this example, the nurse). After the gift is made, go back and work with the same people you did in cultivation (the nurse) and make sure they are part of stewarding your donor.

Offering someone a board, advisory board, auxiliary board, or committee position can be another great way to get the person even more involved and educated with the organization after the gift and investment are made. Usually, this type of stewardship is offered when the person has made a significant-sized gift or investment, or the person can add diversity, expertise, or a cadre of other support from her professional or personal contacts to the organization. It would be advisable if the organization had a committee on trustees or a small group of people within the organization or company who were in charge of bringing and evaluating new candidates for these positions. Usually, there are written criteria, found in the bylaws of the organization, for the term limits of office and expectations for each position. Many advisory and auxiliary boards as well as and committees have written guidelines on the work each board member is expected to do. For instance, many hospitals have auxiliary committees that run many special event fundraisers and organize hospital volunteers. However, when it comes to the "main" board, in my experience, many organizations may have term limits, but very few have written criteria and expectations, *especially when it comes to monetary expectations* for board members. Some have a set dollar amount—for instance, a board member is expected to give $10,000 a year. Some have a "give or get" policy—either make a $10,000 contribution or get that level from someone else or from corporate or foundation support. Others silently hope and pray that the board member's good conscience will miraculously lead them to "make the right decision" and voluntarily give at a significant level each year.

Just be careful not to fall into the trap in which everyone who gives at *x* level should be on the board. Some people are appropriate to place on the board as long as they are willing to be active, help raise money, and can make a meaningful contribution to the present and future health of the organization. This is why it would be so wise to have a committee or small group that sets forth the guidelines and expectations for any board or committee member. So if your current giver would be a terrific contributor to the board or the committee, by all means offer this position as a way to steward the person to active and engaged involvement for your organization.

One of the easiest and least expensive ways to steward a person is to call just to say hello. So often we get caught up in thinking we have to have a purpose to contact the person but there are many people who value the fact that there is no agenda, and that you are just checking in to see how they are, how the family and business are going. Now this is not appropriate for everyone. Very busy and prominent businesspeople, unless you know that they may like this type of call, would probably think this was odd and maybe even a waste of their time. You know the person best, so if they have the personality that may enjoy an occasional call, do it; if not, then think of something else, maybe a card or quick e-mail just to touch base. It shows that you care about them and inevitably they ask how the organization is doing so you will have the opportunity to give them an update or two about what is taking place.

The next stewardship suggestion I have pertains to job-related stewardship. How do you thank in unique ways your boss who either just gave you a raise, promotion, or new job title? You can and should still thank your boss and any other people who were involved in the decision, in person and in writing. There are other things you can do as well. Think if this raise, promotion, or job title gave you the confidence to do things you would never have done before. For instance, maybe you joined a professional organization, wrote for a trade magazine or journal about some advice or best practice that involved your work, were cited in an alumni magazine, or anything job-wise that happened since you received this raise, promotion, or job title. Feedback like this can go a long way with your boss. It reinforces that she made the "right" decision, and that it has rewards well beyond what you asked. Next, try to quantify any successes you have had, extra projects you took on, or additional benefits it has brought to the organization since your raise, promotion, or job title. For instance, maybe with your new job title you felt more confident to suggest some candidate for unfilled positions within the organization. Maybe with your raise you were able to apply to graduate school, which will only enhance the further knowledge you can bring the organization. If this happens you can state:

> *"This raise gave me the financial means to apply for graduate school and I hope within the next few months to be able to report that I have been accepted."*

You can quantify the "value" of what these job-related enhancements have done for you personally and professionally. Many people skip these steps but I assure you if you do them, you have a better chance of receiving more raises and job enhancements than if you just said thank you and went about your job. If you are currently a boss, then you have an appreciation for when an employee goes out of his way to demonstrate that he is living up to your expectations and that he is going to be valuable to the organization for a very long time. If you are not the boss, then place yourself in your boss' shoes and ask yourself, "In what ways can I show my boss that I am carrying out her expectations and priorities and bringing new ideas and energy to the position?" You do not need to go overboard here, but I truly think that if you make the effort from time to time, outside the evaluation process, to express results, your boss will feel really good about the decision and hence, you will have stewarded your boss.

Last but not least, you should have a stewardship plan for each person who says "yes" to your Ask. This is the compilation of everything we have discussed to date, including thanking; consistent communication; recognizing and honoring the person; reporting progress; arranging site visits; calling just to say hello; board or committee appointments; and quantifying what you have brought to the organization with your new raise. In Chapter 3 I said every person must be treated individually, and the same applies for individual stewardship strategies. You can use the stewardship checklist shown in Exhibit 9.2, but then you need to tailor it for each person who gave you a "yes." By tailoring I mean go back to your cultivation and follow-up notes and examine what the person likes and does not like— for instance, contact only by e-mail; does not want any part of the money to be used for meals or token presents; or would really enjoy tickets to the ballet. You get the point. You are now at the apex of all your hard work, time, energy, and strategic thinking. Apply everything you have learned to your stewardship plan. If you do, you have a wonderful chance to be rewarded again and again and again.

Since I am such a strong advocate of stewardship, it merited my last thing to know about any Ask:

10 Things to Know About Any Ask—# 10

A "yes" now will lead to "yes" later if you execute a solid stewardship plan for each person.

CONCLUSION

This chapter is perhaps one of the hardest to get through because it deals with how to handle a "no" answer. Go back and revisit Chapter 1; it may help you brace yourself for a "no" answer and help you understand that the person you asked is not saying "no" to you. In this chapter it was demonstrated that "no" now is not "no" later. For a variety of reasons, most of which are way out of your control, it just did not work out in your favor—for now. If you go through the steps detailed in Exhibit 9.1, you will be positioning yourself for a "yes" very soon.

And speaking of a "yes" answer, we are not home free with the "yes." People who have said "yes" need to be stewarded, that is, they need to be thanked from a variety of people; recognized where appropriate; updated with quantifiable analysis of what their gift, investment, trust, and faith in you has done to date and what it will do in the future; brought to the organization to see their investment "come alive"; offered a position on a board or committee; called just to say hello; and most of all, just kept active, involved, and educated about your organization/company and your progress. Stay close to your new best friends and they will never disappoint you!

LOOKING AHEAD

In the last chapter, we will pull everything together that has been outlined in the previous chapters and see at one glance how the "10 Things to Know About Any Ask" all fit together.

10

Pulling It All Together

L ET US RECAP WHAT WE NOW KNOW WHEN WE want to ask for what we need and deserve. It is always important to go on the journey and ask, "What does money mean to you?" Asking for money and raising money is all psychology, emotions, and past experiences you have had with money. Many times it is these past experiences that make people hesitate, resist, or fear asking for money. Once you have really thought out this very important question, you will want to know how the person you are about to ask for money feels about money. This is a very different question than asking how much money the person has to give. Through your cultivation steps you will learn a great deal about the people you would like to ask for money, particularly through open-ended questions such as "Out of all the organizations you could support, what motivates you to give now or to continue to give?" The answers you hear will provide you with all the answers you need on their views about money.

Asking is all about organization and planning. This is why it is so important to have a well-thought-out plan for what you want. For nonprofits that would be a solid case statement. During a capital campaign, case statements are a must. For businesses, it would be a business plan. A plan, even if it is a "life plan" of the types and levels of jobs you want within a certain time frame, is necessary because it makes your Asks more solid. You now have the answer to questions you may get when you ask, such as: "What are your revenue projections for the next two years?"; "How will the gift be invested by the charity?"; and "What unique skills can you bring to this position?" Furthermore, people may ask you for your plan before they decide on your Ask, so it is always a good idea to be prepared.

After you design your plan and you are ready to do your Ask, it is highly recommended that you "script" out the Ask, particularly if you are going to do the Ask with another person. The last thing you want to do is trip over each other during the Ask so that the person being asked is totally confused and has no idea what you are asking for. Of utmost importance in any Ask is that you ask for a specific amount for a specific purpose and that everyone is *silent* after the Ask; the *only* one who should talk after the Ask is the person being asked.

Now that you are totally organized and prepared to do your Ask, you need to decide who to ask and in what order. This takes a great deal of thought and strategic planning. If you have a group of people that you think may want to support your cause for the first time or continue to support the cause, then it is always a good idea to do some research on each person to determine if the person has the capacity to give and in what approximate amount. Do not fall into the trap of "assuming" that just because a person has a great deal of wealth on paper that it automatically means that person will give a great deal of her wealth. Research and your personal visits and meetings will be the best way to gauge if a person is motivated to give to an organization or business. Once you have done your research, even if that means going out to see them personally without the research search engines or formal research technology, you will need to "prioritize" your prospective pool of givers by creating a top list and next list of people to ask. Of utmost importance here is that you work *comfortably and evenly* with a group of people and not take on too many so that people on your lists are ignored or treated unevenly. It is far better to work with fewer people and be successful than to take on too many people and have little to no success with your Asks because you do not have the time to work with all of them.

Finding the "right" time to ask does not have to be stressful or a guessing game if you walk through the steps of the readiness formula:

Education + Involvement + Cultivation + Inclination + Assets =
The Right Time to Ask

If you think the person is ready to be asked, then apply each element of the formula and see if the person is ready. If you have done all the right cultivation steps and if you took the time to have the pre-Ask conversation, then you will have a really good idea if it is the right time to ask. As always, the best determination is your gut instinct because you and you alone should know and have the best feel for when a person is ready to ask.

A down economy can make many people stop their Asks because it can be viewed as insensitive to people's situations and they think that if they wait, that when the economy gets better, the person will have a better chance of saying "yes." It is highly encouraged that you continue to ask in down economies, *if* the person is ready, but that you do so with sensitivity and compassion. Too often we assume that in a down economy everyone is doing poorly financially and nothing could be further from the truth. If you do not ask when the person is ready and wait until the economy picks up, you will have placed your organization and your Ask low on the person's priority list and it will take a great deal of time to bring that person back to the moment when you wanted to ask but didn't. Ask with sensitivity and be ready to have flexible alternatives as to how the person can give what you asked.

Once you have a good handle on who you want to ask in your top list and next list, you will need to decide who should make the Ask and where the Ask will take place. A few guidelines to keep in mind when selecting the right person or persons to make the Ask are that anyone asking must know the person being asked and must have been part of the cultivation process. It would be a disaster if the person being asked meets the asker for the first time during the Ask. Put yourself in the person's shoes—would you want a total stranger asking you for money or for something you want for yourself or your cause? Equally important, if the Ask is for money, particularly if it is to support a charity, then the asker must have given first in an amount that is equal to the Ask amount or equivalent to the stretch amount being asked for. You never want to be in a situation where you ask for money and the person says to you, "What have you given?" If you have not supported the organization, then why should the person you ask give? Askers who have given first make much more "solid" Asks because they believe in the organization as evidenced by the fact that they have given first.

Anyone who makes the Ask needs to be involved with the follow-up to the Ask, which can take days, weeks, and sometime years. No one wants to be asked and then dropped by the asker. So if two people are doing the Ask, make sure two people are involved with the follow-up. Large Asks should involve someone from the leadership of the organization so if you are planning to make a large Ask, make sure the president, CEO, board member, or someone in an executive or high-esteem position is involved in the cultivation so when it comes down to making the Ask, they can take part.

As we say in real estate, it is all about location, location, location, and the same holds true in making the Ask. You do not want the Ask to be in a place that has the likelihood for interruptions such as a noisy restaurant, an office where prior meetings have been interrupted with telephone calls or office workers needing assistance, or an outside venue where traffic noise and sirens are unpredictable. Select a setting that is quiet and comfortable where the person being asked has met with you before. Always be professionally dressed and be extremely conscious of your body language and tone of voice.

Whether you are asking for a charitable cause, for yourself, or for a creative or business venture, go over the suggested Ask scenarios in Chapters 5 and 6 and see how the selection of words and selection of a person in an authoritative position for large Asks can be extremely effective. Think about the Asks you want to make and once you make them, critique yourself and see how your Asks can go from good, to better, to great. There is no one right way to make an Ask and each one should be tailored to the uniqueness of the situation. Each person you ask is different and should be treated separately and distinctly, which is why each Ask is unique. The troubleshooting tips should give you a good idea of some things that may come up prior to your Ask, especially if you are making the Ask with another person. Hopefully, they will prepare you to deal with the situations very quickly and effectively so that they do not postpone your Ask.

Throughout the book one of the key concepts and recurring themes has focused on *preparation* and it is emphasized again in preparing for the response or responses you will get to your Ask. The best exercise you can do is to go over all your cultivation notes, recall the conversations you or anyone working with you has had with the person you want to ask, and prepare for the answer she may give you. It is all right there, right in front of you. There can hardly be a surprise response, short of something taking place between your last visit or conversation and the time of your Ask. If you anticipate what the person may say, then you can craft your response and be ready when the person gives you her answer. A strong word of caution in doing this exercise: just because you anticipate that the person may say, "it is a bad time," "my finances are down," "you have new leadership so let's wait," if you feel it is the right time to ask, then do it. Anticipating answers that do not lead to a "yes" is merely to prepare you to have a meaningful and focused discussion after the response, it is *not* meant to have you hold off your Ask. Chapter 7 sets forth a variety of responses as well as sample dialog language you can use to keep the Ask alive so that the person will give it her best consideration.

One of my favorite lines is, "So much money is left on the table because no one follows up on the Ask or the follow-up trails off." I cannot tell you how many nonprofits and businesses feel they do the very best they can with telephone calls, e-mails, and letters following up on the Ask and assume that since a certain amount of time went by, the person is uninterested. Every Ask needs to be followed up until you have an answer. The key is to "vary the communication and vary the communicator." If two people did the Ask then they can take the numerous creative steps to follow up, such as telephone calls, hand-written notes, asking for follow-up meetings, or having other givers and beneficiaries write or call or meet and explain the importance of the person's prospective support. Using the Pipeline Tracking Chart in Chapter 8 will ensure that everyone who was asked has solid follow-up steps and will be a visual reminder that more work has to be done if there has not been an answer to the Ask.

When it comes down to it there can only be two answers, "no" or "yes." If the answer is "no" please do not feel discouraged or beat yourself up that you did something wrong or that if you did just one more thing or did it in a different way, the person would have said "yes." Sometimes the person being asked simply does not want to give or invest, or is not interested in giving you what you asked.

That's life. A "no" answer is never a steel door that has closed on you. There will more than likely be a future opportunity for you to revisit your Ask or make a new Ask. This is why it is vitally important when you receive a "no" answer that you thank the person, try to find out through open-ended questions why it is a "no," determine if and when you can revisit the Ask or make a new Ask, and gauge if you want to take something that is less than what you asked for now or if it is better to wait until a later time and make another Ask. With all of this you have *options*, and options can always turn into opportunities.

We saved the best for last—when you receive a "yes" answer. Happy Dance Time! Congratulations, you earned it. It is now time to devise a solid stewardship plan for each "yes" you receive. Stewardship should entail having everyone who was involved with the cultivation and Ask to place a telephone call and send a personal thank-you note. Each organization should have guidelines determining which size gifts or investments receive which types of thank-you acknowledgments from the leadership, but I suggest having the leadership be involved with the acknowledgments to the extent they can handle the volume. Be aware that some people may want tons of recognition publicly, some may want a little recognition, and some will want to be anonymous. Make sure you have that very important conversation with each person to determine what he wants in terms of public as well as internal recognition.

Of utmost importance is that the organization provide the necessary financial updates through quarterly or yearly reports. If the gift or investment was for the organization's endowment or to start up a business, then investment reports may have to be given on a more frequent basis. Your "new best friends" should be brought to the organization to see their gift and investment in action and all the benefits it is bringing and will bring in the future.

Even if your "yes" was something that was asked for yourself, such as a raise, career advice, or for your creative project, you should still do a stewardship plan and do as many of the suggested stewardship steps detailed in Chapter 9 as possible. Stewardship ideas should be creative and hand-tailored to meet the individual needs and desires of the person who just said "yes." Remember, your last "yes" will lead to your next "yes" if the person is properly stewarded.

In pulling it all together, I thought it would be useful to see all at one time the **"10 Things to Know About Any Ask"**:

1. Know your views on money and the importance of raising money before you ask for money.

2. The Ask without a well-thought-out plan will result in no money.

3. A person of great wealth does not always give great wealth.

4. When you ask for money you are not taking something away; you are giving someone the opportunity to feel good.

5. Top-level gifts require that someone in a leadership position do the Ask or be present for the Ask *if* they were present for the cultivation process.

6. Asking for yourself is not asking for a favor—it is asking for what you believe you deserve.

7. The anticipated responses you may receive should not prevent you from asking if you feel the time is right, provided the Ask is done with sensitivity and understanding.

8. The Ask is 25 percent of your time—the follow-up is 75 percent.

9. A "no" now does not mean "no" later.

10. A "yes" now will lead to "yes" later if you execute a solid stewardship plan for each person.

There you have it—your roadmap to any Ask. Please have these on your desk and carry them with you because I really think they will inspire you to make and follow through with your Ask.

I conclude this book with the last exercise to do:

Exercise #10: Right now, list three things you did not know before you read this book and describe how you can implement these concepts right away.

I firmly believe that knowledge is only as good as when it is acted upon and shared. So in this last and very important exercise, take the time to think of the three things you know now. I like this exercise because the three things you select will be the three things you know you need to change. Once you know them, you can implement those changes and you and your organization will have more confidence and be that much more prepared to make your Asks early and often!

Please keep me apprised of your successes. I learn as much from you as you learn from me.

About the Author

LAURA FREDRICKS, JD, IS AN EXPERT fundraising consultant, international inspirational and motivational speaker, and best-selling author. She is the owner of her own boutique consulting company, which provides training, coaching, and proven best practices to a select number of nonprofits and businesses to raise significant money efficiently and effectively from a variety of existing and new sources.

Her best-selling books are *The ASK: How to Ask Anyone for Any Amount for Any Purpose* (Jossey-Bass 2006) and *Developing Major Gifts: Turning Small Donors into Big Contributors* (Jones and Bartlett 2001).

Since 1994, Laura has been teaching nonprofit business management; leadership; fundraising trends; annual, major gift, planned giving, and special events; and capital campaign courses on a certification and master's degree level for the University of Pennsylvania, Columbia University, New York University, Duke University, and the Smithsonian Institution. Her speaking engagements include yearly presentations at the Association of Fundraising Professional's (AFP) International Conference; seven international web conferences for AFP; and keynote speaking presentations for numerous AFP chapters worldwide; the Council for Support for Advancement and Education; Planned Giving Councils; Women in Development; and a Master's Class on the Ask at the International Fundraising Congress in the Netherlands.

In 2009 Laura was invited by the Universities of Australia to make several presentations to the vice chancellors, communications, and marketing and development staffs on how to raise money in a culture and atmosphere that has not traditionally asked individuals in person for money.

She has trained numerous boards and CEOs from national and international organizations to utilize their business and leadership skills to raise unrestricted and restricted money, as well as energized and motivated many small and comprehensive development staffs and volunteers to use their combined talents to work as one cohesive fundraising team.

Formerly, Laura was Vice President for Philanthropy at Pace University in New York, NY, spearheading their centennial $100 million capital campaign where she raised over $92 million in six years, and oversaw all aspects of fundraising and alumni relations for a staff of 40 on five campuses.

She served as Associate Vice President for Development at Temple University, Philadelphia, where she began fundraising toward a $300 million capital campaign; managing and coordinating the major and planned giving programs; corporate and foundation funding; and alumni relations for 15 schools and colleges, two hospitals, and the athletic program. Prior positions include Major Gifts Manager for Deborah Hospital Foundation where she raised $6 million from grateful patients in one year; and Director of the Philadelphia Bar Foundation, where she began a major gift program and bequest society.

Laura is a communications graduate of Rutgers College, New Brunswick, NJ, and holds a law degree from Western New England College School of Law. Prior to her fundraising career, she clerked for an appellate court judge in Pennsylvania and practiced law for over six years as a Deputy Attorney General IV for the Attorney General's Office, Commonwealth of Pennsylvania, specializing in civil litigation.

Her community involvement includes serving as a board member for Cherry Lane Theater, NYC, and for the Greater New York Chapter of AFP; an advisory board member for New York University and Columbia University's Master's in Fundraising Programs; and a volunteer for the Bedford Barrow Commerce Block Association, NYC, and The Caring Community, NYC.

Laura can be reached at www.laura-fredricks.com, (212) 929-9120.

Index

A

Amount of the Ask, 131–132, 171

Annual gifts, 19–20; asking for an increase in the annual fund gift, 115–118

Anticipated response, 42–43. *See also* responses to the Ask

Appointment for the Ask: cancellation, 128–129; making the appointment, 105–107

Ask, the: 10 things to know, 235; amount and purpose, 39–40; components of, 35–42; high-end Asks, 121–128; making the appointment for the Ask, 105–107; the reward of making the Ask, 89–90; written proposals, 107–108. *See also* responses to the Ask; sample Ask dialogs

Askers: giving first, 85–88; ideal characteristics of the asker, 84; personality, 85; time to follow through before, during, and after the Ask, 88–89. *See also* who should make the Ask

Asking: in a bad economy, 18–19; friends, relatives, and colleagues, 68–69; knowing the person you're asking before the Ask, 9–13; in person, 17–18; planning for the Ask, 24–25; why people hesitate to ask, 7–9. *See also* who to ask

Assets, 76–77

Assumptions about wealth, 56–58

B

Benefits of the gift, 40–41

Board of directors: full board participation, 86–88; offering a board position, 224–225; as part of the Ask, 92–96; ways every board member can help raise money, 95–96

Body language, 104–105, 168